D1034336

The Bounds of Reason

THE BOUNDS
OF REASON

Cervantes, Dostoevsky, Flaubert

ANTHONY J. CASCARDI

COLUMBIA UNIVERSITY PRESS
New York
1986

Library of Congress Cataloging in Publication Data

Cascardi, Anthony J., 1953–
The bounds of reason.

Bibliography: p.
Includes Index.
1. Fiction—History and criticism.   2. Philosophy in
literature.   3. Knowledge, Theory of.   4. Skepticism.
5. Cervantes Saavedra, Miguel de, 1547–1616—Philosophy.
6. Dostoevsky, Fyodor, 1821–1881—Philosophy.
6. Flaubert, Gustave, 1821–1880—Philosophy.   I. Title.
PN3347.C47 1986   809.3   85-9994
ISBN 0–231–06212–5

Columbia University Press
New York   Guildford, Surrey
Copyright © 1986 Columbia University Press
All rights reserved

Contents

For
my Mother and Father

Acknowledgments

I FIRST TOOK UP the subject of this book in a seminar on philosophy and literature in the Department of Comparative Literature at the University of California, Berkeley, and I wish to express my gratitude to the students who provided a challenging forum for my ideas. Although none of this material has been published before exactly as it appears here, brief portions of chapter 1 formed the basis for articles written in honor of Stephen Gilman and Edmund L. King. They are "Skepticism and the Problem of Criteria in *Don Quixote*," *Revista de estudios hispánicos: Homenaje a Stephen Gilman* (Río Piedras, 1982), and "Cervantes and Skepticism: The Vanishing of the Body," in *Essays on Hispanic Literature in Honor of Edmund L. King* (London, 1983). Alexander Nehamas kindly reviewed most of chapter 1 from a philosopher's point of view, and while I alone am to be held accountable for any insufficiencies that remain, his scrutiny has lessened the number of faults that may be found. My wife Trish made numerous suggestions for improvement and has generally served as consultant on the text. The University of California, Berkeley, has been particularly generous with financial support toward the preparation and publication of this book, and I am pleased to be able to offer public thanks for it. William P. Germano of Columbia University Press took a keen interest in this work and has been instrumental in seeing it into print.

The dedication is to my mother and father because their support always exceeds the bounds of reason.

Introduction

MY AIM IN THIS BOOK is to reformulate some of the questions conventionally associated with the novelistic representation of reality by viewing them as problems of skepticism and knowledge. Through readings of major novels by Cervantes, Dostoevsky, and Flaubert, in conjunction with philosophical texts, I seek to explain some of the ways in which fiction may be said to engage the problem of our knowledge of the external world and—to name one area which is often overlooked by formalist studies of the novel—our knowledge of others in it. At the very least, one might take these readings of the quixotic novel as providing evidence of a significant prehistory for contemporary "antifoundational" thought. But more specifically, these novelists are not antifoundational but antiepistemological, an epithet which remains valid for them as long as one remembers that the rejection of epistemology only implies a dispute with one account of human knowledge (albeit a dominant one), not a rejection of knowledge as such.

I begin at the point which many have taken to be the beginning of the novel, Cervantes' *Don Quixote*. I find in the *Quixote* an alternative to the classical epistemology which, roughly contemporaneous with it, was developed as a primary response to the threat of skepticism. In turning away from epistemological answers to skepticism, Cervantes, Dostoevsky, and Flaubert cannot themselves be called skeptics. Rather, one finds in their works ways of posing the questions of our knowledge of others and the external world which circumvent epistemological methods. Thus in speaking of the "bounds of reason" I mean to indicate the limits of traditional epistemology, its formulation of the problem of knowledge, and its manner of response to the threats of skepticism, and also the possibility of a range or region of knowledge which might be available where epistemology fails.

[xi]

INTRODUCTION

Throughout my discussions, I draw on and adopt a number of the insights of contemporary philosophy for the purposes of literary analysis. I take my bearings generally from Wittgenstein's *Philosophical Investigations* and from texts written in a post-Wittgensteinian vein. Wittgenstein presents our claims of knowledge not as a priori and analyzable structures of the mind, but as a series of pictures, some of which (the epistemological ones) are said to have "held us captive." The relationship of Wittgenstein's later work to the epistemological tradition of Descartes and Kant is not however one of direct repudiation. As has been shown by Stanley Cavell in *Must We Mean What We Say?* (1969) and *The Claim of Reason* (1979) and by Saul Kripke in *Wittgenstein on Rules and Private Language* (1982)—all of which provide support for my discussions of the novel—Wittgenstein takes skepticism and epistemology to heart; only he develops what Kripke calls a "skeptical solution" to the "skeptical paradox." Something similar may be seen in the way that these novelists find knowledge to be possible in cases where the skeptic would deny its possibility altogether: they find that a response to skepticism involves a dissolution of the very questions which the skeptic wants to ask. In recognizing the possibility of such a response to skepticism, they also recognize a fact which epistemology itself must know, viz., that reason must know limits, as Kant himself was to say in the Preface to the first edition of the *Critique of Pure Reason*. In my final pages, I consider some oblique proofs of this fact; there I examine the disastrous consequences of knowledge which, in its alliance with power, would deny its proper bounds. If such conclusions regarding skepticism can further be considered as representative of the relationship which these novelists bear to philosophy as such, then their work can be seen not as dissolving or deconstructing philosophy, but as rejecting a certain conception which philosophy has of itself, i.e., as a principally epistemological enterprise. (If this is indeed the case, then our notion of a "philosophical novel" must accordingly be revised.) Epistemology is literally the science of knowledge, but in rejecting epistemology it is the science these novelists are rejecting, not the knowledge. Rather, their work redefines the range of possible knowledge in terms of love, of human society, of the body, and of the world of the everyday.

This manner of response to skepticism can be shown to bear directly on the representation of the world, of the self, and of the self's society. To consider one example, any alternative to classical epistemology will entail reconceiving our notion of the subject as privileged knowing agent. And since the quixotic self, unlike the Cartesian self (or "subject"), is founded on the idea of role rather than on (self-)representation, this provides more appropriate terms for discussing character and personal identity in the quixotic novel than have so far been offered by literary theorists. As I go on to point out, founding the idea of the self on the notion of role entails a vastly different vision of the self as moral agent than what we find in the Cartesian tradition. To consider another case, it may be seen that doubts about the existence of the world are shattered as Don Quixote butts up against it with his body. This shows that the world is there and is real, much as Don Quixote would like to deny its materiality; but it also reveals his outsideness to that world and shows that human embodiment is a necessary condition of human knowledge. I take it as significant, in this light, that Don Quixote is figured as a character whose brains have "dried up," for he is a character whose very composition precludes a knowledge of the world by the certainties of the mind. Among *Cervantistas* writing in Spanish, Juan Bautista Avalle-Arce approached a related insight in an essay published some years ago, entitled "Conocimiento y vida en Cervantes" (available in his *Deslindes cervantinos*, 1961). But I have sought here to give some further consideration to what Cervantes might understand by the term "life" (*vida*) especially in conjunction with "knowledge" (*conocimiento*). The topics of knowledge as based on human community, and of embodiment as a condition of knowledge, are twin themes of the pages that follow; at various points I make explicit the ways in which embodiment is also a sign of our outsideness to others, and thus a sign of the limits of our knowledge of others as well.

The problem of reality in the quixotic novel has most often been considered a matter of "perspectivism," a term familiar from Leo Spitzer and Américo Castro but first made famous by Ortega y Gasset. In my reading of the *Quixote* I take issue with this formulation of the problem and make the unconventional claim that the problem of reality is better seen as a problem of criteria, i.e., of our ability to tell whether the world and things in it are one way or another. I follow Wittgenstein in this direction because there is a clear advantage to be gained by seeing perspectivism in terms of criterial judgment, rather than as assembling a sum of viewpoints on the world, as in Ortega y Gasset: it allows for answers to skepticism to be found precisely where these novelists find them, i.e., in the social fabric and linguistic communities in which those criteria inhere.

Once it becomes apparent that skepticism can be answered, if not directly as traditional epistemology had sought, then by some other conception of knowledge, it also becomes apparent that the problem of "reality" and "illusion" in the novel, as conventionally understood, is not well formulated. Although some classic work of lasting value has been done along this line, beginning with Auerbach's *Mimesis* (to mention only the most familiar of the great texts), and with particular reference to the novel as a synthesis of "reality" and "illusions" by Harry Levin (*The Gates of Horn*), the terms of skepticism and knowledge seem to be a more revealing pair. Part of the difficulty in adopting such terms as "reality" and "illusion" lies in making real the force of the "illusion" in this pair, i.e., of the extra-ordinary or quixotic pespective on the world. Can we really, or simply, say that Don Quixote, Prince Myshkin, or Emma Bovary has "illusions" about "reality"? That would of course imply that we knew what "reality" was, which is precisely what skepticism, in its most forceful formulation, will not allow—nor will these novelists, insofar as they remain engaged with the doubts which skepticism suggests. The problem of skepticism in their work is not a straw man, and the problem of reality and illusion cannot be answered by reference to "what the reader knows." Indeed, the force of fiction itself, and the source of its ability to convince (as apart from its verisimilitude) is that in the confrontation of reality by illusion, or vice versa, there is no prior basis for deciding which will prevail or indeed that we know how to tell them apart. I think that these problems are eventually resolved against skepticism, but this takes finding a way to know such things, for instance by finding the uses and limits of reason, and an awareness of its close alliance with power, and by exploring other avenues where reason is discovered to fail. If the work of these novelists is indeed "philosophical," it is so in just this sense: it entails a kind of thinking which will not take for granted, but rather requires a questioning of, the grounds on which claims of knowledge are staked. If this is so, then it may be taken as fulfilling epistemology's best idea of itself.

My approach is "philosophical" to the extent that I have developed my terms of criticism from contemporary and historical philosophical texts. I have allowed my readings of these novelists to be guided by contemporary followers of Wittgenstein (e.g., Saul Kripke and Stanley Cavell) and by major historical texts with which one might naturally expect their work to be in consonance or competition. In the case of Cervantes, I refer specifically to Descartes and Locke; for Dostoevsky I rely largely on Hegel and Kierkegaard; and for Flaubert I look at Kierkegaard and Rousseau. The novels I discuss—*Don Quixote, The Idiot, Crime and Punishment, The Brothers Karamazov, Madame Bovary, Sentimental Education, Bouvard and Pécuchet*—need no introduction except perhaps to say that they are all anchored by the *Quixote*. I take Cervantes' work as my point of departure in part because it was in connection with the problem of "perspectivism" in the *Quixote* that the idea of skepticism first became apparent as a fruitful line of approach, but also because it is an exemplar of the novel as such; it seemed that, whatever else one might want to say about the novel, what one would *have* to say about it would have to be said about this one. The *Quixote* served as a conscious model for Dostoevsky and Flaubert—most notably in *The Idiot* and *Madame Bovary*—but beyond this conscious imitation it sets forth certain paradigms and problems for the genre as a whole. I return to the *Quixote* in my discussions from time to time in order to recall its presence in the work of Dostoevsky and Flaubert, rather than to prove the primacy of Cervantes' answers to the questions they share. The relationship between the *Quixote* and the later novelistic tradition is certainly not news, although it has been overlooked by major critics of the genre such as Ian Watt. I have benefited from Arturo Serrano Plaja's *Realismo "Mágico" en Cervantes* (1967), which pairs Don Quixote with Prince Myshkin and Tom Sawyer, and from the more recent work by Alexander Welsh, *Reflections on the Hero as Quixote* (1981), notwithstanding the disagreements which I express. If my work is in this line, it also moves in a rather different direction, as provided by its more philosophical bent.

Of course there has been no lack of philosophical study of the novel, including the novelists whose work I discuss here. With Unamuno, Ortega, Lukács, Bakhtin, and Sartre, one names only the thinkers of first rank. And yet their work could not be expected to reflect developments of Anglo-American philosophy of the past fifty years or so, especially in the areas of epistemology which I have tried to take into account. Thus despite the debt which anyone who writes on the novel must have to them, I discuss only the early Lukács (*The Theory of the Novel*)—not because I value Lukács over Unamuno or Sartre, but for the tangential reason that Hegel and Kierkegaard, who form an uneasy alliance in *The Theory of the Novel*, are of importance to my discussions on their own. They provide a way for me to say something about *The Theory of the Novel* as a work of philosophical reflection, rather than as literary theory. The presence of the other thinkers named above will remain tacitly understood over the course of what follows. Readers familiar with the essays collected in *The Dialogic Imagination* and with *Problems of Dostoevsky's Poetics* will, for instance, immediately recognize areas of concern which are shared with Bakhtin. My very point of departure in the discussion of criteria in *Don Quixote* might well be set beside Bakhtin's discovery of the dialogic nature of truth in the novel (i.e., that truth is not a "property" of statements or of objects, but is itself social). We diverge once I come to draw conclusions from the communal nature of truth, and in particular the vision of our separateness in society which I find these novelists to hold. But since my conclusions can be drawn independently of any argument I might have with Bakhtin, I would not be adding to those conclusions to invoke his example at length. Beyond this, my concern with skepticism and epistemology in the novel operates mainly at the thematic level, whereas Bakhtin is concerned primarily with form, so that our interests do not exactly mesh. Moreover, an engagement with Bakhtin would require the introduction of a special vocabulary, and I have my work cut out for me, following Wittgenstein and the example of "ordinary-language" philosophy, in clearing free of special vocabularies. In this way, and in the preoccupation with the nature of community, there are perhaps closer affinities with Raymond Williams' *The English Novel, From Dickens to Lawrence* (1970).

As I mentioned above, my thinking about the novel, at least in its first stages, was stimulated by Ortega y Gasset and by what I found to be the limitations of Ortega's approach. In spite of the fact that in philosophy Ortega is no longer much read, the *Meditations on "Quixote"* and the *Ideas on the Novel* continue to be challenging books, especially when taken in tandem, each one having strengths where the other may be found lacking. For Ortega, the problem of reality and illusion in the novel (which on his account may be said to be the novel's guiding theme) begins from questions about the existence of the world and about the representation of the world to the mind. Yet I begin, following Wittgenstein, by taking skepticism first as a problem of criteria, and only in secondary and isolated cases as a problem of existence. My justification for this is that it is illuminating of certain veins of the novel which Ortega had to ignore. The problem of our knowledge of others, for instance, has a large place in my discussions, as do questions of "social epistemology," i.e., of that knowledge which is founded on the existence of social groups.

Because I am concerned to give due weight to the quixotic dimension of these novels, at various points of cross-reference in the text I indicate the filiation of questions of skepticism and knowledge from the *Quixote* to the work of Dostoevsky and Flaubert. Cervantes stands at an early point in the novelistic tradition, and I see the *Quixote* as a seminal text in raising these questions, but I should also say why I have chosen the novels of Dostoevsky and Flaubert as my specific points of comparison. I can perhaps best approach the substance of my reasons by reference to Iris Murdoch's *The Sovereignty of Good* (1970) and in particular to the essay "The Idea of Perfection" published there. It is said that the conception of philosophy exemplified by Wittgenstein is incapable of providing an acceptable morality—a fact which is similarly evident, she says, in the "empty will" of the Romantics (she names Dostoevsky in particular). If what I say here is right, then it is indeed possible to find a moral vision which is compatible with Wittgenstein's anti-foundational position (although, to be sure, it is not present in it); the implications of the present study are that this morality is fundamentally a humanist one, one which finds the possibilities of ethical conduct in and through the twin facts of human embodiment and human community. Since embodiment can be taken as a sign of our isolation from others, I should again underscore that the forms of society or communion which these novels project must necessarily recognize limits. This is exemplified in the friendship of Don Quixote and Sancho, who over the course of the novel gradually come to know each other but who also grow apart, or in the marriage of Charles and Emma Bovary, in which communion is more radically suppressed. What I would call our "separateness-in-society" is shown throughout Dostoevsky's novels, and may legitimately be seen as one of their major themes.

Finally I should say that I speak of *Don Quixote* as the "first novel," as if this were a question beyond dispute. Candidates for this particular distinction have been so numerous and so diverse—ranging from Menippean satire (which is in fact a ghost) to Defoe's *Robinson Crusoe*—that some may find it cause for concern. Calling anything the "first novel" of course implies a claim about the genre and not simply about a single work, and my interest here is not with the genre but with a particular group of novels which, seen together, are illuminating of shared concerns. Hence one may take this phrase as nothing more than a matter of convenient legislation on my part and as reflecting the fact that of the novelists I study Cervantes is in fact the first. As long as one sees that the apparent breadth of this description does not impute a similar scope to my claims, and takes those claims as limited to the contexts and cases in which they arise, this should not prove exceptionally problematical and may stand without further explanation here.

The Bounds of Reason

I.
CERVANTES

SKEPTICISM AND THE PROBLEM
OF CRITERIA

ANY READER of the *Quixote* is likely to be struck by the fact that objects and events as encountered in the novel are one thing for Don Quixote, another for Sancho, and perhaps still another for the townspeople of La Mancha. Certain episodes capture these incongruities especially well, and have become emblematic of the Cervantean perspective on reality. When Sancho sees windmills, Don Quixote sees giants; when the Squire sees a flock of sheep, the Knight sees an army; what Sancho takes to be a barber's basin, Don Quixote takes to be the fabulous Helmet of Mambrino. Critics of the *Quixote* have taken these episodes as evidence of Cervantes' "perspectivism," or of the fundamental "ambiguity" of the book.[1] I want to suggest, however, that these incidents all raise the problem of skepticism by questioning the usefulness of criteria in making identifications. I hope to show that whereas the skeptic will find that criteria fail to function, and that we lack the capacity to judge whether things are one way or another, the *Quixote* shows the opposite, viz., that there are grounds for agreement about what we claim to know, hence that knowledge *is* possible. The necessary caveat to add is that knowledge may not be rational, as the skeptic would lead us to expect, and that the criteria at work are not necessarily mental entities. The *Quixote* is both antiskeptical *and* antirational. In it, Cervantes points up the limits of reason and of epistemology, the science of knowledge.

Philosophical skepticism is justly famous for some of the more radical consequences to which it can lead—Montaigne's Pyrrhonian doubts ("Que sçais-je?"), for instance, or Descartes's worry that he may not be able to know wakefulness from dreams. But the first and perhaps the most powerful step in skeptical argument has nothing to do with any of these charges, however troubling they may seem. The general complexion of skepticism is best captured in the problem of criteria; these are the means by which we judge things, the standards which enable us to tell what things are. The objection that the skeptic will want to raise is not whether things exist at all but whether we can *tell*. What the skeptic questions is whether we have any way of discerning; he doubts that there are criteria that can tell the identity of things.

The pervasive importance of criteria to Cervantes' novel shows up first in the presentation of distinct, often contradictory, identifications of the world. Consider how Cervantes raises the question in a typical episode of the book. Early in the novel, Part I, chapter 2, Don Quixote arrives at an inn. He sees two women whom he takes to be beautiful damsels; he takes the roadside inn to be a castle:

> By chance there stood in the doorway two lasses of the sort known as "of the district"; they were on their way to Seville in the company of some mule drivers who were spending the night in the inn. Now, everything that this adventurer of ours thought, saw, or imagined seemed to him to be directly out of one of the storybooks he had read, and so, when he caught sight of the inn, it at once became a castle with its four turrets and its pinnacles of gleaming silver, not to speak of the drawbridge and moat and all the other things that are commonly supposed to go with a castle. As he rode up to it, he accordingly reined in Rocinante and sat there waiting for a dwarf to appear upon the battlements and blow his trumpet by way of announcing the arrival of a knight. The dwarf, however, was slow in coming, and as Rocinante was anxious to reach the stable, Don Quixote drew up to the door of the hostelry and surveyed the two merry maidens, who to him were a pair of beauteous damsels or gracious ladies taking their ease at the castle gate. (I,2)[2]

Certain questions suggest themselves: Does Don Quixote actually see a castle (he says he did), or does he just *imagine* that he saw a castle? Does Don Quixote see the same thing as the innkeeper when he appears and looks at the inn? How can we tell whether the thing which looks like an inn to the innkeeper and like a castle to Don Quixote is in fact an inn or a castle? How are we to judge? The importance of these questions to the problem of skepticism is this: if there are no grounds for deciding what a given thing, such as an inn, actually is, then the skeptic may well claim that criteria fail to function; and if this is the case, he will want to deny the possibility of knowledge altogether. Taking problems like the identification of the inn to be problems of criteria and judgment, rather than problems of perception, means that their solution will be philosophical, not empirical. The difficulty does not stem from a lack of information which empirical inquiry could supply, but from an uncertainty about how to reconcile two conflicting judgments.

With the inn, as in most cases in the *Quixote*, there is a ready answer that is quick and pat. One might say that while Don Quixote and the innkeeper identify the inn/castle differently, the reader is able to choose between their judgments and to identify the object in question correctly as an inn. This is true, and it would be a good reason to conclude that criteria do work in the *Quixote*. But it leaves inexplicit certain doubts that the skeptic will want to voice—doubts which Cervantes' text seems to suggest. The skeptic is likely to point out that the narrator, who seems reliable here, may be mistaken or lying, and he is likely to reinforce this objection by reminding us that the unreliability of the narrator becomes a prominent and explicit concern in the novel; this is particularly true after chapter 8, as we learn that the text is a translation of a suspicious Arabic history. The skeptic will remind us that the entire narrative is couched in uncertainty and feints. The name of the hero is in doubt ("They will try to tell you that his surname was Quijada or Quesada—there is some difference of opinion among those who have written on the subject—but according to the most likely conjectures we are able to understand that it was really Quesada," I,1). The exact nature of the first adventure is uncertain ("Certain authors say that his first adventure was that of Puerto Lápice, while others state that it was that of the windmills," I,2). Our author has drawn his information from the annals of La Mancha and from a translation of the Arabic history written by Cide Hamete Benengeli, but there is no evidence that the first source is reliable, and there is every reason to be suspicious about the second. If this is the case, if we are dealing with an account the entire text of which may be unreliable, then there is reason to consider the bases on which one might claim to make any distinction at all. I am not of course saying that there are no such grounds, and I do not wish unnecessarily to mystify the nature of the fictitious authorship device, but I am saying that Cervantes is extremely careful in crafting the *Quixote* to make sure that we are aware at every level of the difficulties entailed in finding stable grounds for knowledge.

This is especially the case where one might seek such grounds outside the text, on some "transcendental" level. But how might we solve a problem of identity that occurs inside the book by recourse to an external judgment? To resolve the problem of criteria in the *Quixote* by appeal to "what the reader knows" is to forget that the characters in the book are sealed inside it, that they cannot hear tell of our judgments, and so cannot avail themselves of our certainties. To say that the reader knows how to identify the inn is to say nothing that might resolve a dispute between Don Quixote and the innkeeper, for instance. Cervantes himself works consistently against a "transcendental" solution by placing the characters and events of the novel at a textual level that eludes such determinations. A critic like Leo Spitzer, who thinks that the author of the book is a kind of demiurge, a stable point of appeal on such matters, has failed to consider just how evasive the "author" of this text really is; (he says that "Cervantes, while glorifying in his role of the artist who can stay aloof from the 'engaños a los ojos,' the 'sueños of this world,' and create his own, always sees himself as overshadowed by supernal forces"; "the transparence of language is a fact for God alone"[3]). He misunderstands that when we are asking about the identification of an object, we mean to limit our answers to the field in which the questions were put (i.e., the world of the characters). (I am assuming here that the problems of skepticism and criteria as seen in the *Quixote* are instructive of general philosophical problems: we want to be able to identify the things of our world by reference to our world alone, and not to any other; we want to decide for ourselves what things are, not have to ask God, for instance, about them.)

The skeptic is insistent on doubting that we can know whether a given thing is what we identify it as, but it is not clear whether he could advance a coherent proof that our customary identifications of the world are wrong. In order to do so, he would have to show that something—an inn, for instance—is not what we ordinarily take it as, but is in fact something else. This would mean discovering something about it, something which we did not know or about which we were (he says) mistaken. He might for instance show that the innkeeper is in error, that what he sees as an inn is really a castle in disguise, as Don Quixote says it is. The skeptic may or may not be able to make such discoveries; we have no way of telling in advance whether he can or not. The question is important because it places a corresponding burden on the skeptic's opponent, the epistemologist. In order for him to be successful against the skeptic, he must construct a proof to the contrary; he must show us our ordinary identifications of things as discoveries about them. He must show us, for instance, that the tautological identification of the inn as an inn is not in fact a tautology, that it is not hollow. And this is something his own grammar will not allow him to do. Consider that where it might make sense to say that Don Quixote sees a castle in the guise of an inn, we could not meaningfully say that the innkeeper sees an inn "in the guise of an inn." Wittgenstein gave some attention to this problem in *Philosophical Investigations,* and one of his remarks may reinforce the point: "One doesn't 'take' what one knows as the cutlery at a meal *for* cutlery"[4]—just as one does not "take" an inn as an inn. At some point, notably at the point where we cease to think that the problem of knowledge can be conclusively decided by a proof in the form of a discovery or demonstration, we find that there are no grounds for *doubt* about whether things are what we take them for; we find that the question does not make sense.

I have characterized the skeptic and the epistemologist as adversaries, each with certain arguments available to him in a dispute over our identification of things. But they share the belief that the matter of our knowing is dependent on rational arguments, proofs, discoveries. In the *Quixote,* however, we see certain ways of knowing which are grounded more deeply than the skeptic's doubts can penetrate and which are shored up at a point beyond the epistemologist's ability to claim as a proof. The *Quixote* points up the bounds of reason, but this does not mean that the skeptic wins the argument, that knowledge is not possible. On the contrary: it means that there are types of knowledge which lie outside the purview of rational proof or contradiction.

When Don Quixote approaches the windmills in chapter 8 of Part I, Cervantes prepares for a similar clash of perspectives, and for the same apparent breakdown of criteria, as in the episode of the inn. The narrator leaves no reasonable grounds for doubt about the identity of the windmills; yet Don Quixote judges them to be something quite different from what we ordinarily take them as ("At this point they caught sight of thirty or forty windmills which were standing on the plain there, and no sooner had Don Quixote laid eyes upon them than he turned to his squire and said, 'Fortune is guiding our affairs better than we could have wished; for you see there before you, friend Sancho Panza, some thirty or more lawless giants with whom I mean to do battle,'" I,8). The perspectives of Knight and Squire are no less divergent here in the second sally than earlier, at the inn, in the first. The misalignment is direct, almost schematically drawn. Here, as at the inn, Cervantes contrasts Don Quixote's extraordinary interpretation with Sancho's perfectly ordinary vision, that is, with a perspective immune to doubt that the windmills are windmills ("'What giants?' said Sancho Panza. 'Those that you see there,' replied his master, 'those with the long arms some of which are as much as two leagues in length.' 'But look, your Grace, those are not giants but windmills, and what appear to be arms are their wings which, when whirled in the breeze, cause the millstone to go'").*

The question again is: how do we tell—how might the characters tell—whether the thing in question is a windmill or a giant? This time the answer comes for Don Quixote in a painfully physical way: his identification of the windmills as giants leads him to a brutal clash with them. This provides him with evidence about the windmills that no rational argument could refute or, conversely, prove more strongly: "being well covered with his shield and with his lance at rest, he bore down upon [the windmills] at a full gallop and

*Throughout, I omit references where the source is identical to that of the immediately preceding citation.

[8]

fell upon the first mill that stood in his way, giving a thrust at the wing, which was whirling at such a speed that his lance was broken into bits and both horse and horseman went rolling over the plain, very much battered indeed." This is one of the first and most memorable times that we see Don Quixote actually butt-up against reality while trying to deny some ordinary identification of it; this is all the more reason to say that there are no grounds for doubt that the windmills are what they are. Their very physical presence should make it difficult for Don Quixote to mistake them or to question whether they are what they seem to be.

For Don Quixote, though, the things of the world are not to be so easily accepted. He insists always on seeing the world as mediated by the identifications he gives to it, as sheathed in some guise, some appearance. This is what Ortega meant, in his meditation on the windmills, by the duplicity of things—their brute materiality, and their interpreted (poetic) nature: "Riding over the Plain of Montiel with Don Quixote and Sancho, we come to understand that things have two sides. One is the 'sense' of things, their meaning, what they are when interpreted. The other is the 'materiality' of things, the positive substance that constitutes them before, and independent of, any interpretation."[5] The revelation of this double nature in the ordinary things of the world would be reason enough for crediting Cervantes with the invention of a poetry of the commonplace. But Oretga overlooks most of the slapstick and irony in this poetic "transformation" of the world of the everyday. He imputes to Cervantes a vision that is Don Quixote's. For Sancho, who does not share this vision, any "interpretation" of the world, any "explanation" of the windmills, for instance (as windmills), would be superfluous, a tautological and hollow statement which he would not make unless prompted by Don Quixote's mad ideas. Don Quixote, for his part, must find ways to explain the most ordinary identifications of things; he accounts for the world as the work of evil demons and enchanters ("'I am sure that this must be the work of the magician Frestón, the one who robbed me of my study and my books, and who has thus changed the giants into windmills in order to deprive me of the glory of overcoming them'"). Unlike Sancho, Don Quixote requires an interpretation of the world, an

[9]

accounting of what Ortega calls its "sense" ("el 'sentido' de las cosas, su significación"). His interpretations of the world are animated by his commitment to the values of knight-errantry, which command him to action beyond the bounds of reason. Thus he is an un-intellectual character, even anti-intellectual, but he has the effect of a philosophical catalyst: his function is to unseat the false confidences of those who have failed to take stock of their relationship to the world or adequately to question their lives.

With the episode of the windmills we move beyond the initial problem of criteria to several complicating concerns of skepticism. Because the skeptic claims that we cannot tell whether reality is one way or another, he can threaten that we have no way of getting beyond our different interpretations of the world to an independent reality. He claims that the world is *only* our (different and incommensurate) interpretations of it, and in so doing he denies what Ortega would call its other, material, side. Through Don Quixote's painful experiences, such as we see in the episode of the windmills, Cervantes takes pains to resist this skeptical reduction; the episode is important in part because this clash with the world sets a pattern for later adventures in the novel which affirm the existence of the world. But there remain the vexing problems of relating our different interpretations of the world to a world beyond them and of reconciling these interpretations with one another. We do not yet know for instance whether Don Quixote sees something different from Sancho when they look at the windmills, or whether Don Quixote simply gives a different interpretation to what Sancho also sees. At what point do the seeing and the interpretation become distinct? How is it that Don Quixote can look at an inn and notice a certain aspect of it—whatever that aspect might be—and see it as a castle, or notice a certain aspect of the windmills and see them as giants? How can we be sure whether this discrepancy is located in Don Quixote's vision or interpretation and not in some ambiguity of the world itself?

I want to begin an investigation of these problems, and give them a more accurate formulation, by reference to the later writings of

Wittgenstein, in particular the *Philosophical Investigations.* Especially in the second half of that book, Wittgenstein provides an approach to those questions which Ortega would pose in terms of "perspective" and "point of view" but which is preferable to Ortega's formulation because it permits the recognition of different interpretations or "readings" of the world while at the same time avoiding the nihilistic consequences of skepticism by differently *locating* those differences. Since Wittgenstein would admit that it is relatively senseless to speak of knowing the object "itself" or the world "itself" (but would rather see the concept of "world" redefined in terms of our contextual arrangement of objects, and of course our dealings with them) he can take the neo-Kantian vocabulary of "concepts" and "aspects" which Ortega would use and transform it in terms of the practical (and imaginary) projections we make of objects *into* a world. Consider the distinction which Wittgenstein draws between "seeing" and "seeing as." Two famous examples provide the sense of "seeing as": the first is a drawing of a duck-rabbit, a configuration of lines that can appear either as a rabbit's head, or as a duck, depending on which aspect of the figure one keeps in focus. But as a second example shows, "keeping an aspect in focus" will mean projecting the figure into different conceptual contexts, as in the case of the triangle which is, so to speak, rotated through a series of different projections:

This triangle

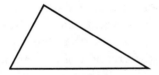

can be seen as a triangular hole, as a solid, as a geometrical drawing; as standing on its base, as hanging from its apex, as a mountain, as a wedge, as an arrow or pointer, as an overturned object which is meant to stand on the shorter side of the right angle, as a half-parallelogram, and as various other things. (II, p.200e)

I take the force of Wittgenstein's example as follows. Seeing an "aspect" of something does not mean seeing one (predominant) facet of a many-sided thing. This is because there is no essential "thing" of which to predicate those aspects. It is not, therefore, the same as seeing a "perspective" of something. It means seeing something in context, against a background, seeing it, as it were, *under* an aspect. The older (Kantian) word for this would have been "concept," but the danger of speaking of concepts, as of the still older talk of "ideas," is that we are led to believe that these are things which lie somehow in our heads, rather than in the world. The skeptical difficulties which follow therefrom are legendary. Once given the vocabulary of "concepts," "perceptions," and "ideas," the skeptic will take the question of our seeing the "same thing" to require a comparison of perceptions or ideas, so that seeing the "same thing" would mean having the same numerical perceptions and ideas, one wants to say sharing the ideas *themselves*. If the skeptic is allowed this vocabulary, then he will draw conclusions not only about "subjectivism" or "perspectivism," but about the radically private nature of experience.

My suggestion, however, is that the skeptic need not be given this vocabulary to work with. Certainly the *Quixote* does not offer it. We may begin instead with Gilbert Ryle and say that this notion of "ideas" is a ghost in the machine and start instead from the more pragmatic and antifoundational terms which Cervantes' novel suggest.[6] The reformulation of "perspectivism" in terms of seeing things "under an aspect," as Wittgenstein meant it, draws us immediately away from the hoary idea of "subjectivism" which perspectivism is thought to support and instead draws us to see the ways in which we can conceive of the world, and our lives in the world, as that which we fashion *together*, so that the creation of a world, which I shall later say is the creation of a common ground, is that which we make among us. This is the task which Cervantes sets for his characters in the novel, and the means which have conventionally been seen as supporting "perspectivism" (e.g., language, especially in Spitzer's approach) can instead be seen as providing a basis for the discovery of that common ground.

Before turning to a critique of Spitzer's idea of linguistic perspectivism, however, I would suggest that Cervantes is continuously at pains to show, and to have his characters discover, that there are ways to bridge disparate worlds and "private" (subjective) experience. This is possible because in the *Quixote* there are no radically disparate worlds, but one world, which the characters struggle to create or to repair after Don Quixote's threats upon it; their experiences are part of it. Don Quixote and Sancho have the capacity to take an interest in each other, to become involved in common pursuits, to adopt characteristics of one another's behavior and outlook. Cervantes understands "experience" not as private and subjective, but as something which in principle can be shared. The characters in the *Quixote* travel together; most important, they talk. Don Quixote and Sancho are companions who come to share a language, and language, as Wittgenstein said, is a "form of life." At the start, Sancho has had little experience in adventures, as Don Quixote is quick to say,[7] but by the end of the book it is Sancho who is thirsting for adventures and who understands them so well. Of course, to think of knowledge in these terms, as based on contexts and the shareability of a common ground, is to think of knowledge as provisional; contemporary antifoundational thinkers like Richard Rorty might describe it as "pragmatic." At any rate, it *begins* by granting that knowledge in human contexts will not admit of perfect (some would say "transcendental") success. Cervantes recognizes this in one particular moment of Part II, when Don Quixote at last gives up knight-errantry and Sancho pleads with him to continue their adventures. I will return to this moment in my concluding remarks, but would suggest here that Cervantes is willing to face the limitations which such a conception of human knowledge entails: if the two characters deeply know and influence one another, so that each one takes on the other's traits, then this knowledge will leave them once again apart and so will prove the incompleteness of their knowledge and their outsideness to one another's lives.

It is common among critics of the *Quixote* to say that the characters use language in the form of dialogue to bridge their experiences, to change not just themselves but each other over the course of their adventures together. Rather than examine the dialogue here, I want to look at one very special instance of Cervantes' use of language to this end, the hybrid formation *baciyelmo*, which

[13]

Sancho invents in order to name the barber's basin (*bacía*) that Don Quixote takes to be the fabulous helmet of Mambrino (*yelmo*). The episode is worth considering in some detail because it exemplifies and deepens nearly all of the questions that have so far been raised in connection with skepticism in the *Quixote*: the difference between what a thing is and what we take it as, the nature of the difference of our individual perceptions of reality, and the problem of knowing and communicating those perceptions.

In a famous study of Cervantes' linguistic "perspectivism," Leo Spitzer said that language generally in the *Quixote* was responsive to the individual's particular experience and circumstances, to his "point of view" on the world. Spitzer found this perspectivism in the instability of common and proper names in the novel: Sancho is called Zancas in one chapter and Panza in another, his wife is called Teresa Cascajo at one point, Teresa Panza at another, and Teresa Sancho at still another. Spitzer takes Cervantes' "perspectivism" as a warning against false confidence in reality, a reminder of the deceit of the senses:

> There is one case in which Cervantes' perspectivism has crystallized into a bifocal word-combination; in Don Quixote's remark "eso que a ti te parece bacía de barbero me parece a mí el yelmo de Mambrino, y a otro le parecerá otra cosa" ["what seems to you to be a barber's basin seems to me to be the helmet of Mambrino, and will seem something different to someone else"] (I, 25), there is contained a Weltanschauung which Américo Castro has, in a masterly fashion, recognized as a philosophical criticism (typical of the Renaissance) of the senses ("el engaño a los ojos"); and this vision finds its linguistic expression, highly daring for Cervantes' time, in the coinage, with which the tolerant Sancho concludes the debate about the identity of the shining object—as if he were reasoning: "If a thing appears to me as *a*, to you as *b*, it may be, in reality, neither *a* nor *b*, but *a* + *b*" (*Linguistics and Literary History*, p.60).

Spitzer's allusion to Américo Castro is a reference to *El pensamiento de Cervantes* and in particular to Castro's chapter on the critique of reality in the *Quixote*. Spitzer generally follows Castro's notion that Cervantes wants to show us that reality varies according to the way in which it is perceived, that the "what" of reality is determined by the "who" perceiving it, by the vital ambit into which the things of the world are drawn (one can see Castro's indebtedness to Ortega y Gasset in judgments like these).

But by the time we come upon the *baciyelmo* in the *Quixote* we already know that the world is susceptible to different interpretations, that Sancho will identify it in terms of his ordinary experiences and that Don Quixote will identify it differently, in terms of his experience as knight-errant. We know, from the clash of perspectives of Don Quixote and Sancho, that we must guard against taking reality to be any one way without pausing to question its alternative identifications or to account for the personal histories which might alter any perception of it. This amounts to saying that the kinds of questions the skeptic may raise are live issues in the *Quixote*; indeed, they constitute the existing problem, not a solution to it as Spitzer implies in the final lines of the passage quoted above. The question which the *baciyelmo* prompts is not whether reality has more than one side but whether language can negotiate the different identifications we give to it, whether it can serve the intercourse of the personal "perspectives" which anchor our visions of the world. By framing the problems which the skeptic raises in this way, the nettled task of comparing mental judgments or inner perceptions is shown to be unnecessary and the assumptions which underlie it are revealed to be ill-formed.

In order to attack these questions, I want to turn once again to Wittgenstein's *Philosophical Investigations*. (Wittgenstein's method, it might be added, which consists largely of the analysis of ordinary expressions, is not so different from Spitzer's; where Spitzer looks for an author's general outlook in the details of his style, Wittgenstein looks to what we "ordinarily say" as a justification of the philosophical claims we make.) In the *Investigations*, Wittgenstein distinguishes between a "public" and a "private" language, the one responsive to our shared agreements and judgments ("If language is to be a means of communication there must be agreement not only in definitions but also [queer as this may sound] in judgments," I, §242), the other responsive to the perceptions, experiences, and intended meanings of the speaker alone. These distinctions, I think, will clarify the role of language in the episode of the

[15]

baciyelmo in particular and the matter of knowledge and criteria in the *Quixote* in general. I want to suggest that the difficulties outlined above have their roots in some ill-conceived notions about language itself and about the ways we use it to judge things (i.e., to "employ" criteria). Wittgenstein's discussion of the impossibility of a "private language" will help point up these flaws.

We could conceivably resolve the question of criteria by saying that Don Quixote simply means something "special" when he uses language and calls objects by their names—something different from what we ordinarily mean by those denominations (for example: when Don Quixote calls something an inn, he really means that it is a castle in disguise; when he calls something a barber's basin, he means that it is Mambrino's helmet transformed by some enchanter). The question, which the *Philosophical Investigations* helps focus, is whether such a language is in fact imaginable. Could there be a language where there is agreement *neither* in definitions *nor* in judgments? How could language be private, responsive to the intended meaning of one individual alone?

Wittgenstein begins his assault on the notion of a "private" language by noting that "A human being can encourage himself, give himself orders, obey, blame and punish himself; he can ask himself a question and answer it. We could even imagine human beings who spoke only in monologue; who accompanied their activities by talking to themselves . . ." Then he asks, "But could we also imagine a language in which a person could write down or give expression to his inner experiences—his feelings, moods, and the rest—for his private use?" (I, §243). Imagine, as Wittgenstein does, that a person might make a mark, an "S" for instance, or some sound, to be indicative of something which *he alone* means; perhaps this is what Don Quixote intends when he calls a castle an "inn" or Mambrino's helmet a barber's basin. How do we or can we know that this is not what he is doing when he calls things by their ordinary names?

I do not ask for conviction about Wittgenstein's arguments against a private language on the basis of these remarks alone, although I do think that the *Quixote* leads us to a similar position. A large ingredient in what Don Quixote, or the user of a "private

[16]

language" does, is to pursue his practices in a repeated way: he always, on certain occasions, marks "S" in his diary or always, on certain occasions, calls an "inn" a "castle." What this private-language user might say *grounds* his language is this fundamental coherence, this process of repeating the "same" mark or word. He would say that this establishes a "rule" for his language as deep as the "rules" (the conventions) which form the basis for ours. But the fact which exacerbates the problem of Don Quixote's private language, or of his private use of language, is that while his rules are different his words are the same as ours. Thus apart from the simple confusion which it might entail, there seems to be no hope for understanding him if he insists on using "public" words to follow a private rule (e.g., calling what he means as a castle by the name of an inn, or what he takes to be giants by the name of windmills). The difficulty with his private use of language is that there can be no such thing as a "private rule."[9] And since it is the rules, or conventions, of language and not the words which we share, there is no way for Don Quixote to share his language with others, and there is no way that he can mean what others mean when he uses their words. The idea of a private language might be interpreted as embodying a wish for total responsiveness; this is because such a language would be entirely one's own, expressive of an exact and peculiar perspective on the world, or of one's unique inner moods, states, and feelings. But it is also suggestive of a radical *inex-pressiveness*, of a communicative paralysis, of the fact that Don Quixote's meanings, feelings, perceptions, are his and his alone. These observations are meant to indicate that language must be "public," an expression of what is common among us, if it is to work at all. (To look ahead to Flaubert, language is in crisis when instead it is in the service of private interest, when the expression of the common becomes ridden with cliché.)

If we think of criteria as a list of conditions or tests intended for some kind of "application," they will no doubt be unable to compress two numerically distinct perspectives into one; but language, taken as a network of usages held in common, as "public" in this sense, is capable of negotiating our different "perspectives" and judgments. This aspect of language is imaged in the neologism

[17]

baciyelmo. The coinage suggests a view of language as a tool, as an instrument of communication, not as something that mirrors the world "out there" or our mental images of it ("in here"). The hybrid formation suggests that language is not a mirror, map, or copy of reality, and that it does not tie our "mental states" to the world. The word (*baciyelmo*) is not a synthesis of aspects of reality in the sense that Spitzer intends because language, on this view, does not *represent* the world or our perceptions of it. Language is a tool of social interaction, a means in which people bear witness to their agreements. This is what Wittgenstein meant to warn against when he said that "A *picture* held us captive. And we could not get outside it, for it lay in our language and language seemed to repeat it to us inexorably" (§115); instead, we should think of language as a practice, its use as following a (common) rule.

If we follow what I take to be the sense of the *baciyelmo* and cease to regard language as a representation of the world, then we learn something significant about the usefulness of criteria, as they come forward in language. At the start, I said that criteria are the "standards" which enable us to tell what things are, that they are the "means by which we judge things." But if we think of criteria as being formed by matching judgments to mental forms or moulds, then the skeptic will be right in his effort to denounce knowledge in favor of claims of the radical privacy of experience. He will insist that there is no exact, numerical identity between our words and the world, or between my words and yours (and therefore who can say about the correspondence of my world and yours). Criteria, so conceived, could not possibly do all the work we would wish of them. They are unable to unite two distinct views, or two individuals in their views of the world. I adduce Wittgenstein's arguments against a private language, and his conception of language as a (common) practice, in order to suggest that these views are flawed. Wittgenstein asks us to think of criteria inhering in language only to the extent that their functioning is part of the way we are able to carry on in language and the world. Language is practice and custom, and understanding is participation in a language game, and so the skeptic's charges that it is impossible for us to get "behind" our words to our perceptions, or "outside" of language to its verbal referents, are falsely based. Cervantes' image of the *baciyelmo* finds support in this view: words are a way of dealing with the world rather than representing it; they are tools of collective interaction. The judgments people form about the way things are (their "criteria") are not held in some inner mental space; rather, they are made known in the way people behave in the world. If we want to tell a story about what caused criteria to inhere in language in the way they have, we would have to write a universal history of *human* knowledge. Instead we say (with Spitzer, for example) that these judgments have accumulated over time, and we explain them by etymology; or we say that they were put there by a succession of "ingenious" creatures (such as happens before our very eyes in the case of the *baciyelmo*), in which case we call the development of language a process of continuous verbal invention.

In the episode of the *baciyelmo*, however, as in all the episodes I have considered so far, Cervantes wants very much to raise the problem of identification, and to question our judgments of reality, by showing us instances of skewed "use." The question he suggests is this: if our identification of things is determined by human custom or practice, then could we change what things (really) are by changing their use? Apparently this is what Don Quixote does in the case of the *baciyelmo*. Consider how he accounts for the "missing piece" of the fabled "helmet":

"Do you know what I think, Sancho? I think that this famous piece of that enchanted helmet must by some strange accident have fallen into the hands of someone who did not know, and was incapable of estimating, its worth, and who, seeing that it was of the purest gold and not realizing what he was doing, must have melted down the other half for what he could get for it, while from the remaining portion he fashioned what appears, as you have said, to be a barber's basin. But be that as it may; I recognize its value, and the transformation it has undergone makes no difference to me; the first village that we come to where there is a blacksmith, I will have it repaired in such a manner that the helmet which the god of smithies made and forged for the god of battles shall not surpass or even come up to it. In the meanwhile, I will wear it the best way I can, for something is better than nothing at all, especially seeing that it will serve quite well to protect me from stones." (I, 21)

[19]

Don Quixote can say that a barber's basin is Mambrino's helmet in disguise, or under a spell, or transformed, because he takes it as such. His "taking as" conflicts with Sancho's taking the basin as an ordinary object (which is, of course, no "taking as" at all). In the context of ordinary identifications, the object is unquestioned; in part because it is a common, everyday thing, the barber's basin fits easily into the grammar of the world. This does not mean that Don Quixote cannot *use* the basin as a helmet, that he cannot in fact *take* it as one; but that will not, for all the world, *make* it one. Cervantes wants to explore the possibility that the identifications we have given to reality may be mistaken, that we may be focusing on or noticing odd aspects, but his purpose is to affirm their everyday value and use.

What Cervantes shows through the eccentric practices of Don Quixote is what Wittgenstein would call points of logical "grammar." What it means, for example, for an object to be a basin, or a helmet, or, as Wittgenstein chooses on occasion, a chair, is that it fits into the conceptual scheme of the world implicit in our everyday dealings. You can of course sit on almost anything you like, just as you can put a basin on your head, but it is part of what Wittgenstein calls the "grammar" of a word that *this* is what we call a chair, and that *this* is what we call a basin, that each fits like the piece of a puzzle with what we call "the use of a chair" (for sitting) and "the use of a basin" (for shaving). And you can of course sit on a chair almost any way you like, but as Wittgenstein says in the *Blue Book*, "It is part of the grammar of the word 'chair' that *this* is what we call 'to sit on a chair' " (p. 24).

With this juxtaposition one can also see how far from what thinkers since Ortega y Gasset have called "perspectivism" Cervantes in fact is. (Bakhtin's description, from a purely formal point of view, of the "dialogic" nature of the novel, would more closely fit the case.) One may feel that if these problems do not yield something like a "perspectivism" the *Quixote* is no longer rich in insight or ambiguity (which are sometimes thought to be the same) or that Don Quixote represents merely a comic or otherwise trivial eccentricity. But what I take Cervantes to have seen is that the logic of our everyday practices has its own peculiar depth and that to under-

[20]

stand this depth will take a *simpler* form of thinking than what epistemology implies. What it takes to know a barber's basin from a helmet is for us to put epistemology, with its characteristic concern for the analysis of "perspectives," aside.

The barber's basin appears again in the *Quixote,* in chapters 44 and 45 of Part I. In the spirit of a joke on a local barber, the Barber decides to fall in with Don Quixote. The Barber begins by establishing his credentials as an expert witness, and tells him that the basin is really a helmet:

> "Master barber," he said, addressing the other one, "or whoever you may be, I may inform you that I am also of your profession and have held a license for more than twenty years, being quite familiar with each and every tool that a barber uses. And in my youth I was a soldier for some little while, and I likewise know what a helmet is, and a morion, and a closed helmet, along with other things having to do with a soldier's life. And I can tell you—standing always to be corrected by those of better judgment—that the piece we have before us here, which that worthy gentleman holds in his hands, is as far from being a barber's basin as white is from black or truth from falsehood; and I further assert that it is a helmet, though not a whole one." (I, 45)

In his naiveté and innocence, the barber is struck by the marvelous fact that this ordinary basin seems suddenly to have been turned into the helmet of Mambrino ("The one, however, who was the most desperately bewildered of all was the barber, whose basin, there in front of his eyes, had turned into Mambrino's helmet, and whose packsaddle, also, he had not the slightest doubt, was due to turn into the rich caparison of a steed"). Don Quixote succeeds in elevating the world of the ordinary to a plane of special valuation by seeing the ordinary as extraordinary, as surrounded by an aura of magic. But the circumstances surrounding this appearance of the barber's basin are more complex than before. Part of the problem is that there is general agreement among Don Quixote and the others, even if they are contriving to fool the barber. The episode anticipates an important group of adventures in Part II of the novel where, through various forms of sham or pretend, things are made to seem as Don Quixote expects them to be. In the episode of

Maese Pedro's Puppet Show, for instance, or at the palace of the Duke and the Duchess, the world conforms to Don Quixote's expectations of it. But it is far from clear that the problem is any longer one of identification, or that the issues these episodes raise can be settled by appeal to criteria.

Maese Pedro's puppets represent the legendary Gaiferos' freeing of Melisendra from the tower of Sansueña (Zaragoza). The events call forth Don Quixote's intervention as knight-errant because he senses that they are part of his world; he senses that his virtues are well matched to these dangers:

Upon seeing such a lot of Moors and hearing such a din, Don Quixote thought that it would be a good thing for him to aid the fugitives; and, rising to his feet, he cried out, "Never as long as I live and in my presence will I permit such violence to be done to so famous a knight and so bold a lover as Don Gaiferos. Halt, lowborn rabble; cease your pursuit and persecution, or otherwise ye shall do battle with me!"

With these words he drew his sword, and in one bound was beside the stage; and then with accelerated and unheard-of fury he began slashing at the Moorish puppets, knocking some of them over, beheading others, crippling this one, mangling that one. Among the many blows he dealt was one downward stroke that, if Master Pedro had not ducked and crouched, would have sliced off his head more easily than if it had been made of almond paste.

"Stop, Señor Don Quixote!" cried Master Pedro. "Those are not real Moors that your grace is knocking over, maiming, and killing, but pasteboard figures. Sinner that I am, if you haven't destroyed and ruined all the property I own!" (II, 26)

As a staged representation, an organized instance of "pretend," Maese Pedro's puppet show is paradigmatic of a new set of problems relevant to the question of criteria and their place in human knowledge. In ordinary contexts, the identity of something and its essence are too close to permit much useful distinction; recall Wittgenstein's remark adduced earlier: "One doesn't 'take' what one knows as the cutlery at a meal *for* cutlery"; that is because cutlery *is* for cutting. But the context of pretend blocks the proximity between what things are and what we take them for: the puppet is a puppet, but it is of the essence of the puppet show that we not take it so; we must take it as Don Gaiferos, Melisendra, or some other hero. For this reason, the staged representation raises the question of the *existence* of things, apart from their identifications. What we need is not the means to give the proper identifications of the puppets, but a way to explain to Don Quixote that they are not alive. Identification and existence are different questions, and require different formulations. Where the issue is identity, the appropriate question to ask is about a thing's being *so*, e.g., about an inn's being an *inn* (as opposed to a castle), or a windmill's being a *windmill* (as opposed to a giant), or a barber's basin being a *basin* (as opposed to a helmet). But in instances of pretend, as in Maese Pedro's puppet show, we want to ask about a thing's *being* so, not about its being *so*.[10] This difference is crucial: the issue is not one of identity but of existence. When we ask, for instance, about an actor's or a puppet's "seeming" or "appearing," we do not mean to distinguish it from all others of its kind; the question is not whether Gaiferos is Gaiferos and not Montesinos, but whether this is *Gaiferos*, alive and real, or only a puppet, a representation of Gaiferos. As I said in connection with the inn and the windmills, the *Quixote* leaves no room for the reader to doubt such things; there is never any pretense to the reader that Don Quixote is not watching Maese Pedro's puppet show; in this sense, the distinction between reality and illusion in the *Quixote* is crystal clear for us. But this ignores again that the most important questions the book raises are those with which the characters must deal. There is nothing particularly wrong with saying that the reader is able to tell that Don Quixote is watching a puppet show, except that this looks past everything that is significant and engaging about the episode— the fact that Don Quixote can be and is mistaken on the matter: just as he confuses windmills and giants, he takes the puppets for real.

The question before us now is whether criteria can insure our knowledge of existence, and if not, whether there is any other basis to claim we know the existence of the world. My opening observation was that the problem of criteria was the first and most important concern of skepticism because our ability to judge things, and to come to agreement about our judgments, underwrites many of the claims to knowledge that we make; we want to maintain the viability of criteria because the skeptic is likely to argue from one instance of the failure of criteria that knowledge in general is impossible. One way to refute this objection, in an effort to shore up knowledge, might be to try to produce some criteria and to evaluate them—for example by asking J. L. Austin's purposefully ordinary question "How do you know?" in response to some factual claim; his claim is that "There's a bittern at the bottom of the garden."[11] There are several possible answers one might supply as criteria in support of such a claim, such as "From the booming noise," or "From its color," or "By its size." One might list any number of characteristics, depending on what we thought would be sufficient to distinguish a bittern from every other bird, or in relation to what we thought was doubtful or suspicious about this example. But these are all criteria of identity; they presume that the matter of our knowing is dependent on some aspect of the object under consideration, on some facet of the thing we are judging; they leave the existence of the object unexamined and unquestioned. However, we want criteria that will tell us definitively that the bittern is real and that Don Quixote's puppets are fake, criteria to tell us which of the birds on the branch can fly and which figures are stuffed with straw. One might reasonably come up with a provisional list of such criteria; but could they give us information about the *reality* of the thing in question? Is that a question which can be satisfied by a piece of information?

Addressing this question, Stanley Cavell said that " . . . the question of reality is not settled the way questions of identity are settled. I haven't got a set of routines or features or cautions to appeal to in settling questions of whether the thing is live" (*The Claim of Reason*, p. 63). Why not? Why could we not check the temperature of the thing, wait to see whether it moves, examine its gait or flight, and so on?

There is this thing wheeling right overhead. I ought to be able to settle whether it's real right now, and from here; or anyway, from not very much closer. It is part of my equipment as a knowing creature to be able to do that; knowing it from here is what I want to know. Then what question can I ask myself now? "Is its flight pattern quite right?" But now that means not "Is that the way *goldfinches* fly?" (as contrasted, perhaps, with larks, if they are similar in this respect), but rather "Is that the way a *living creature* flies (as contrasted with even the best mechanical contrivances)?" On what ground might I conclude one way or another? In what "way" do living creatures fly (or walk, or cough, or cry, or kiss, or request, or assert . . .)? What general answer to this is there other than, "The way living creatures I've known do these things"? And of course that is no answer. In what "way" do I know this? I might say: If I didn't know it I would have none of the concepts which apply only to living things . . . Am I implying that we do not really *know* the difference between hallucinated and real things, or between animate and inanimate things? What I am saying is that the differences are not ones for which there are criteria. (*ibid.*)

If there are no criteria which will tell us about the existence of the world, this is because it is the existence of a world which enables criteria to operate in the first place; recall that in discussing the *baciyelmo* I said that criteria are interactive judgments which inhere in the common language; this language, to paraphrase the earlier Wittgenstein, is one of the limits of our world. That we cannot cite a list of criteria to decide questions of existence does not mean, however, that we are left groundless in making such claims. There is another possible set of answers to Austin's question ("How do you know?") which we have not yet considered: for example: "I was brought up in the fens" (p. 79), or, as Don Quixote told Sancho in the episode of the windmills, he knew it by "experience." Here, the responses do not name or describe an aspect of the thing under consideration; they are not criteria of identity, but tell us something about a practice or usage, about how we deal with the world. Because they describe a relationship between knowledge and knower, they suggest that the justification of a claim to knowledge depends not only on its correspondence to the world but on the position of the person who advances the claim. This is the sense of the explanation that what may be deficient in a claim to truth is not its correspondence with the facts but the claimer's right to the claim, or his position with respect to it. It is said in this regard that knowledge is *justified* belief; in my discussion of Dostoevsky, I shall describe this as the mode of conviction. Thus one may argue for the existence of the world on the Kantian grounds that one has in one's understanding the "concepts" to which it will necessarily conform, but one must also be willing to stake the value of a "world" as such on those same concepts. Such claims and justifications are not possessed only of the force of reason. There is no list of criteria which can be cited in their support so, for all we know, we may be wrong—even if we are as "certain" as Don Quixote when he takes the puppets to be real. But in this case one can say that his claims have the full strength of his world as their justification, which is all the justification they may have.

If our knowledge of the world depends as much on our relationship to the claims we make as on its correspondence to the facts, the consequences of possible error must still be closely considered. How would we explain a mistake? What would we say if we were wrong? If we had erred about the identity of an object (called it a thrush when it is a bittern, or a castle when it is an inn), we would say that we had missed some important aspect of it (say the size of the bird's wing, or the fact that this "castle" had no turrets); we would say that we had not seen or noticed all of the object. What we lack (because what we want to know) is a piece of information. But what if we had erred on the question of reality, judged something to exist and then found that it did not, or vice versa? What could we say (short of reference to magic, which is the choice that Don Quixote makes)? Whatever our reaction, whether awe or wonder or amazement, we could not just say that we were missing a piece of information because there is no piece of information that could be so significant; and some things we know (e.g., the existence of the world) overwhelm any information we might have. We can only explain that we were mistaken about the bittern's existence, or that Don Quixote took the puppets for live figures, on pain of denying the coherence of the world (grounds for insanity), or by denying the world altogether. The point is that our assertions about reality and existence place at risk whatever it is we have at stake in the world, whatever our deepest interest in it may happen to be. Don Quixote banks his conviction that the puppets exist on what the existence of their world means to him, on the sum of interests that he has in it—the values of knight-errantry: "In order to fulfill the duties of my profession as knight-errant, I wished to aid and favor the fugitives, and with this in mind I did what you saw me do . . . I willingly sentence myself to pay the costs of my error, even though it did not proceed from malice" (II, 26).

One might think that the question of identity, by contrast, does not seem to entail stakes this high. That may be an excuse for our failure to take responsibility for who we are, or it may be our way of insuring the coherence of our world. Imagine the anxiety of an existence where every identification, every judgment or act of discernment, required us to stake our world on the outcome. Nonetheless, this is just what Don Quixote does. He makes no distinction between the support he lends to claims of identity and that which he lends to claims of existence. His reaction to the misidentification of the inn, or the windmills, or the barber's basin, could well be that he had failed to notice a certain aspect of the object, that he was lacking in information; certainly, there are characters in this novel whose desire for knowledge can be satisfied in this way (e.g., the Humanist Cousin, the Barber, the Canon of Toledo). But since Don Quixote refuses to deny that the world is the way he thinks it is he finds explanations which will leave his world intact; hence his frequent recourse to thoughts of evil demons and enchanters:

"I am now coming to believe," said Don Quixote, "that I was right in thinking, as I often have, that the enchanters who persecute me merely place figures like these in front of my eyes and then change and transform them as they like. In all earnestness, gentlemen, I can assure you that everything that took place here seemed to me very real indeed, and Melisendra, Don Gaiferos, Marsilio, and Charlemagne were all their flesh-and-blood selves. That was why I became so angry."

He insists on seeing the everyday world as the heroic world in disguise, or transformed, because the admission of error on this point would jeopardize the very existence of his world and what it means to him: the values of knight-errantry.

This is a mode of knowledge, and a way of justification, that one would call heroic, not rational. Don Quixote's defense of what he

[27]

claims to know is a sign from Cervantes that our knowledge of the world may involve significant risks. There is no proof, no guarantee, that our most firmly held beliefs will correspond to the facts; there are no final assurances, even where our knowledge is underwritten by courageous convictions; nor is there "certainty" of the sort the skeptic denies or the epistemologist seeks to find. There are times when our knowledge cannot be described within rational bounds.

THE CONDITIONS OF BODY AND MIND

WHEN Ian Watt published *The Rise of the Novel* in 1957, he was among the few critics to give an accounting of the philosophical conditions which surrounded the novel's rise. Watt said that the epistemological basis for the emergence of the genre was the same which allowed for literary "realism." This, he said, was a realism of "presentation," dependent not so much on the fact that it might show the seamy side of life as on the fact that the form of imitation was transparent, invisible between perceiving subject and the object of perception. As a definitive answer to these questions, *The Rise of the Novel* is limited in several ways; it has already been repudiated by critics, and Watt himself has had occasion to modify some of his views.[1] What is striking about the book nonetheless is that Cervantes is largely ignored. The omission is especially conspicuous because the first English novelists—Richardson and Fielding in particular among the writers Watt studied—owed major debts to Cervantes. Today, we would see those debts largely in terms of the "form of presentation"; but that is precisely where Watt's understanding of novelistic form becomes difficult to accept. Especially in the quixotic tradition, among writers of what Robert Alter called the "other great tradition," it seems that the nature of reality, and our perception of it, is not as unproblematical as *The Rise of the Novel* would suggest. For novelists writing, as Fielding, "in the manner of Cervantes," the representation of reality *is* a problem, perhaps the central problem; the form of the presentation does indeed intrude between us and our perceptions.

This is another way of saying that the novel gives us re-presentations of reality, not presentations; and that, in turn, is a crucial part of what skepticism has to say about our relationship to reality. Among the threats of skepticism, the one which is made most forcefully and disturbingly by the novelistic form of representation is not that reality is a dream (although that too may be one of its worries), and it is not that reality limits our dreams. It is that reality is *withheld* from us, and we from it: the issue of the representation of reality turns on our presentness to that reality. The self-conscious, playful form of the quixotic novel embodies this truth. It is made real for the reader of these fictions in the seemingly infinite layers of representational apparatus which are imposed between him and reality—in the case of *Don Quixote*: narrator, translator, copyist, and Arab historian. The French psychoanalytical critic Marthe Robert was hinting at this when she said of the *Quixote* that "Imitation here does not challenge the objective reality of the external world but rather its accessibility, the possibility that it can be penetrated and possessed." "The quixotic imitator," she says, "begins by invoking the enormous mass of books that impose an invisible screen between himself and real things. At the same time he warns the reader that what he describes is not reality, that his novel is not a faithful reproduction but a fictional construct based on one of the exemplary books in which the real world sees its own reflection."[2] A reality that is mediated by historians (faithful or false), by translators, copyists, narrators, and their books, is one whose presence is screened from us. It is one to which we are outside and cannot know in the seamless, direct ways that Watt supposed. As I want to explain, this caveat to *The Rise of the Novel* is important for several reasons, both because it points up certain flaws in the philosophical tradition to which Watt is referring and because it ignores the counterexample of Cervantes, who influenced the literary tradition to which he refers.

In my discussion of criteria in the *Quixote*, I said that Cervantes was resistant to the view of human understanding which takes our knowledge to be a matter of mapping mental states and the world. This is true in part because the notion of the human mind necessary to such a view only became fully developed with the rise of rationalist psychology after Cervantes' time. An explanation here of how Cervantes provides for knowledge in the case of Don Quixote (and I would underscore that my focus here is on Don Quixote the character rather than on *Don Quixote* the book) on the exclusion of such a view will thus allow me to deepen the line of argument which I began in connection with criteria and Wittgenstein's views. Through a discussion of *The Rise of the Novel* and a critique of Ian Watt's reliance on the "new" epistemology to explain characterization and personal experience in the novel, I hope to reinforce those arguments and to show how, in this very specific sense, Cervantes' principal character is anti-epistemological in composition. This will in turn lay the groundwork for my discussion of the role of the body in human knowledge in the remainder of this section, and for a description of the moral basis of Don Quixote's personal identity in the next.

Watt identified the philosophical conditions of the rise of the novel with rationalist philosophy and, in particular, with philosophical psychology current in seventeenth-century England and France. The basis for the new realism was "that truth can be discovered by the individual through his senses: it has its origins in Descartes and Locke, and received its first full formation by Thomas Reid in the middle of the eighteenth century" (p. 21).[3] The novel, he says, challenged literary tradition by taking as its primary tenet "truth to individual experience—which is unique and therefore new" (p. 13). "The various characteristics of the novel [thus] all seem to contribute to the furthering of an aim which the novelist shares with the philosopher—the production of what purports to be an authentic account of the actual experience of individuals" (p. 27). *The Rise of the Novel* is, in large measure, a study of cases which seem to justify this claim and its implications—that the novel gives us *individuals* as characters, persons with particular names, who exist at specific, and specified, times and places, whose existence is certified in the Cartesian or Lockean way, by continuity through time in the course of a plot; the plot is not an arbitrary or merely symbolic arrangement of incidents, but an interconnected whole, a succession of occurrences with a causal basis.

Looking for congruence between this rationalist-empiricist philosophical tradition and the novel, Watt should naturally be unable to account for the *Quixote,* insofar as Cervantes wrote the book

[31]

before that tradition was fully formed. The philosophical "psychology" which has direct influence on the *Quixote* is largely derivative of the medieval interest in the humours, as exemplified in Juan Huarte de San Juan's oft-cited *Examen de ingenios*. Yet there are enormous difficulties even in accounting for the "private character of experience" in the novels of Richardson on the basis of psychological empiricism as instances of the direct, unmediated form of presentation which the novel supposedly exemplifies. The novels of Richardson epitomize the very *private* character of experience, the fact that it is not available for unmediated public inspection. The feminine readership and urban setting of these novels were doubtless important factors, and the epistolary form may indeed give a semblance of *intimate* personal experience ("The letter form . . . offered Richardson a short-cut, as it were, to the heart, and encouraged him to express what he found there with the greatest possible precision," p. 195). But the very nature of these letters, their goals and techniques of execution, ordered toward the expression of "the ideas passing in the mind at the moment of writing" (p. 194), hint that they are *not* "direct" presentations of personal experience, but mediated presentations thereof, even if the mediating factor is the seemingly transparent "mind" to which Watt refers.

It is common to claim the invention of the mind for the rationalist tradition, especially for Descartes and Locke. But similar notions are antique. What was new in the "age of reason" was the location of the boundary between mind and body and the primacy of the mind in matters of knowledge. As Richard Rorty explained,

There were, to be sure, the notions of taking tacit thought, forming resolutions in *foro interno,* and the like. The novelty was the notion of a single inner space in which bodily sensations ("confused ideas of sense and imagination" in Descartes's phrase), mathematical truths, moral rules, and the idea of God, moods of depression, and all the rest of what we now call "mental" were objects of quasi-observation."[4]

What was different and new about seventeenth-century conceptions of the mind was that now there was a way to divide conscious states, or states of consciousness, from events in the external world;

[32]

the implication is that, in ancient thought, even where the notion of "mind" does occur, the "mind" was so placed within the spectrum of the human and the natural that these two states were not distinguished. The new placement of the division is one way of explaining how seventeenth-century epistemology had the effect of removing man from immediate presence to the world, of blocking his presence to it, and thus of fomenting skepticism.

The notion of the mind as either a reflecting surface—a "glassy essence," the kind of presumably transparent locus suitable for the thoughts of the characters of Richardson's novels—as a wax tablet on which impressions are made, or as an internal theater in which such things as "ideas" are displayed for examination and judgment by some inner eye—are among the various mechanistic models invented to account for human knowledge by this tradition. What is significant to my discussion about these mechanisms is that through the "inner eye" or "mental theater," it is thought that one has *direct* knowledge of one's mental states, which cannot be claimed for one's knowledge of others or the external world. It is this fact which furthers skepticism's aims, in effect distancing mind from world.

Along with the invention of the mind, it was the currency of the Lockean notion of "ideas," in part derivative from Descartes, which was central to the new epistemology of the seventeenth century. Here again the antiskeptical aims of epistemology were ill-served. Accepting a rationalist model of the mind, it is natural to think, as Locke implicitly did, that ideas are in some ways "copies" derived from the things of the world, re-presentations of them. If the world is not *directly* present to us, certainly our ideas are, and a Lockean view will suppose that there is no difference between our ideas and the world; but in fact there may be *every* difference. The point is that there is no way of knowing this difference, no way for us to stand, as it were, beside our ideas, or beyond them, to see if they match the things of the world; as Berkeley said, ideas are comparable only to ideas. The task would be that of "judging that the ideas which are in me are similar or conformable to the things which are outside me"[5] (Descartes), but in order to do so we would have to conceive of some sort of absolute Outsider, someone outside not only to the human mind but outside also to the external world in order to know whether something like an "idea" is an accurate copy of a thing.[6]

Furthermore, if we think of knowing something as having an idea "in" our mind, or of our mind being in a certain "state," and thus of the inner life as composed of objects of some sort or other, then these states or objects are bound to be private ones; but the privacy to which they would consign us would be an *absolute* privacy, in the sense that if ideas and mental states are ours, they are ours alone, and are withheld from all outsiders. Accepting the association of epistemological psychology and the rise of the novel should lead to the idea of an unknowable inner life, not the kind of personal sentiments and emotions which, *The Rise of the Novel* seems to imply, are actually public, knowable directly by the reader from the privileged vantage point he is given on the character's experience. In a certain sense, the failure of *The Rise of the Novel* is that it looks at these things from the reader's "God's-eye" point of view, instead of from the characters'; it fails to take full account of the fact that the world of a novel is the characters' world and that they are sealed inside it, not present to us.

So seen, there are reasons why an accounting of the nature of the novel in terms of the epistemological tradition is a warrant against *both* the self-confident "realism" *and* the claim of the faithful portrayal of intimate experience which are supposed for the genre: on the one hand, the external world is not directly available to the knower, and on the other, intimate experience is necessarily private, sealed inside the mind. Thus the tenets of the new epistemology left it open to skepticism's worst threats, rather than countered those threats. The answers to skepticism were not to be found in the mental models of knowledge which the new epistemology had to offer; rather, as the *Quixote* shows, the fact of human embodiment plays a major role in human knowledge: these are the conditions which Cervantes will not allow his characters to escape. Philosophy from Descartes onward learned to take the mental as the privileged basis for knowing and thus swept aside any other "interfering" qualities; certainly there is no reason to err in the opposite direction, to make the body entirely responsible for what we know. (Seen from one angle, that was exactly what the epistemologists wanted to claim they had done: they wanted to explain mental phenomena in terms of a physical mechanism, to account for our ideas in terms of impressions on a wax tablet, for instance.) But still there is reason to reopen the question, particularly for the *Quixote,* and to examine the role of the body, this other part of the human, in the work of knowing.

The *Quixote* is the best counterexample to the line of thinking representd by *The Rise of the Novel* and to the philosophical psychology which Watt leaves unquestioned, if only for the reason that the book was written wholly apart from that tradition. As Cervantes makes plain from the very start, Don Quixote is a character with no mind ("se le secó el celebro," "his brain dried up") and hence with no place in which to "have" any mental states. Don Quixote vitiates any dualistic account of human knowledge; through him, Cervantes explores what we can or cannot know by what some would call the senses, or the body, or, in echo of Montaigne, "experience." Whatever we call it, Don Quixote sets the conditions of knowledge outside the bounds of reason. What I want to show for a few key episodes of the novel is that we may *try* to refuse the knowledge that our bodies give us, but that this refusal becomes untenable—as in the case of Don Quixote's relationship to the external world—or involves the refusal of other human beings. The episodes I shall discuss are those of Part I, chapter 17, where Sancho is blanketed at the inn; the episode with Maritornes (chapters 16–17); and chapter 43, where Don Quixote is hung from the window on his return visit to the inn. This series of events anticipates the sequence of chapters in Part II where Don Quixote and Sancho fall victims to the practical jokes of the Duke and Duchess.

While Sancho is at the inn in Part I, some itinerant tradesmen, in a mood for mischief, stop and haul the Squire off his donkey; they pull a blanket from a bed: "Throwing Sancho into it, they glanced and saw that the roof was a little too low for the work in hand; so they went out into the stable yard, which was bounded only by the sky above. Placing the squire in the middle of the blanket, they began tossing him up and down, having as much sport with him as one does with a dog at shrovetide" (I, 17). The scene is clearly comic, and the reader is inclined to laugh, especially because Don Quixote maintains a tenor of high seriousness: "He saw Sancho going up and down in the air with such grace and dexterity that, had the knight's mounting wrath permitted him to do so, it is my opinion that he would have laughed at the sight." There is something right, or apt, about the way that Sancho falls (which Cervantes describes as *"con gracia y presteza"*), something natural about his submission to the physical forces at work on his body. All this happens irrespective of his will in the matter—in sharp contrast to Don Quixote, who refuses to accept what he sees, much less admit that his own body might be subject to similar forces.

Upon returning to the inn in chapter 43, Don Quixote becomes the butt of the joke. He is left hanging from his wrists, precariously balanced over Rocinante. As the horse moves away, he is suspended just a few inches above the ground. The effects on the body are remarkable; in the *Quixote*, the animals themselves acknowledge that their corporeality is in fact beyond their control:

. . . one of the horseman's mounts came up to smell Rocinante as the hack, sad and melancholy, with his ears drooping, stood there motionless, supporting his well-stretched master's weight; and being, when all is said, only flesh and blood though he appeared to be of wood, Rocinante could not but weaken and in turn smell the one that had come to court him. In doing this, he moved ever so little, and at once Don Quixote's feet slipped from the saddle and he would have fallen to the ground if his arm had not been held fast, a circumstance which caused him so much pain that he thought his wrist would be cut off or his arm torn from his body. For he was left hanging so near the ground that he could touch the earth with the tips of his toes, which was all the worse for him since, being conscious of how little he lacked of being able to plant his feet firmly, he wore himself out by stretching himself as far as he could in an attempt to accomplish this. He was like those who, suffering the strappado and placed in the position of touch-without-touching, merely add to their pain by the effort they make to stretch their bodies, in the vain hope that with a little more straining they will be able to find their solid footing. (I, 43)

These are classic themes and techniques of comedy. If Don Quixote could, he would refuse the hard reality of the world; that was his intent at the beginning of the episode, calling on the sword of Amadís, on Lirgandeo, Alquife, and Urganda to disenchant him and remove him from the evil "spell." At the same time, though, he has to admit defeat ("He now cursed himself for his lack of judgment and sound sense in having ventured to set foot there a second time after having fared so badly before; for it was generally accepted by knights-errant that, when they had essayed an adventure and had not succeeded in it, this meant that it was not for them but for others, and there was no necessity of trying it again").

What is remarkable about these events is Cervantes' insistence, almost brutally it seems, on his characters' submission to the natural world outside them. There is no suggestion of inner, "private" experience or knowledge. Indeed, there is nothing at all about the knowledge seen here which would require Cartesian or Lockean mental models; knowledge is understood as a function of the human body and the way it fits, or fails to fit, with the world about it. From Don Quixote's slender, wan figure ("with little flesh on his bones and a face that was lean and gaunt," I, 1), one might expect an animation, like the heroes of cartoons; but the forms and shapes of cartoon drawings are *disembodiments*, and are animated as if from without. By contrast Don Quixote's body always intrudes, no matter how much he might wish otherwise or try to ignore it. It is resistant to his will and rejects the heroic postures he would impose on it. If what the *Quixote* gives us is representative of the new "realism" of the novel, then it is useful to say that it gives us a world in which humans are destined to have both minds *and* bodies, a world whose creatures are corporeal, one in which there is death and sex, and in which the conditions of human embodiment, rather than human reason, set the bounds of knowledge. It may not matter that the *Quixote* does not begin at birth, though it does start with a baptism of sorts; but it is crucial that it should end at death. That is Cervantes' way of recognizing the fact that being human means being in a human body, of acknowledging that the body is not simply a guise that can be donned and doffed at will, but that all who are "in" such bodily guise are, as Ortega said, sealed inside for life.

When the body is displaced in awkward ways, or thrown out of joint, as is typical in comedy, we see that we do not fit with the world outside us at every instance, that there is no perfect mesh of body and world. This is evidence of our outsideness to the world; the body is proof of a seam between us and it, evidence of our incongruence to what is external to us. These apparently slapstick episodes of the *Quixote* would have us modify the skeptical conclusion that we are neither present to reality nor it to us, by the awareness that we cannot *penetrate* that reality, cannot possess it or mould it to our will. In a recent study, Alexander Welsh drew a parallel between the practical-joke-like character of these incidents and philosophical skepticism. The effect of the joke, he said, lies in the fact that "it shatters faith in the external world,"[7] that when Sancho is blanketed or Don Quixote suspended from the window they find reason to doubt the stability of the world around them. But just the opposite seems to be the case. The characters who fall victim to these practical jokes have no choice but to acknowledge the existence of the world.

Thus while the characters of the *Quixote* may be sealed inside their bodies, seamed outside the world, their knowledge of the world goes beyond rational certainty. The hardness with which the comic hero falls is itself evidence that the world exists. Yet Don Quixote's mission is to deny the world, to refuse the fact that Dulcinea is anything but a peasant girl or that he is subject to the conditions of his body, that if he drinks a noxious potion, which he thinks to be the elixir of Fierabrás, his stomach will rebel, as in I, 17. His *askesis* in Sierra Morena (I, 25) is further evidence of this fact. Don Quixote tries to deny that he will go hungry if not supplied with food and thirsty if not given drink; that episode is a benign parody of the conditions of holiness, a sign that the human condition makes our will to overcome it a thing worthy of blessedness in the first place. Each time that Don Quixote is slapped down or knocked over or in any other way submitted to the conditions of his embodiment, he learns what it means to live without escape from the world ("'you must know that the things I do are not done in jest but very much in earnest. Otherwise, I should be violating the rules of knighthood. . . My head-knockings, therefore, have to be real ones, solid and substantial, with nothing sophisticated or imaginary about them,'" I, 25); in the comic clash, Cervantes shows us certain types of knowledge which can be refused only on pain of refusing our human conditon.

It was these *human* conditions of knowledge that the rationalist tradition was unable to, or loath to, accept. A rationalist would make physical sensations knowable in the same way that mental states are knowable—through the mechanisms of the mind. Making mental states the basis for knowledge, explaining knowledge in terms of "mind" and "idea," had the effect of elevating every case of knowledge to the status of a "best case," of ensuring that everything we know could be known under the conditions of perfect knowing. But this is a further reason why traditional epistemology opened itself so widely to the threats of skepticism: the skeptic has only to show that knowledge can be discovered to *fail* in such (best) cases (e.g., the case that I am in my dressing gown, seated by the fire), cases accessible to ordinary human beings, not just experts, in order to claim that human knowledge is insufficient to its task or incapable of achieving its goals. But the knowledge that seems to come from the comic situations in the *Quixote* would counter both skepticism *and* traditional epistemology. Certainly, there is a special logic of comedy that absorbs skepticism. It requires, in one description, "that we discover outer and inner aptness with objects to *succeed* in the *worst* cases, and by means of a precision and beauty of conduct in principle open to any normal human being."[8] In other words, what happens to Don Quixote and Sancho in the way of physical, not mental experience, *cannot* fail; that is because the world is *there* in every case. It is this natural buoyancy which comedy shows.

Sancho's blanketing at the inn in Part I which I mentioned is thematically related to his flight on Clavileño in Part II. Literarily, the flight is patterned on the model of the *somnium scipionis*; the hope it expresses, which turns out to be illusory, is that we might be able to see the world from a transcendental perspective, look out on it as spies of God, thus know it in its true size and shape ("'it was by enchantment that I was able to see the whole earth and all the people on it, no matter which way I looked,'" Sancho claims, II, 41). The idea of a super-human knowledge as connected with the ability to fly is an ancient motif; Leonardo da Vinci expressed it, and it is reiterated in the myth of Faust. That Sancho's adventure not only fails but was from the start a sham, that the hopes it promised were illusory, are signs that there is no such thing as the superhuman conditions of (human) knowledge, that we delude ourselves, as the rationalist or traditional epistemologist does, in seeking the "best" or the "perfect" conditions of knowledge (whether we expect, with the epistemologist, that knowledge is bound to succeed in these cases, or whether we threaten, with the skeptic, that it may fail). In so doing we avoid the *only* conditions in which knowledge is possible at all: it is a matter for human agents in a world of lived experience, not the business of someone who might transcend the bounds that those conditions set.

Nowhere in the novel are those conditions more deeply engaged than in the early episode in Part I with Maritornes at the inn. Even in the first description of her, Cervantes recognizes the bodily conditions which define her existence ("broad-faced, flat-headed, and with a snub nose; she was blind in one eye and could not see very well out of the other. To be sure, her bodily graces made up for her other defects: she measured not more than seven palms from head to foot, and, being slightly hunchbacked, she had to keep looking at the ground a great deal more than she liked. This gentle creature in turn aided the daughter of the house, and the two made up a very uncomfortable bed for Don Quixote in an attic," I, 16). When that night she stumbles into Don Quixote's arms, dressed only in a nightshirt, he first does not see just who she is. Cervantes describes their contact, their groping in the dark, and completes the description of Maritornes' appearance—her clothing, her hair, the bracelet she is wearing. In the face of these descriptions, the comedy turns on Don Quixote's willingness to ignore the plain physical reality that confronts him; he would take Maritornes for one of the "*fermosas doncellas*" he has read about in books:

As he lay there, . . . the hour that had been fixed for the Asturian's [Maritornes' lover's] visit came, and an unlucky one it proved. . . . Clad in her nightgown and barefoot, her hair done up in a fustian net, Maritornes with cautious silent step stole into the room where the three were lodged, in search of the muleteer. She had no sooner crossed the threshold, however, than the knight became aware of her presence; and, sitting up in

[40]

bed despite his poultices and the pain from his ribs, he held out his arms as if to receive the beautiful maiden. The latter, all doubled up and saying nothing, was groping her way to her lover's cot when she encountered Don Quixote. Seizing her firmly by the wrists, he drew her to him, without her daring to utter a sound.

Forcing her to sit down upon the bed, he began fingering her night-gown, and although it was of sackcloth, it impressed him as being of the finest and flimsiest silken gauze. On her wrists she wore some glass beads, but to him they gave off the gleam of oriental pearls. Her hair, which resembled a horse's mane rather than anything else, he decided was like filaments of the brightest gold of Araby whose splendor darkened even that of the sun. Her breath without a doubt smelled of yesterday's stale salad, but for Don Quixote it was a sweet and aromatic odor that came from her mouth.

His refusal to see Maritornes for what she is, a disheveled prostitute, parallels the darkness of the scene and Don Quixote's blindness, which Cervantes mentions in the following passage ("he pictured her in his imagination as having the same appearance and manners as those other princesses whom he had read about in his books, who, overcome by love and similarly bedecked, came to visit their badly wounded knights. So great was the poor gentleman's blindness [ceguedad] that neither his sense of touch nor the girl's breath nor anything else about her could disillusion him, although they were enough to cause anyone to vomit who did not happen to be a mule driver"). So staunch a reluctance to accept the world as it is, so dogged an unwillingness to come to terms with reality on its terms, are themes of tragic potential which Cervantes seems to intimate through the detail of the blindness. Yet the comic effect of the episode is unmitigated, as if to show that the wisdom of comedy and tragedy is at bottom the same.

In the episode with Maritornes, what is at stake is not just knowledge of the external world but knowledge of other persons. Thus the episode raises a deep question: is there any difference between Don Quixote's refusal to acknowledge the physical body of Maritornes and his refusal to acknowledge *her*, as a person? Is blindness to other bodies different from blindness to others themselves? To think so would suggest that there might be something other than a human body to which a human soul might be attached; at some point, our knowledge of others (of other "souls," as it were) depends entirely on our ability or willingness to recognize them as other bodies; that is a matter to which I will return in later pages. Part of the complex irony of these particular scenes is that it is precisely Maritornes, the prostitute, whom Don Quixote should refuse, for by profession she had chosen to make her body something which cannot be given, only bought, and hence something which should not be the object of a refusal. As in all these episodes, Don Quixote's position becomes untenable at some point. Eventually, Maritornes' lover the mule driver discovers the pair in apparent embrace and deals Don Quixote a brutal blow to the jaw. The episode concludes as Maritornes falls on Sancho; they brawl and this in turn leads to the spasms and convulsions that Sancho suffers from having drunk of his master's "elixir of Fierabrás."

Critics have insisted on the dignity with which Cervantes depicts Maritornes, especially at the end of chapter 17. There, she brings Sancho some wine to console and heal him, "paying for it out of her own money; for it is said of her that, although she occupied so lowly a station in life, there was something about her that resembled a Christian woman." Over the course of these two chapters, Maritornes' actions resemble those of the repentant sinner of the New Testament. Cervantes' emphasis on Maritornes' Christian goodness seems to suggest that he was aware of the Biblical resonances of the episode; he must understand that sinning and forgiveness run parallel to the refusal and acceptance of the body. If initially Maritornes is incapable of giving of herself, she is in the end able to give a gift to Sancho. Cervantes thus recognizes that Maritornes' error, the fault of prostitution, lay in taking her body in too *private* a way, taking it as a personal possession, as chattel, as something which is owned and which therefore could have been sold but perhaps not given.

To be sure, prostitution is not the only situation in which the body can be treated in this way. "Privacy" is a danger in all relationships with others. There is an important parallel in this respect between the episodes at the inn with Maritornes and the story of Marcela and Grisóstomo (I, 13–14)—she, who refused him her love, out of hardness of heart, and he, who committed suicide as a result. Whereas Maritornes gives her body too freely, which is no real giving of it at all, Marcela refuses Grisóstomo *and all others* her body; that is why Cervantes describes her as made of marble, as cold and impenetrable ("[Grisóstomo] loved well and was hated, he adored and was disdained; he wooed a wild beast, importuned a piece of marble," I, 13). For exactly the opposite reasons, both women are unseducible (the prostitute may seduce, but she cannot, as such, *be* seduced). The Marcela-Grisóstomo episode is a classic case of love unrequited; and for that reason it highlights by contrast Maritornes' actions, whether with her lovers or in her final gesture of generosity toward Sancho: she is an example of love unrequitable, love which does not expect to be loved back. Maritornes' lasciviousness contrasts with Marcela's severe chastity; Marcela refused to marry because she "did not feel that she was equal to bearing the burdens of matrimony" (I, 12). Both conditions indicate an inability to accept the body, which in turn places limitations on love.

Yet in the Marcela-Grisóstomo episode the fault is not the woman's alone. Grisóstomo has, after all, committed suicide. He too must have thought of his body as his possession, something over which he had ultimate control; that is why he felt he had the right to treat it as he wished, and to destroy it in the end. Spurned and disdained by Marcela, he grew desperate; jealous of her body, which she would not yield to him, he lost hope. If her fault was the refusal of love, his was the expectation that love would be granted. In contrast to the Christian goodness of Maritornes and the comic outcome of the scene at the inn, the story of Marcela and Grisóstomo has all the makings of a tragic plot.

Taken together, this group of incidents is one of the surest signs we have of Cervantes' resistance to mind-body dualism. But the wisdom they offer is more subtle still. On a deep level, what they show about human knowledge is that the conditions that the body sets, wholly apart from rational bounds, are virtually undeniable. We can, like Don Quixote, try to refuse what the body teaches us. Where the knowledge we refuse is knowledge of the external world, we are bound eventually to be brought to physical awareness, convicted by the world outside us. With regard to the knowledge of others, though, we can refuse the human body only on pains of refusing the human soul. As these cases, taken together, suggest, the pre-emption of the mind-body dualism of rationalist philosophy masks a deep concern for the conditions in which we are given to the world, a concern for the specially human ways in which we are made present to others and to the world outside us, or for the ways in which our presence to them, and theirs to us, is blocked or withheld. Yet these concerns show also that the possibilities we have for "publicness," for socialness, for community, are limited by the facts of our privacy, our apartness, our isolation—facts of which the body, in which each of us is sealed, is a sign.

The themes which gather around the fact of human embodiment as a primary condition of human knowledge, and the wish to deny those conditions, become more explicit still in one of the *Novelas ejemplares, El Licenciado Vidriera (Master Glass)*. I want to conclude my discussion of the role of the body in knowledge in Cervantes with a brief discussion of this text and the peculiar variety of skeptical madness that Cervantes envisions in it. The affliction that the Licenciado suffers is complementary to Don Quixote's. After travels in Italy and studies of law in Spain, Tomás Rodaja falls victim to the designs of a Toledan woman well versed in "wiles and intrigue" ("una dama de todo rumbo y manejo").[9] She is amorously attracted to Tomás, but he is "more interested in his books than in other diversions," and resists her advances. She gives him a potion, "thinking thus to bend his will to love her." As a result of the serum, the Licenciado imagines that he is made of glass, that he is, in a sense, the exact opposite of Don Quixote—all mind and no body. Throughout, the story is laden with philosophical suggestions. The potion itself is reminiscent of the Platonic *pharmakon*, a drug whose powers were reputed to be both salutary and harmful (Cervantes' narrator explains that "Those who administer such love potions are rightly called envenomers, for what they do is to administer poison to their victims, as experience has repeatedly shown"). Like the *pharmakon*, the serum is an inducement to thought, ostensibly a boon to philosophy's goals: it renders the Licenciado a mouthpiece of truth, capable of speaking otherwise unspeakable truths to society. That the potion is administered in the interests of love is a suggestion of the seductiveness of truth, and a reminder of the deep alliance between philosophical and sexual knowledge— concerns which have been linked since at least Plato's *Phaedrus*—a sign that the philosophical pursuit ought to resemble the most intimate forms of knowing.

Cervantes' direct source for the germ of *El Licenciado Vidriera* was probably the passage in Erasmus' *The Praise of Folly* which talks about those forms of madness in which the soul and the body split apart, where the soul breaks loose from its bodily ties ("As long as the soul uses the physical organs only," Erasmus wrote, "it is called sane; when, however, breaking away, as it were, from its imprison- ment, it is called insane"[10]). But the fiction of the disappearance of the body and the image of someone who is pure mind, or who worries that he may only be a brain awash in a vat, responding to neural stimuli, are old and recurrent themes of skepticism. The classic formulation of the disappearance of the body as a philosoph- ical problem was stated just after Cervantes, in the first of the Cartesian *Meditations*. There, Descartes says "I shall consider my- self as having no hands, no eyes, no flesh, no blood, nor any senses, yet falsely believing myself to possess all these things" (*Meditation I*, p. 148). The Licenciado's madness falls precisely in line with those forms of lunacy from which Descartes hoped to be free (i.e., the maladies of persons "devoid of sense, whose cerebella are so trou- bled and clouded by the violent vapors of black vile, that they constantly assure us that they think they are kings when they are really without covering, or who imagine that they have an earthen- ware head or are but pumpkins or *are made of glass*," p. 145; my italics). Descartes went on to imagine himself to be a person with no body, to consider that his idea of the body might be a case of false belief and not certifiable knowledge, because he hoped to make the certainty of his existence and identity dependent on strictly mental criteria. He wanted to sweep away any interfering material qualities and so to eliminate the possibility of sensory error. In order to know what we know with certainty—which is what the skeptic, in his rigor, asks—we must know it by mental criteria. Descartes assumed that the kind of knowledge needed to demonstrate certainty would be found in perspicuous (i.e., "clear and distinct") ideas; the fiction of the disappearance of the body is emblematic of his wish to make those ideas not only perspicuous but absolutely lucid, virtually transparent.

Descartes was particularly interested in the relationship between himself and his body because he wanted to find out whether his body was an *essential* part of him, whether his relationship to it, although remarkably close, was in fact necessary. "Nature teaches me," he wrote, "that I am not only lodged in my body as a pilot in a vessel, but that I am very closely united to it, and so to speak so intermingled with it that I seem to compose with it one whole" (p. 192). Is it that human beings are simply beings in human guise? Am I, or am I *in,* my body? As the *Discourse on Method* makes clear, Descartes concluded that his existence was not contingent on the body; instead, he derived existence from the capacity for thought, which was made manifest in his ability to doubt:

I saw that I could conceive that I had no body, and that there was no world nor place where I might be; but yet that I could not for all that conceive that I was not. On the contrary, I saw from the very fact that I thought of doubting the truth of other things, it very evidently and certainly followed that I was; on the other hand, if I had only ceased from thinking, even if all the rest of what I had ever imagined had really existed, I should have no reason for thinking that I had existed. From that I knew that I was a substance the whole essence or nature of which is to think, and that for its existence there is no need of any place, nor does it depend on any material thing; so that this "me," that is to say, the soul by which I am what I am, is entirely distinct from body, and is even more easy to know than is the latter; and even if body were not, the soul would not cease to be what it is. (p. 101)

The Licenciado's madness shows some of the same traits that are marked in the Cartesian *Meditations* and the *Discourse*. Considering that he is made of glass, the Licenciado thinks that his spirit, his essence or soul, is untrammeled, that it is free from material limitations and can be known directly ("glass, being a thin and delicate

[46]

substance, permits the spirit to operate through it more quickly and efficiently than through the sluggish, earthbound body," p. 71). The Licenciado's body of glass is the key to his intelligence and insight, the source of his enlightenment, an image which satisfies the skeptic's wish for perfect knowledge ("they put many and difficult questions to him, to which he replied at once with proof of the keenest mind. The most learned members of the University and the professors of Medicine and Philosophy were astonished that an individual possessed of such a rare madness as to believe that he was made of glass, should be endowed with such great intelligence as to be able to answer every question correctly and with insight").

Glass, with its suggestion of transparency, intimates the yearning for a seamless presence to the world which the embodied characters of the *Quixote* do not find. Cervantes' purpose in *Master Glass* is to portray the disastrous consequences of the wish for an escape from the body and the false hope of transcendental knowledge that it might bring. Among the immediate consequences of the Licenciado's idea that he is made of glass are a fear of the finitude which the body imposes on members of the human species—a fear of death—and an aversion to others ("He begged them to talk to him *from a distance,*" my italics). As if in recognition of the fact that embodiment is of mortal importance, that it is a condition necessary to being human, the transparent glass of which Tomás believes he is made is remarkably fragile; it becomes a source of division between him and the world. Thus in contrast to the perspective of a professional epistemologist, of someone like Descartes, Cervantes sees that we will *not* be made immediately present to the world simply by removing the bodily veil. Our distance, our separateness, our isolation from others, do not decrease with our denial of the body. The man of glass is wrapped in dark cloth, shielded from the world ("Tomás asked them to give him some kind of covering with which to protect the brittle vessel of his body, lest in donning a tight garment he might break it. They provided him with a brown suit and a loose shirt, which he put on with great care, fastening it with a cotton rope," pp. 71–72).

For an epistemologist like Descartes, the will to transcend the body is sustained by a desire to attain a knowledge uninhibited by any earthbound constraints; it is consequent on the idea that man is defined as a thinking thing, and on the wish to place the mind in a position of transcendence. *Master Glass* proves a rather caustic commentary on such aspirations. The dream of an incorporeal existence is not sufficient to guarantee that we can possess transcendental knowledge. Cervantes finds a latent arrogance in the notion that man should be described as pure mind, or in terms of his "glassy essence," as the phrase went,[11] and thus likened to the angels and spirits; he saw too many opportunities for godliness, too easily avoided, in our embodied condition. His recognition that we are fated to inhabit our bodies should be set beside the fact of the Incarnation and what that teaches us, viz., that the Christian God was also meant to inhabit a body, that there is something divine about the bodily state, and not that we achieve holiness in transcending it. Unlike the epistemologist, Cervantes is interested in the body because it is the specifically *human* condition in which we are given to know one another and the world, or to fail in that knowledge.

Cervantes finds that the skeptic's arguments (e.g., Descartes's insistence on the possibility that he may be deceived about his body) entail a retreat from the world and an avoidance of others. The miserable failure of the man of glass suggests that, unlike Descartes, Cervantes saw that there is nothing else for human beings to be (in) except their bodies, that, as a famous tag from Wittgenstein's *Philosophical Investigations* (II, p. 178e) puts it, "The human body is the best picture of the human soul" (Cervantes would say: not only the best picture, but the only picture). To say that the body simply *is* the image of the soul, is to say that its physiognomy, its aspects, show what it is to be human. The questions implicit in Descartes's *Meditations* about my relationship to my body are thus better expressed by saying that I am bound by the body, in its possession, that the body has claims upon me.[12]

If Tomás got outside his body by some sort of bewitchment, by the demonical lady from Toledo and her potion, then he finally gets the demon out of him—and gets himself back into his body—by something akin to exorcism ("a monk of the order of St. Jerome, who had great gifts and skill in making the deaf hear, and even talk after a fashion, and in restoring the mad to their senses, took it upon himself, out of the kindness of his heart, to cure Glass. He treated him and cured him, restoring him to his former wits and reason," p. 88). His body is returned by an act of mercy, as if to say that humans can direct such acts only toward the body, that if we want to help heal other souls, then we ought look to their bodies.

As long as Tomás thinks he has no body, he denies the fact that man is an animal among others like him, that he is an inherently social being, not simply a sapient one. Thematically, Cervantes' view that the body is the human and social condition in which knowledge is possible provides the link between the Licenciado's mad idea that his body is made of glass and the long list of truths which Tomás sets out to preach. Much of what he has to say deals, ironically, with the specifically *social* aspects of society, with various forms of evidence of the fact that none of us lives alone. The institutions and arrangements which attract his attention center around the bonds of authority and control, around the tacit and explicit constraints which hold us together in groups. He is drawn to consider the relations of masters and slaves, doctors and patients, lawyers, convicts, social servants. He points out to people that they are of necessity defined as social beings, that their existence and identity derive from their ties to others, even if those ties are not products of their own will. (A muleteer for example proclaims that he is a decent man; Tomás answers that "'The honor of the master reveals that of the servant; therefore, look on whom you serve, and you will see how honorable you are. You serve the lowest scum on the face of the earth,'" p. 78). Through the Licenciado's dicta, Cervantes hints at the central fact of human existence as social existence—the same fact that was later given definitive formulation by Rousseau in the *Social Contract*, viz., that "Man was born free, and everywhere he is in chains." His point, like Rousseau's, is that these two conditions *necessarily* accompany one another, that in order to free man from his bonds we must free him from society, which of course we cannot do. I will discuss this formulation of the problem of "social epistemology" further in connection with *Madame Bovary*; here, I simply want to point out that Cervantes, like Rousseau, sees that the social order is everywhere present, that

[49]

it is there before we are, and that we are bound to it even where it derives no apparent authority from us (i.e., where our will and our consent in the social contract are purely tacit).

The manifest irony of the Licenciado's remarks is that he tries to refuse the social aspect of his own condition. In his diatribe against the doctors, for instance, the Licenciado inveighs against the visitation of any unwanted pain or suffering on the body. The sense of what he says is that the body ought not be made subject to an alien will ("The judge can pervert or delay justice; the lawyer may, for his own benefit, defend an unjust cause; the merchant may gobble up our property; in a word, anybody with whom we must have dealings may do us a hurt; but to take our lives without fear of punishment, none of them. Only doctors can and do kill us without let or hindrance or unsheathing any sword except a prescription. And their crime is never discovered, for the ground covers it up," p. 80). Yet the Licenciado himself lives under the influence of the will of another, and for as long as he does, for as long as he is under the sway of the potion, resistant to the socializing influence of love, he is an ineffective spokesman of the truth. Thus rather than bind him to others in society, the truths which Tomás recites estrange him.

What Tomás has to say—much of it drawn from Scripture—may be true, but it fails to convince. This is because truth, which was Descartes's concern, matters less to Cervantes than truthfulness, the means by which we render ourselves exemplars of what we know. Authentic wisdom requires finding the right relationship to truth, recognizing that others cannot see or hear the truth in us if we do not first erect it in ourselves, build ourselves up in its image. The Licenciado had set out in life to pursue learning because he wanted specifically to make something of himself, to *become* someone ("'I have heard it said that bishops are made of men,'" he says, p. 62). But he fails to see that mere learning, the simple acquisition of knowledge, must be subordinated to the personal appropriation of what we may learn: what matters is not simply to know, which is what the skeptic wants, but to be edified, to be commanded by what we know, as Don Quixote is.

This is not to say that the possession of such self-commanding knowledge will allow us to fare any better in the world, or that we will be able to erase the seams which mark our finitude and our outsideness to the world, by the simple grace of wisdom; everything about Don Quixote, as about Socrates, as about Christ, suggests otherwise. At the close of *Master Glass*, Tomás recovers his sanity, regains possession of his body (or allows his body to retake possession of him); yet even as he becomes "at one" with himself he remains "at odds" with the world about him ("He was losing much and earning nothing. Seeing himself threatened with starvation, he made up his mind to leave the Court and return to Flanders where he hoped to use the strength of his arm, inasmuch as he could make no headway with that of his wits. And suiting his action to the thought, he said, as he turned his back on the Court: 'Oh, Court, which crowns the hopes of the audacious and blights those of the modest and upright, which fills the cup of shameless charlatans to overflowing, and starves the modest man of worth,'" pp. 88–89). The hard fact is that society may never be ready for the truth, that it may always resist what we have to tell it. But against this there is no recourse. At the end of the novella, where the Licenciado is in possession of his body, in command of who he is, yet deeply at odds with the world, his destiny crosses that of Cervantes' knight. As the story suggests, the condition of embodiment bears not only on knowledge but on self-understanding, on each of us knowing and being who he is. It is the basis for moral and ethical conviction, which outstrip the rational bounds that the mind imposes.

PERSONAL IDENTITY: THE MORAL GROUND

IN THE PREVIOUS SECTION, I outlined certain ways in which knowledge in Cervantes' novel is a function of bodily, and not only mental characteristics. Those are instances of intercourse with the external world and with others in which the body yields knowledge which is beyond the scope of certainty, unassailable by the claims or objections of reason. The relationship between knowledge and the body, and the considerations that this entails—the nature of the self, the nexus of body and mind—are of still greater consequence in the *Quixote* for the question of personal identity. Admittedly, the problem is complex. Any explanation of personal identity in Cervantes' novel must distinguish the identity of a novelistic character from that of characters in earlier fiction; and it must recognize the apparent contradictions in the fact that Don Quixote is persistent in claiming to know who he is ("sé quien soy") while knowledge in this novel is not reducible to purely mental criteria.

For the greater part of its history, criticism of the novel has taken a predominantly Cartesian-rationalist perspective on the question of personal identity; in that sense, *The Rise of the Novel* is a wholly representative text.[1] The critical tendency to distinguish novelistic characters on the basis of individuality, inward experience, the capacity for personal change and self-determination, presupposes the existence of something like a Cartesian "subject," a knowing entity with a privileged, first-person vantage point on his own experiences. These assumptions pervade modern philosophical reflection on the *Quixote*. They show up not only in *The Rise of the Novel* but in important studies by Unamuno and in América Castro's best essays on the book. Only Ortega y Gasset's early *Meditations on "Quixote"* (in which he had already begun to distance himself from German phenomenology and its roots in the rationalist tradition, thus anticipating Heidegger's later work), along with Marthe Robert's *L'Ancien et le nouveau,* are free from a subjective understanding of character. The image of a solitary hero, almost melancholic in his subjective inwardness, pervades Unamuno and Lukács. For Unamuno, Don Quixote goes into the world to "prove" his soul; and in so doing, the hero suffers the gnawing malaise of solitude ("Don Quixote traveled, alone with Sancho, alone with his solitude"[2]). In *The Theory of the Novel*— written under the joint influence of Kierkegaard and Hegel, as I will discuss in my opening pages on Dostoevsky—Lukács saw Don Quixote as the image of a suffering soul, of a troubled personal inwardness, incommensurate to the world about him. He saw the novel as the hero's adventure of interiority, and the *Quixote,* the first novel, as "the first great battle of interiority [*Innerlichkeit*] against the prosaic vulgarity of the outward life."[3] Lukács took Don Quixote's attitude as that of "inner certainty [*innere Sicherheit*] and the world's inadequacy towards it" (p. 110). We have already seen that Don Quixote's attitude toward the world cannot be summarized in terms of certainty; it may be tragic in a way, but the tragedy does not derive from the failures of reason or from the defeat of his "inner certainty." Don Quixote outstrips the limits of certainty; his posture toward the world goes beyond convincedness; as I suggested earlier, in his clashes with the world he is inexorably *convicted* by it. It will be my task in this section to show how at the same time Don Quixote's personal identity is fashioned apart from any subjective inwardness, especially as such "inwardness" implies a Cartesian-rationalist notion of the subject.

Granting that the *Quixote* is the first modern novel, and granting that it has roots which intermingle with those of picaresque fiction, literary critics have sought to link the development of novelistic character with the first-person vantage point on human experience supplied in those pseudoautobiographies. Américo Castro said that the *Lazarillo de Tormes* was essentially the first modern novel because it gave us the "illusion of observing human life directly, without any intermediary, of being invited to enter the individual's inner consciousness and to contemplate his actions from that viewpoint."[4] This implies two things: first, that the picaro does have an

inward life, a consciousness, which we know by his direct observation; and second, that this inward life, in its self-consciousness, is
the defining trait of novelistic characters. But as Arnold Weinstein
pointed out in a recent study, Lázaro does not display a continuous
self-awareness throughout the book.[5] As Lázaro acquiesces to the
demands of society, the voice of inward awareness is repressed.
Because the picaresque "novel" is a circularly structured autobiogra-
phy, it yields a self that is severely constrained; Lázaro is consigned
to the verbal space in which he has summarized himself *beforehand*.
As a consequence of its structure and of the ordering that this
imposes on human life, the *Lazarillo* gives no novelistic characters;
the narrator, the character's alter ego, is intent on presenting a
"complete picture of me."

The kind of identity which we associate with novelistic characters, which Don Quixote and Sancho are the first in literature to
exhibit, has nothing to do with the closed, futureless selves of the
picaresque novel. Their identity is a product of self-knowledge that
is in fact impossible to summarize, the kind of knowledge which
seems elusive as we look for it. How well do picaresque heroes know
themselves? Consider the question of Lázaro or of Mateo Alemán's
Guzmán de Alfarache: Lázaro is so intent on giving a complete
picture of himself, a narrative snapshot of his life, that he has
nothing of a self to know at the end of the book. The story is a
Bildungsroman that is underwritten by caustic irony, one that moves
forward and backwards at once. Stephen Gilman saw Lázaro as
"dead" after the middle of the book;[6] if this is so, then he buries
himself at the end. Lázaro succeeds in opening a total window on
himself and as a result he has no character, no identity at all.
Guzmán de Alfarache seems to know himself well enough to turn
his whole existence into a topic for sermonizing observation and
critique. In this respect, the *Guzmán* resembles *Tristram Shandy*
(e.g., as Tristram Shandy says "You must have a little patience. I
have undertaken, you see, to write not only my life, but my opinions also, hoping and expecting that your knowledge of my character, and of what kind of a mortal I am, by the one, would give you a
better relish for the other"). But the structure of the *Guzmán de
Alfarache* is quite different: the "opinions" are written *over* the auto-

biographical text.[7] Critics of the book have never really known how to take the promise of conversion at the end. Should we believe Guzmán or not? The answer depends on whether we will want to believe an inveterate sinner. As a character, Guzmán offers himself up for mercy—ours and his own. What kind of identity, then, corresponds to a "character" whose entire life is subject for pity and sermonizing? Only someone whose existence was spiritually dead anyway. In the Guzmán, there may be hope for spiritual regeneration, but that hope turns on the slim promise of a third part of the novel, which was never written. As in the Lazarillo, the totalizing closure of the story places strictures on the identity of self and precludes the kind of self-knowledge which novelistic characters seem to possess.

In the Quixote, this changes. Much has been made of the fact that by a subtle mirroring device in Part II, Don Quixote and Sancho are made to stand out from the book into which they are written, as if in bas relief. This has been taken as Cervantes' suggestion that these characters are autonomous. That may be true, but it is not the crucial matter. What was important was to give the impression of characters whose identities could not be circumscribed, *even to themselves.* Unlike the characters of picaresque fiction, the lives of Don Quixote and Sancho overflow the limits of the book. It is the very incompleteness of identity, the openness of the self, which makes deep self-knowledge and learning possible. Such a conception of personal identity necessarily eschews a subject-centered Cartesian perspective which would privilege the self as center of a world, as a unique and private vantage point on personal existence; it recognizes the ways that self-knowledge surpasses even those bounds.

As I have said, Cervantes is reluctant to render inner states of consciousness in the Quixote; the centrality of the body in the project of knowledge is meant to point this up. As an element of novelistic characterization, that technique is carried on in the "quixotic" tradition, in Richardson and Fielding, for instance. At one point the narrator of Tom Jones says that "It would be an ill office in us all to pay a visit to the utmost recesses of his [Bilfil's] mind, as some scandalous people search into the most secret affairs

of their closest friends, and often pry into their closets and cup-
boards, only to discover their poverty and meanness to the world"
(IV, 3). It has been said that Richardson's use of the epistolary
device was ordered so as to present the inner states of his characters, but we have already seen the difficulties involved in maintain-
ing that position. Literarily, it will not account for the formal
intricacies of novels in the "quixotic" vein; and philosophically it
suffers from the limitations of the rationalist tradition. Here, I want
to discuss in detail the Cartesian roots of that tradition in order to
show the constraints of an understanding of personal identity and
characterization in the novel as defined by "individuality," the presentation of "inner states," and the continuity of consciousness
through time. These are central concepts which the British tradition—Locke and Hume in particular—developed on the basis of
Descartes's work. Starting directly with Descartes and his understanding of the subject as the privileged knowing agent, I want to
offer in contrast key incidents in the *Quixote* and propose an explanation of personal identity and character in Cervantes' novel as
based on the moral notion of role. This, in turn, will allow me to
conclude with a discussion of "quixotic" justice.

In the *Discourse on Method*, where Descartes takes up his most
famous discussion of knowledge, he recounts how he vowed to
doubt the truth of everything he could, "to reject as false everything
as to which I could imagine the least ground of doubt, in order to
see if afterwards there remained anything in my belief that was
entirely certain" (p. 101). He saw that "whilst I thus wished to think
all things false, it was absolutely necessary that the 'I' who thought
this should be somewhat [sic], and remarking this truth 'I think,
therefore I am' was so certain and so assured that all the most
extravagant suppositions brought forward by the skeptics were incapable of shaking it" (*ibid.*). It was on this basis that Descartes
defined himself as a subject, a "thinking thing," "a substance the
whole essence or nature of which is to think" (*ibid.*). Even if he
could imagine himself to have no material substance, no body, even
if he could imagine there to be no place for him to be, he could not

imagine himself not to be a thinking thing. This is the point beyond which his doubt could not recede; once it touched the point of self-reflecting thought, it was catapulted back into self-affirmation.

The consequences of the definition Descartes gave of himself, in his words, are this: "That this 'me,' that is to say, the soul by which I am what I am, is entirely distinct from body [sic], and is even more easy to know than is the latter; and even if body were not, the soul would not cease to be what it is," which is to say that his essence as a thinking thing would be no different. I do not want to investigate the consequences of mind-body dualism any further here; but I would call special attention to the way in which Descartes accounts for his identity; what he says, in effect, is that to be Descartes (and to know that existence) is the same as what it is like *for Descartes to be Descartes* (for *him* to know that existence). He defines himself out of mental scrutiny, out of observation from within; this is also why his "subjective" philosophy is potentially solipsistic. To reduce personal identity to the criteria of the mental, to circumscribe identity by the limits of rational thought, leads to serious impasses with regard to the nettled problem of our knowledge of, and by, other minds. While Descartes cannot alone be held responsible for that problem, it is unlikely that he would have come to the same conclusions regarding personal identity had his meditations been taken up in a different setting. Along with Montaigne in the circular reading room, the image of Descartes huddled in his dressing gown before the fire is one of the most powerful emblems of the solitary thinker, of a personal identity that was conditioned by private circumstances, of a thought which took root in the silence of the mind. For Descartes, the evidence of his own thinking was sufficient grounds to take the first, all-important step, against skepticism. But, to take the example invoked by G. E. Moore, and later by Wittgenstein, there is little doubt that Descartes's answers would have been markedly different if he had, for instance, held up an envelope for public view, or asked a group of peers whether there was room for doubt about the existence of this hand, these feet, this flesh.[8] Cartesian "privacy" is not only mental; it is determined by the solitary setting in which thought is engaged. As the nature of language and criteria in the *Quixote* shows, the general conditions

[57]

of knowledge as Cervantes conceives them are public and communal rather than solitary and private. On this essential point the *Quixote* is irreconcilable with Cartesian thought. Cervantes' characters find instances in which, as Wittgenstein would say, "grounds for doubt are lacking" (*On Certainty*, §4). Instead they find grounds for agreement and disagreement—for dialogue—about what we take things to be, largely because Cervantes imagines their interactions as taking place in an open, public sphere.

Seen from a certain angle, Don Quixote does bear some resemblance to the Cartesian subject, to the knower who knows "from within." He makes important statements about himself—claims not only to existence but specifically to identity, assertions not only *that* he is, but of *who* he is, and perhaps most important, to *know* who he is ("sé quien soy"). But as we shall see, for Don Quixote this knowledge of self depends on his ability to assume roles, whereas for Descartes it means to recognize himself as the subject of thought—and that, as Nietzsche famously criticized in *Beyond Good and Evil*, was not necessarily grounds for establishing personal identity: "I shall never tire of underlining a concise little fact which these superstitious [logicians] are loath to admit—namely, that a thought comes when 'it' wants, not when 'I' want; so that it is a falsification of the facts to say: the subject 'I' is the condition of the predicate 'think.'"9 Others, Wittgenstein among them, have said that the proposition "I am I" is not so much false as empty, that it could not say something meaningful about the self. But for some, knowledge of this emptiness is the height of bliss; that is what Nietzsche, at least, saw in Don Quixote.

But how is it that Don Quixote's claim to know who he is, if it is a tautology and hence empty, provides such a crucial clue to his identity? The tautology of personal identity "I am I" (or, as Don Quixote would formulate it, "soy quien soy") is backed by a claim of knowledge "I know who I am" ("sé quien soy"). This bespeaks a personal integrity. It is a sign of the absolute confidence with which he maintains the bond between "inner" and "outer"—or between "subject" and "experience," to choose other terms—between *being* who he is and *knowing* who he is. The claim suggests a bond so tight as to render such distinctions virtually useless, conventional as they might be.

The first crucial proof of self-identity in the book comes in chapter 5 of Part I. In response to the pleas of his neighbor Pedro Alonso, Don Quixote insists that he knows who he is; yet he is reluctant to fix his identity and, in fact, insists on its indeterminacy:

> "Sinner that I am, cannot your Grace [Don Quixote] see that I am not Don Rodrigo de Narváez nor the Marquis of Mantua, but Pedro Alonso, your neighbor? And your Grace is neither Baldwin nor Abindarráez but a respectable gentlemen by the name of Señor Quijana."
>
> "I know who I am," said Don Quixote, "and who I may be, if I choose: not only those I have mentioned but all the Twelve Peers of France and the Nine Worthies as well; for the exploits of all of them together, or separately, cannot compare with mine."

Don Quixote's reply has given critics pause. Few have understood that Don Quixote's ability to imitate, to take various roles upon himself, is itself the source of his identity. By this protean imitative ability, Don Quixote places himself on the brink of annihilation (indeed, until the very end of the book, the figure of Alonso Quijano is in eclipse). It is as if, peering in to the emptiness of the tautology, "I am I," Don Quixote were filled with the conviction that it is up to *him* to fill that space and to take responsibility for the claim to be who he is. If, as Don Quixote's reply to Pedro Alonso shows, his identity is fashioned by his inexhaustible capacity to imitate, that means not just to play roles but to take them upon himself, almost as if to assault the self by its roles. Sancho, in following the Knight, likewise learns to take certain things upon himself and thus to define his own identity, his life.

To address Sancho first, Américo Castro was certainly right when he said that Sancho "takes upon" himself the "dangerous office" of squire.[10] Castro cites a crucial passage from the book:

> "decoyed and beguiled by a purse with a hundred ducats that I found one day in the heart of the Sierra Morena; and the devil is always out putting a bag of dubloons before my eyes, here, there, not here, perhaps over there until I fancy at every step I am putting my hands on it, and carrying it home with me, and making investments, and getting interest, and living like a prince; and so as long as I think of this I make light of all the

hardships I endure with this master of mine, who, I well know, is more of a madman than a knight." (II, 13)

As Sancho says, to take something upon oneself means to make an investment in it, not only to take an interest in it but to draw interest from it—the kind of interest he has in his life because of his decision to follow Don Quixote—and to "carry it home" with him.

What Sancho does in a limited field of concerns, Don Quixote does with his whole existence. To say that he plays one or several roles will not indicate what it means for him to take those roles upon himself. When he imitates Abindarráez, Amadís, Roldán, or any of the others, he does so with such unstinting conviction that there is a practically infinite distance between the character and the role: the "self" never gets in his way because he acts unselfconsciously.[11] When Castro saw that in Don Quixote's prodigious ability to be imitative there were potential threats to his identity, that his affirmation of self through the role was a manner of self-preservation against hostile worldly forces, he continues a line of thinking already evident in Unamuno and, outside Spain, in Lukács; it is congruent with the appraisal that Don Quixote has a personal "inwardness" incommensurate to the world about him. But to a greater degree, Don Quixote's imitations are premised on the extrarational standards of role-playing which demand an assuredness of purpose and a knowledge of self gained through active engagement, far beyond the bounds of subjective, inward experience.

What Castro saw and admired as Cervantes' recognition of the autonomous value of human existence depends on Don Quixote's ability to forego reasons, to go mad without cause, "desatinar sin ocasión," to act out of an unimpeachable self-knowledge, one that is not gained from within but that is conferred from without. Indeed, the fact that Don Quixote is worthy of concerns that should, rigorously speaking, be limited to the identity of persons, is indicative of the depth of his self-knowledge. It is summarized, in Castro's words, by the fact that "To live, for Cervantes, is not to know, nor to make distinctions between this and that; nor is it a search for the ultimate truth behind the fleeting, uncertain appearance of all that surrounds us" (p. 28, my emphasis).[12] When Don Quixote says, "I know who I am" he is not interested in answering the claims of a skeptic who would doubt it. His neighbor Pedro Alonso is one such skeptic; but Don Quixote's energetic reply is indication that his identity, the knowledge of who he is, is rooted more deeply than the skeptic's doubts can probe. In the *Quixote*, self-identity is given as a function of taking an identity upon oneself, charging oneself with it, making it fully one's own. What Don Quixote knows of himself is knowledge that no skeptic could doubt or refute; relative to it, the skeptic's doubts give no purchase. That Don Quixote can be Amadís *and* Orlando *and* Abindarráez, that he can be any or all of the Nine Worthies *and* the Twelve Peers, and that he, as who he is, *exceeds* all those identities, means that the world cannot give him a true and complete picture of himself. His task is to be the character that takes all those roles upon himself, and whose existence remains greater than their sum.

Don Quixote confirms his identity at two further moments in the novel, once in successful battle and once in defeat, both of them episodes with Sansón Carrasco. In Part II, chapter 14, Don Quixote wins an important, if accidental, victory over the Caballero de los Espejos (Sansón disguised as the Knight of the Mirrors). In return, Don Quixote is able to extract an avowal of the nonpareil beauty and value of Dulcinea del Toboso; he is able to counter Sansón's false claims to have already defeated a certain knight by the name of "Don Quixote," telling Sansón that that knight-errant could not have been he "but was some other that resembled him, just as I am convinced that you, though you appear to be the bachelor Sansón Carrasco, are another person in his form and likeness who has been put here by my enemies to induce me to restrain and moderate the impetuosity of my wrath and make a gentle use of my glorious victory" (II, 14). By defeating the Knight of the Mirrors, Don Quixote succeeds in unmasking him; the incident runs parallel to Sancho's unmasking of the squire Tomé Cecial (Tosilos). The unmasking points up the sham role-playing of Sansón Carrasco and his squire, the fact that they do not know what it means to take on a role as an *identity*. Don Quixote refuses to accept that the Knight of the Mirrors is Sansón Carrasco, for he cannot imagine that everyone does not have his kind of constancy; besides, this would deprive him of the satisfaction of having defeated "so valiant a knight as he imagined the one of the Mirrors to be" (II, 15); Don Quixote always gives the world credit for being as heroic as he is. Sansón's masquerade was designed to bring Don Quixote to reason, but there is no greater moral or ethical purpose behind the intent. In *The Tragic Sense of Life*, Unamuno saw Sansón Carrasco as pragmatic European man, who relates to the world by logic and planning and who upholds the rationality of society and its cultural institutions. Insofar as Sansón is emblematic of inauthentic, unheroic role-playing, the juxtaposition with Don Quixote, and Don Quixote's victory here, are indicative of Cervantes' understanding of the function of role as a viable ethical mold, as a basis for the formation of character (in the moral sense) and personal worth.

But identity is not only conferred in victory. Sansón Carrasco returns again in Part II, now disguised as the Caballero de la Blanca Luna (Knight of the White Moon). This time, Don Quixote is defeated, and Sansón exacts a promise that he will return home for at least a year's time. The defeat is crucial because it comes so near the end of the book and Don Quixote's divestment of his chivalric role. Sansón's victory appears to be a triumph of reason over ecstatic, quixotic heroism; superficially, at least, it seems that Don Quixote's identity is threatened here. Since this encounter with Sansón drives Don Quixote back home, our decision to regard this defeat as a conclusive weakening of identity will ultimately depend on how we regard Don Quixote's assumption of the identity of Alonso Quijano in the final chapter. But as Don Quixote takes the name of Alonso Quijano at the end of the book, he knows who he is with more conviction than at any other point: "'I was mad and now I am sane; I was Don Quixote de la Mancha, and now I am, as I have said, Alonso Quijano the Good" (II, 74). He prepares his last will and testament to seal his identity for posterity, to signify his command over who he is and will be.

In *Reflections on the Hero as Quixote*, Alexander Welsh argued that for Don Quixote the experience of defeat as such—not only at the hands of Sansón Carrasco here, but continuously throughout the novel, as he clashes with the world—serves to strengthen personal identity. Don Quixote is bound to be defeated because his

[62]

ability to be himself outstrips the circumstances and conditions which the world could possibly supply him; thus his abrasive encounters with the world are like trials and tests which confirm his identity. This is not to say that defeat at the hands of Sansón Carrasco is not filled with a certain anguish or remorse; it is. But in a very real sense, it is this defeat which makes Don Quixote's identification with Alonso Quijano at the end of the book possible; in contrast to the opening of the novel, where the hidalgo of La Mancha was floating vaguely in a nebulous sea of names (Quijada, Quesada, Quejana), his name is fixed at the end. The episode with Sansón is a significant indication that Cervantes sees the difficulties involved in the winning of identity—that for Don Quixote to be in the world, and for him to be who he is in the world, will necessarily mean for him to be at odds with the world.

The ethical individualism that Cervantes constructs for his character should not be confused with "subjectivism." Don Quixote's individualism, as Cervantes portrays it, means that Don Quixote will find that the world does not bend to his will, that his designs on it do not succeed. It is knowledge as old as Socrates that the gaining of identity in this ethical way—which is stated in the *Gorgias* as the condition of being "at one" with oneself, morally whole—may well entail being "at odds" with the world; we have already seen that happen in the case of Master Glass. In the very conception of his novel, in the idea of a knight who sets out to revive the age of chivalry, Cervantes is preparing for such a clash. Apart from Don Quixote's virtue, this conflict shows Cervantes' recognition of the world *as such*, apart from the designs of his hero: the creation of a character of unimpeachable moral fibre who is defeated at the hands of the world shows that there is indeed a world there to reckon with. This is what I think Heidegger meant by his comments about the anxiousness of our being "thrown" into the world. The implication is not that this anxiety, or what Kierkegaard would call "dread," is a revelation about my inner mood, but rather that it proves that the world is outside me and is there (and hence proves the validity of moods in advising us of the world).[13]

In the *Quixote*, a willingness for this kind of anxiety is thus not an existentialist concern, at least not in the vulgar meaning of that

[63]

term. It refers to the openness of the self to the world, which serves as the possibility or "condition" around it. What the self finds, however, is that the rule of its existence is change, so that knowledge of the self as it is always seems a betrayal of the self as it was. Don Quixote's defeat at the hands of Sansón Carrasco is a form of "self-revelation" which marks the crucial juncture of his self-knowledge. It is the moment at which Don Quixote's mission, the idea of his role as knight-errant on which he has staked his identity, seems to betray him. And the process by which Don Quixote takes on certain characteristics of Sancho Panza's role, and vice-versa, which Salvador de Madariaga described as the "Sanchification" of the one and the "Quixotification" of the other,[14] is further evidence of growth into mature identity by a willingness to relinquish the claims of a former self.

It is only at the end of the book, when such self-revelations are done, that selfhood is finally earned; yet for Don Quixote this means the discovery of his "average everydayness," the recovery of his identity as just another man, Alonso Quijano el Bueno. Personal identity, which must be lived out, is not submissible to sovereign totalization and cannot be summarized, least of all *beforehand* as in the earlier picaresque. Thus Don Quixote's death is not the singular, heroic event which stands on the other side of his life. Personal identity is achieved in, and in obedience to, the context that Heidegger and Ortega call the "world": the context sets limits, which are its horizon; that horizon is death, which in Don Quixote's case corresponds to the return to the world of the everyday. In some striking but finally unexistentialist ways, thus, Cervantes anticipates what Heidegger meant to say by the fact of our being "towards death." The resistance to any vulgarized existentialism is shown in the *Quixote* by the remarkably unheroic nature of Don Quixote's death.

With regard to personal identity, Don Quixote's death at the end of the novel, and his defeat at the hands of Sansón Carrasco which anticipates his death, are not spiritual failings. Don Quixote may be weak of body, unable physically to attain the full heroic potential which he imagines for himself, but even in defeat he is resolute on affirming that he knows who he is. This tenacious adherence to the idea of personal identity, more than to any one role, in the face of physical defeat, endows Don Quixote with a sense of moral and ethical commitment. He says to Sansón Carrasco, for instance:

"Dulcinea del Toboso is the most beautiful woman in the world and I the most unhappy knight upon the face of this earth. *It is not right that my weakness should serve to defraud the truth.* Drive home your lance, O knight, and take my life since you already have deprived me of my honor." (II, 64; my emphasis)

This encounter costs Don Quixote a full six days mending in Barcelona; but still, as he and Sancho leave the city to return to La Mancha, the Knight can affirm that "each man is the architect of his own fortune," as he tells his disheartened Squire. Don Quixote's identity is strengthened in defeat because he calls on the ethical individualism which guides his actions and shapes his life:

"each man is the architect of his own fortune. I was the architect of mine, but I did not observe the necessary prudence, and as a result my presumptuousness has brought me to a sorry end. I should have reflected that Rocinante, weak as he is, could not withstand the Knight of the White Moon's powerful steed. In short, I was too daring; I did my best but I was overthrown. However, although I sacrificed my honor, I cannot be accused of failing to keep my word. When I was a knight-errant, valiant and bold, my deeds and the might of my arm supported my reputation, and now that I am an ordinary squire I will back up my word by keeping the promise I have given. Proceed, then, friend Sancho, and let us go to fulfill the year of our novitiate in our native province, for during that period of retirement we shall obtain fresh strength." (II, 66)

The adherence to the word of honor, the knight's sacred promise, is not just a hollow invocation of an outmoded chivalric code. It is evidence that Don Quixote must be an exemplar, in his actions, of the knowledge of who he is. To be the product of one's own works, the architect of one's own fortune, and to win identity in this way, means that it is up to us to invest our lives, to take an interest in them and to reap the profit therefrom. The claim that he is the maker of his fortune echoes the Counter-reformation debate over faith and good works; but in Cervantes' text it has more the ring of a challenge than of an admonition. Of the characters in the book, it is only Sancho who responds to the call. That money should be one of his motives is an appropriate enough sign of the value he places on the enterprise, and of the interest he takes in it. It does not mean that money will necessarily be enough to wake people up to their lives; the Knight of the Green Greatcoat is as well-off as any of the characters in the *Quixote*, but he has not sallied forth, he has not ventured and risked as Don Quixote and Sancho have. Likewise, simply dressing up as a knight-errant is no proof of a real investment in living; Sansón Carrasco can disguise himself as a knight, but he is not the product of his works in the way that Don Quixote is; the true investment in living is funded only by ethical commitment.

The economic metaphors which the *Quixote* suggests to explain personal identity highlight the ethical individualism which underlies Cervantes' evaluation of his characters. But I want to emphasize that these are metaphors primarily representative of value and worth, not wealth. In *The Rise of the Novel*, Ian Watt saw a more literal parallel between novelistic characterization and the socioeconomic conditions which prevailed during the period of the novel's rise in England. Watt identified economic individualism and the advent of capitalism together as factors central to the triumph of the genre. Particularly in Defoe—in Moll Flanders, in Roxana, in Captain Singleton, in Colonel Jacque, and above all in Robinson Crusoe—we have characters whose lives are directed by financial pursuits. Their ability to make their own lives is dependent on their ability to seek and determine their fortunes in the world. They are not bound to the static, feudal order of things; and they are virtually free from the limitations of family structures. They are thus able to accept the basic principles of capitalism—of investment, profit, and growth—and find in these principles the necessary resources to create their own lives. By its very nature, capitalism works a continuous transformation on its objects; it fiercely resists economic stasis; when the "objects" involved are novelistic characters and their world, it can provide conditions favorable to personal growth.

In certain ways, the socioeconomic circumstances of Spain at the height of her Golden Age match those which prevailed during the time of the rise of the novel in England. Cervantes wrote the *Quixote* in advance of the serious economic decline, at a time when the caste values of medieval Spain were being eroded by the ascendant values of class. Because of economic expansion in America and wars in Europe, a nation with a feudal economy was being pulled into capitalistic economic circumstances; caste life among Christians, Moors, and Jews, had become disrupted and grew intolerant because of the gradual advances, and now the effective dominance, of the Christians. Even before the *Quixote*, in the romances of chivalry on which Cervantes drew, there is a visible spirit of adventure which drives the heroes; and in actuality, from the first encounters with the New World—in the diaries of Columbus, for instance—there is an economic fire, a material acquisitiveness, which approximates those actual adventures to the fictional paradigms which Cervantes had in mind when writing the *Quixote*.

Yet Don Quixote purifies these motives; his spirit of adventure is not driven by dreams of wealth. In Cervantes' novel, the economic interest shows up more literally in Sancho than in Don Quixote. It is Sancho who forsakes his family, who seeks financial reward and economic independence; he is moved to follow Don Quixote by the promise of social gain, the governance of an island. In this regard, Sancho is more typical of later novelistic heroes than Don Quixote is. Certainly he is prototypical of the bourgeois class of readers who saw their own desires for financial and social independence mirrored in the novel. This is not to condemn Sancho; it is simply to say that the *Quixote* stands apart from the English novelistic tradition because the *hero* dissociates himself from such motives. Cervantes sees that the enterprising spirit may promote individual responsibility, as for Sancho; the desire for financial and social independence may instill a certain personal autonomy. But if Sancho embodies the bourgeois wish to be free of economic constraints and class limitations, then Don Quixote represents that wish fulfilled; he seeks to transcend, to go beyond the boredom which follows on the financial independence that characterizes his idle condition at the opening of the book. He leaves the relatively secure surroundings of his library to strike out in the world. His individualism is of an ethical sort, which means that it entails actions which transcend material circumstances or causes. Don Quixote is a character struck with the idea of self-knowledge and self-determination in an instinctual way; he knows who he is and he is able to determine his existence and his fortune apart from consid- erations of estate or class. If his identity is a function of the models he imitates, the roles he plays, then that must be taken as a sign of the nearly religious nature of his self-knowledge. His penitence in Sierra Morena, his self-imposed asceticism, the ritual of having himself dubbed a knight, are clues that his role-playing and heroism are matters of moral import; they cannot be limited to purely finan- cial concerns.

The natural danger for the man of bourgeois circumstances is that the same factors which prompt his aspirations to independence may prove liabilities and may compromise him ethically. Because of the way in which he takes his roles upon himself, because he transcends the given economic conditions of life, Don Quixote is free from those dangers. Again in this way, the *Quixote* distinguishes itself from the European novel of the eighteenth and nineteenth cen- turies and the moral dilemmas of the surrounding bourgeois culture. As Alasdair MacIntyre wrote in regard to Henry James (*The Portrait of a Lady*), Diderot (*Rameau's Nephew*), and Kierkegaard (*Either / Or*)

The unifying preoccupation of that tradition is the condition of those who see in the world nothing but a meeting place for individual wills, each with its own set of attitudes and preferences and who understand that world solely as an arena for the achievement of their own satisfaction, and who interpret reality as a series of opportunities for their enjoyment and for whom the last enemy is boredom . . . the problem of enjoyment arises in the context of leisure, in which large sums of money have created some social distance from the necessity of work.[15]

As a consequence of these material conditions, the economic indi- vidualism which may have prompted the first growth of the novel has become little more than moral emotivism, an attitude which takes the subjective self as the highest court of appeal in ethical decisions and in which the world is, as a consequence, a "meeting place for individual wills" rather than as a place for public agreement and dissent. Superficially, the scenario that MacIntyre describes might seem to match that of the *Quixote*. Cervantes' knight is in certain ways like Kierkegaard's "A," who is rich, or Rameau, who is a parasite on his patrons and clients. But Don Quixote's individualism is not limited to the possibilities or opportunities supplied by wealth or free time; and, as I have discussed, the general conditions of knowledge in the book are public and communal rather than private. Those romantic characters often lose their moral integrity and capacity for ethical choice because the leisured social and economic environment in which they flourish, which demands them to seek or protect personal status, mandates ethical and moral subjectivism to the disadvantage of ethical individualism. Unlike Don Quixote, they easily degenerate into what Kierkegaard called the aesthetic stage of life, forsaking altogether the responsibility of choosing right and wrong except as such decisions will foster their private comfort; Flaubert's Emma Bovary will offer such a case. As if in response to this tradition *avant la lettre*, Don Quixote fashions an identity for himself, wins his self, achieves his individuality, without forsaking moral choice; conversely, he is able to act ethically without sacrificing his personal autonomy. For these reasons, Cervantes' conception of personal identity as reflected in his hero offers an important window on larger moral problems, problems which are in the end far greater than the novelistic tradition itself.

The staunchly individualistic characters of that tradition, like the aesthetes MacIntyre describes, are not immoral or amoral characters, at least not ostensibly so. But they are likely to base their choices on the values set by the individual's subjective consciousness, apart from concern for the larger social good or even for the public (communal, political) contexts in which choice and action necessarily occur; their ethical lives are ruled by the vagaries of personal choice. They may take themselves to be the products of their own works, but they fail to place their "works" in any interpersonal, public sphere. Cervantes breaks the patterns of moral subjectivism into which ethical individualism can so easily degenerate because he bases the moral aspect of his hero's identity on the socially derived category of *role*. In this, Cervantes registers his greatest distance from Descartes. In the *Quixote*, the hero can play many roles and still not be compromised by the contradictions among them; roles are social structures through which the individual engages values responsibly, thus transcending purely subjective concerns. For Descartes, as for any thinker espousing a subject-centered understanding of personal identity, the very possibility of multiple roles is inconceivable. Indeed, the subject of the *Meditations*, the thinker committed to rigorous self-doubt, is bound to slough off all roles as inauthentic or self-deceptive; he seeks a stable point of personal identity, in order to define his personal essence (in Descartes's case on the basis of the *cogito*, of his status as a *res cogitans*) rather than in terms of social function. The private, isolated conditions in which the thought of the *Meditations* takes place are designed to insure such a monistic conception of personal identity.

Because we have, as a post-Enlightenment culture, largely forgotten what role-playing means and what value it has, we are surprised by the fact that Don Quixote shapes an identity of profound moral integrity through his imitations and that his role-playing in turn gives him a self-knowledge which lies beyond the claims or the caveats of rational thought. Contemporary philosophical and popular thinkers alike view role-playing with a substantial degree of circumspection. Role-playing rings of Sartrean "bad faith"; for sociologists (e.g., Goffman), the role dissolves the self; it offers no basis of moral support. Certainly, the vulgarized interpretations of Don Quixote in our century run directly counter to the sense of Cervantes' novel: they make Don Quixote a champion of selfhood *over and above* the self's roles, of "sincerity" over virtuous action. But all the evidence of the novel suggests that Don Quixote gains personal identity and value through the role, not the "self." One of the immediate advantages of Alasdair MacIntyre's *After Virtue* in this regard is that it revives the notion of role-playing in a positive moral sense, one which is able to account for personal identity as we see it in the *Quixote*. In what he rightly calls "heroic" societies

[70]

(which would be an apt description of the setting that Don Quixote imagines for himself), individual value is judged in conjunction with the values of a social group. The self is responsible, to itself and to the group interdependently, but is not the "center of a world" as a Cartesian subject is. Action is unmediated by self-consciousness and is spawned by the heroic virtues. As Don Quixote demonstrates in his valorous response to defeat by Sansón Carrasco, his principles of action are congruent with this way of being; he is bound to keep his word of honor even though there may be other possible paths of action which might gain him more immediate personal benefit or pleasure.

To consider the virtues that Don Quixote exhibits is to give a descriptive portrait of his identity and role. As a character, he is a focus for the engagement of an ethos, that of chivalric knighthood. What Don Quixote is and, moreover, *who* he is, depend on his practice of the virtues; these cannot remain abstract, theoretical paradigms or categories. Especially in the episodes where Cervantes shows Don Quixote in the foreground—where he fights the army of sheep, or attacks the "giants" (windmills)—Cervantes maps out the profiles of his character in terms of a code of traditional behavior. Don Quixote is courageous; he is a gentleman of honor, who keeps his promise; he is temperate; he is just; and he is the character defined by these virtues because he practices them, engages them, puts them into play. (*Pace* Iris Murdock, it is significant and enlightening to note that *moralis* in Latin, like *ethikos* in Greek, referred to a man's character, his disposition to lead a certain kind of life.) Don Quixote is virtuous, and unlike the lesser townspeople he is a "character" because he applies the moral knowledge inherent in the virtues. The minor figures in the book all have roles in the society—the Barber, the Curate, the Renaissance Gentleman of the Green Greatcoat, the Duke and the Duchess; each has a certain identifiable status. But none of them makes his role the focus of moral concern; none engages his social position ethically. Don Quixote strikes out to practice the virtues. Of him it could be said what Marx challenged in his eleventh thesis on Feuerbach, that he is not content simply to interpret the world; he knows that the time has come to change it, regardless of the fact that the project may be hopeless and thankless. Seen in this way, the *Quixote* raises serious doubts about the conventional notion that a novelistic character is someone who is unique and inimitable, someone who knows himself subjectively, as Descartes did. Self-knowledge and personal identity in Cervantes' novel at least are not founded on the fruits of a mind's project of pure enquiry but on the ethical and moral bases of character and role.

An awareness of the importance of role in the *Quixote* is a virtual requirement for understanding one of the novel's main themes: justice in the world. Justice, as Don Quixote practices it, is the product of his will to accommodate his actions to the heroic virtues, not to rational principles or subjective norms. With quixotic justice, as with all facets bearing on personal identity, Cervantes is well aware that what Don Quixote does is at odds with the state of the world as he finds it; this incongruity between Don Quixote and the world points up a refusal to allow reason to stand him over against the world, a reluctance to be placed in a position of detached judgment. To act heroically, to engage the virtue of justice, means for Don Quixote to *ignore* the difference between a transcendental point of view and the immediate situation or circumstances which call for action.

The problem of quixotic justice (that is to say, as exemplified in the *Quixote* and as carried on in the later novelistic tradition) has recently drawn attention from Alexander Welsh. In *Reflections on the Hero as Quixote*, he saw certain parallels between quixotic justice and the fundamentally Enlightenment conception of justice which runs through Hume, Mill, and Kant, and which is continued in the more recent work of H. L. A. Hart, John Rawls, and Robert Nozick.[16] But if what I have been saying about the bounds of reason in the *Quixote* is right, then there should be some important discrepancies between this tradition and the quixotic sense of justice. It is especially the sense of rationality underlying that tradition, which is wholly inimical to justice, the heroic virtue, as Don Quixote practices it.

[72]

The apparent similarity comes from Don Quixote's speech to the goatherds in Part I, chapter 11, where he gives his version of the origins of society. Holding a few acorns in his hand, Don Quixote expounds at length about the mythical "Golden Age," so called

"not because gold, which is so esteemed in this iron age of ours, was then to be had without toil, but because those who lived in that time did not know the meaning of the words 'thine' and 'mine.' In that blessed era all things were held in common . . . All then was peace; all was concord and friendship . . . Fraud, deceit, and malice had not yet come to mingle with truth and plain-seeking. Justice kept its own domain, where favor and self-interest dared not trespass, dared not impair her rights, becloud, and persecute her as they now do. There was no such thing then as arbitrary judgments, for the reason that there was no one to judge or to be judged."

But at some time in between this "Golden Age" and the present age of iron the order of knights-errant was instituted, according to Don Quixote, "'for the protection of damsels, the aid of widows and orphans, and the succoring of the needy.'" Don Quixote's idea of the Golden Age certainly sounds like the notion of a "state of nature" as Hume invoked it in A Treatise of Human Nature, a fictional moment at the very dawn of history, prior to the competing claims which a situation of limited goods or scarce resources will incite and which subsequently will erode the benevolence of men. And his conception of the age of knight-errantry as an intermediate moment certainly resembles the "original position" of society advanced by John Rawls in his influential A Theory of Justice (1971). What is significant to my argument are the ways in which they differ.

The "original position" in Rawls' theory is a fictional moment invoked in order to imagine the best possible social arrangements. It describes a time before anyone is aware of what procedures will be used to distribute their limited goods, hence a time when the members of society live behind what he calls a "veil of ignorance." The proponent of distributive justice wants to be able to apportion the limited goods of the world to the members of society fairly; and he especially wants to devise a procedure which will provide for this. In order to do so, he assumes that members of society in the original position are all equal and freely choosing, rational agents. And in order to insure that none is privileged over the others in making the first, procedural, choices, he imagines all behind a veil of ignorance, deprived of knowledge about the choices and personal histories of the others.

The question which may likely arise in connection with the idea of an "original position" is how society progressed from the state of nature to its present, "intermediate" position. This is not a problem for Rawls, because the "original position" is a heuristic device; and it has been recognized that the idea of the "veil of ignorance" is introduced by him because the idea of justice as modeled on the principle of rational choice, exemplified in a competitive bargaining game, is unprovable as a theorem.[17] In the *Quixote*, however, Don Quixote seems not to recognize the fact that the state of nature is a fiction, and he offers an explanation of how the present state of society has developed from it. His explanation is that the state of nature was corrupted, in large part, by the acquisitiveness signaled by the possessive words "mine" and "thine." Faced with society in its present state, Don Quixote abandons the assumptions operating in the fictive "original position." He has no concern to imagine the equality of all members of society (his world is sharply divided into good- and evil-doers), and he has less interest still in the matter of just procedure. The idea of the original state and the veil of ignorance together are motivated by a deep awareness of the "costs" of justice, which is to say by an awareness that every act of justice may require the readjustment of claims, counterclaims, and future expectations on all sides. But as the encounter of Don Quixote and the punished servant-boy Andrés—the next case I want to consider—shows, Don Quixote has little or no concern for these costs.

To approximate quixotic justice to the tradition which is exemplified by Rawls, as Alexander Welsh has done, is questionable because it ignores the discrepancies between Don Quixote's nature as a moral agent—a nature which I have described as founded on his personal identity and social *role*—and the rational basis of choice and action which that tradition entails. That basis has its roots in Descartes, in his conception of mind; but it reaches its peak in the philosophy of Kant. (There are close ties between Rawls' theory of justice and Kantian moral philosophy—a relationship which Rawls acknowledges.) In Don Quixote's will to act in accordance with his role, he may seem to behave as a Kantian agent, guided by a morality of austere command; but his actions are less consistently "principled" in any rational way, more subject to arbitration by "quixotic" caprice or velleity—what he calls faithfulness to the virtues of knight-errantry. There is, in the end, something terribly un-Kantian about the quixotic sense of justice and, vice-versa, something wholly unquixotic about rational, Kantian choice. In *The Foundation of the Metaphysics of Morals*, Kant said that he wanted to make every action accord with transcendental moral principles, to act in such a way that everything he might do would conform to the rationally unimpeachable norms he called "maxims." But in order to do so, one must have the ability to judge situations from a coolly critical perspective, to go beyond the point at which sensibility is a limitation on the understanding. What the *Quixote* shows, if anything, is the *untenability* of such a perspective.

To qualify as an agent in a model of distributive justice, one must be free to choose and one must have the rational ability to judge situations with the pure mind, from the position of the sovereign subject. As Alasdair MacIntyre explained, "to be a moral agent is, on this view, precisely to be able to stand back from any and every situation in which one is involved, from any and every characteristic that one may possess, and to pass judgment on it from a purely universal and abstract point of view that is totally detached from all social particularity" (*After Virtue*, p. 30). This is exactly what Don Quixote does *not* do. Never does he act or judge circumstances apart from his *role* as knight-errant. And this role, because it is a viable and valuable way of engaging his individuality, is wholly determined by society and culture. These are the factors which support his campaign for justice in the world, not reason or judgment in the Kantian sense. At this point, it may be apparent that a rejection of the notion of criteria as abstract entities, to be compared to our mental "states" and to the world, in favor of the idea of our dealing with the world as a practice or usage, as I discussed earlier, would naturally support the foundation of justice on the basis of role rather than on the grounds of reason: the words of a language, and the criteria which inhere in them, are themselves determined as "playing a role."

One of the troubling consequences of an ethics like Kant's is that the reliance on the subject's powers of rational judgment elevates the categories of right and wrong to normative status. Right and wrong, as the basis for the maxims of action, become absolutes and in effect supplant the categories of good and evil. As Charles Fried, a recent thinker in this line, wrote, "the norms which express deontological judgments—for example, Do not commit murder—may be said to be absolute. They do not say: 'Avoid lying, other things being equal' but 'Do not lie, period.'"[18] A sense of justice based on normative right and wrong in effect enforces a cleavage of deontology and teleology, because the categories of good and evil are taken to be too distant and abstract to be engaged in human conduct. Don Quixote's encounter with the servant boy Andrés in Part I, chapter 4, all but lays bare this difficulty. Seeing the punished boy, Don Quixote immediately charges his master to pay the back wages owed him. Don Quixote does not stop to consider that what is right and wrong in this case may differ from what is good and evil in general, much less look at the social costs of his actions. Right and wrong are not cleft from good and evil in Don Quixote's world. His project is to ignore that distinction, to collapse right and wrong with good and evil—to make every state-of-the-world an end-state, and to revive the kingdom of ends, the age of knight-errantry, in the present state.

There are understandable reasons why one might today see Don Quixote's actions as the epitome of Kantianism, rather than as opposed to all that it implies. Certainly, Don Quixote is as inimical to compromise as the Kantian moral agent, as reluctant to add the tag "all things being equal" to the admonition or principle (the "maxim") "Do not lie." But Don Quixote is not worried about moving from the specific case to the general, from the injustices done to servant boys to some conclusion about how we should act toward them, or about how master-servant relationships should be arranged or abolished. He has no such need; those "principles" are inherent in his role. What he does to win his personal identity is to engage them, to channel them into virtuous action as knight-errant.

This is not to say that Don Quixote's sense of justice is problem-free or that Cervantes thinks it might ever successfully be established in the world. There is a coda to the episode with Andrés which illustrates forcefully, and painfully, otherwise: after Don Quixote leaves the boy and his master, taking the master's promise of mercy at face value, the boy is punished again, and more severely. But in this respect, quixotic justice is no different from any other aspect of the novel. The world teaches hard lessons (e.g., that justice has costs) and is often better off, imperfect as it may be, *without* Don Quixote's intervention. We live in an age which is not the state of nature; our society is no longer in its "original position." There are competing claims to be adjudicated, compromises which must be made. We live in a state which is not so much beyond as *after* good and evil. But where the rationalist tradition would substitute normative right and wrong for those terms, Don Quixote is blind to the reasons for so doing. One might contrast him to Nietzsche's equally unrational moral agent: Don Quixote exists in a world not "beyond good and evil" but *before* their severance from right and wrong. Conceived from any rational point of view, his work of justice is bound to seem absurd.

II.
DOSTOEVSKY

THE CONTRADICTIONS OF SKEPTICISM: EXISTENCE AND EXECUTION

> "every man on earth was under the sentence of death"
> —Camus, *The Stranger*

IN MY DISCUSSION of personal identity in the *Quixote*, I said that self-knowledge in Cervantes' novel is not established by a project of pure inquiry, in the way that Descartes sought, but by the engagement of values through the hero's role as knight-errant. Cartesian epistemology and, later, British philosophical psychology, placed the subject as the privileged knowing agent, and Don Quixote resists this understanding of the self; the winning of personal identity requires an ethos that is not submissible to the bounds set by human reason; this is why, I argued, self-knowledge in the *Quixote* is not an epistemological affair. In these pages, I want to extend my discussion of personal identity to Dostoevsky's *The Idiot* and to texts directly influenced by it (Kafka's *The Trial* and Camus's *The Stranger*) and to mark their relationship to the pattern set by *Don Quixote*. What I expect will emerge is this: that while in Cervantes' novel we can say that personal identity depends more on bodily than on mental factors, this is not so in *The Idiot*. The reason is not that Dostoevsky's characters are any less finite than Cervantes', or sense the conditions of their embodiment with any less force, but because the question of the self's identity is sparked by the problems and contradictions which ensue from its nature as a self-aware, thinking thing; the point of contact with Cervantes emerges in the way these contradictions find resolution outside the bounds of reason and prompt foolishly ethical actions.

Thinkers earlier in this century—Lukács in *The Theory of the Novel*, for example—saw the *Quixote* as exemplary of the hero's personal identity in the novel, but gave a different accounting of it

[81]

than the one I have been proposing. Lukács saw the novelistic character as one whose redoubtable inwardness is, tragically or comically, incommensurate to the world about it. The troublesome word in this description is, of course, "inwardness" (*Innerlichkeit*), which seems to posit a subjective consciousness for the novelistic character and for that reason appears inapplicable to Don Quixote. As my discussion of *The Idiot* I hope will make clear, the difficulty with Lukács's terminology can be traced to his adoption of some of Kierkegaard's ideas, which were prominent in his thinking as he wrote *The Theory of the Novel*. What Kierkegaard meant by subjectivity is the appropriation of wisdom, the process of edifying oneself in the light of what one knows. Yet what Lukács says in *The Theory of the Novel* about the hero's "inner certainty and the world's inadequate attitude toward it" (p. 110) fits as a description of the "quixotic" strain in Dostoevsky quite well. His characters do have the kind of consciousness that such self-certainty presupposes, and they find themselves repulsed by the world; consider Prince Myshkin, who is a near saint, the embodiment of the idea of a "beautiful soul" thrown into a world that is stubborn, vile, base—supremely real.

The appropriate starting point for a discussion of personal identity in Dostoevsky, whose characters are so clearly self-aware, is not Descartes or Locke, but the German tradition of Fichte, Schopenhauer, and Hegel. In the *Phenomenology of Spirit*, Hegel characterized a particular stage of consciousness which I think describes the basic predicament from which Dostoevskian characters achieve self-knowledge. He called this stage Skepticism, and explained it is a moment of self-consciousness in which the self is aware that it is a thinking thing ("A consciousness which, as the infinitude of consciousness or as its present moment, is aware of itself as essential being, a being which *thinks* or is a free self-consciousness"[1]) and has confronted the world outside it as a freely acting, independent consciousness. This consciousness seeks to preserve its independence, its freedom, *itself*, and is thus led to deny the world and its relationship to it: "What Skepticism causes to vanish is not only objective reality as such, but its own relationship to it" (p. 124). But this denial, conceived to maintain the independence of self-consciousness and thought from the world, entails serious contradictions, and these ultimately lead to the abandonment of skepticism. As Hegel describes, these contradictions are of two general types. First, this Skeptical moment is self-contradictory in whatever pronouncements or determinations it may make ("It pronounces an absolute vanishing, but the pronouncement is, and this consciousness is the vanishing that is pronounced. It affirms the nullity of seeing, hearing, etc., yet is itself seeing, hearing, etc. It affirms the nullity of ethical principles, and lets itself be governed by these very principles," p. 125). Second, it is indeterminate and vacillating. In order to preserve its independence, it refuses to admit the decidability of questions, and maintains only that it cannot know:

Point out likeness or identity to it, and it will point out unlikeness or nonidentity; and when it is now confronted with what it has just asserted, it turns round and points out likeness or identity. Its talk is in fact like the squabbling of self-willed children, one of whom says A if the other says B, and in turn says B if the other says A, and who by contradicting *themselves* buy for themselves the pleasure of continually contradicting one another. (pp. 125–26)

The advantage of *The Phenomenology of the Spirit* to explain self-knowledge in *The Idiot*, over Fichte for example, or Schopenhauer's *The World as Will and Representation*, which probably show more superficial affinities with Dostoevsky's text, is that Hegel recognizes these contradictions explicitly.[2] He lets us see, as I think Dostoevsky does, that there may be serious difficulties with the notion of self-identity as pure idea (e.g., as the Fichtean "I-am-I," which Kierkegaard mockingly called a "rendezvous in the clouds"[3]), or as given by the "empty" will (as for Schopenhauer) of which the world is the "idea" or representation (*Vorstellung*). In Dostoevsky, the will and the "idea" constitute one term (but one term only) of a more englobing and recurrent dialectic: Raskolnikov, for instance, spends hours in thought and reflection on his crime, but his dilemma stems from the conflict of his idea of the crime with the crime itself, which has visible effects in the world; the Karamazov brothers, to take another example, can discuss the problem of evil in the world, but they are implicated in the murder of their father, and Dimitri is arrested for the crime. In these and other cases, a character's self-identity is given crucial determination by the friction between its idea of itself and its actual displacement in the world.

Hegel recognizes the contradictions of an independent self-consciousness which, in its skepticism, denies the world; he expects that a thinking thing will recognize those contradictions for itself and seek their resolution. In Hegel's plan, this resolution is part of the progression of consciousness toward Absolute Knowing, toward Reason knowing itself as such—a moment of consciousness which he calls Spirit. This, however, is where Dostoevsky's likeness to Hegel ends. As Dostoevsky's individuals relinquish their contradictory modes of consciousness, they direct their concerns away from rational knowing and seek, sometimes to achieve, self-illumination. They become less concerned for the preservation of freedom and the independence of thought from the world and seek instead to be edified in their human circumstances and mortal condition; they find that *knowing* who one is requires *being* who one is, or as Nietzsche put it in the subtitle to *Ecce Homo*, "becoming" who one is. Dostoevsky's characters figuratively learn to incorporate Kierkegaard's critique of Hegel into their lives (Kierkegaard wrote that "Hegelian philosophy, by failing to define its relationship to the existing individual, and by ignoring the ethical, confounds existence"[4]). They are guided by what Kierkegaard meant in the *Concluding Unscientific Postscript* by the easily misunderstood phrase "truth is subjectivity"—the source for Lukács's notion of Don Quixote's "inwardness"—a personal appropriation of whatever they may come to learn.[5] As Kierkegaard described it, and as I think the examples from *The Idiot* which I will discuss show, this kind of "subjectivity" is not achieved by the submergence of consciousness into itself, but by a process best called "alienation," in effect by tearing the self away from its subjective self-images, allowing the self to be open to public anxiety and ridicule. As I want now to discuss in greater detail, it is this Kierkegaardian-like response to the contradictions of skepticism which best describes Dostoevsky's perspective on personal identity.

The contradictions of skepticism, and the transition from this freedom of self-consciousness to authentic self-knowledge, are marked on several prominent occasions in *The Idiot*: in the Prince's accounts of the execution that Dr. Schneider took him to see at Lyons about a month before his return to Russia at the opening of the narrative, in the intervening account of the case of a reprieved prisoner, and in Ippolit's threats of suicide, which he never manages to bring off. The Prince's first retelling of the execution at Lyons, in the presence of the Yepanchin's footman, is typical of the significant content of these events. The Prince is morally aghast at what he calls "murder by legal process," and "an outrage on the soul,"[6] as we might well expect. But he is less struck by the torture, or the spectacle, than by the fact that execution renders death an absolute certainty. What he finds harrowing is the condemned man's *knowledge* of the fact that he will die:

"take, for instance, torture: you get suffering, wounds, bodily agony, all of which distracts the mind from mental suffering, for up to the very moment of your death you are only tormented by your wounds. Yet the chief and the worst pain is perhaps not inflicted by wounds, but by your certain knowledge that in an hour, in ten minutes, in half a minute, now, this moment your soul will fly out of your body, and that you will be a human being no longer, and that that's certain—the main thing is that it is *certain*." (I, 2; p.47)

"here you have been sentenced to death, and the whole terrible agony lies in the fact that you will most certainly not escape, and there is no greater agony than that. Take a soldier and put him in front of a cannon in battle and fire at him and he will still hope, but read the same soldier his death sentence *for certain*; and he will go mad or burst out crying." (pp. 47–48)

As he recognizes that he will die ("for certain"), the condemned man achieves personal illumination, a complete and lucid recognition of his condition ("his face is as white as paper, the priest is holding up the cross, the man greedily puts out his blue lips and looks and—*knows everything* [sic]," I, 5; p. 93). My claim about what happens here is twofold: first, that the condemned man passes from a state of conscious self-awareness to a state of self-knowledge; and second, that this dramatic change is prompted by the contradictions of skepticism.

In *Reflections on the Hero as Quixote*, Alexander Welsh discussed these near-death episodes and said that they reveal the question of existence to be more fundamental than the question of identity: "In *The Idiot*, 'Am I?' is an even more basic question than 'Who am I?'"[7] But it is difficult to see how the question of personal identity might *not* be preceded by the question of existence. What we need to know is why the question of existence necessarily entails the question of identity, why a free-consciousness, aware of itself and able to deny the world or its relationship to it (thus able to raise the question of existence in the first place) *must* incite the question of personal identity. Welsh expresses something that is so readily assumed about these accounts of execution and near-death in *The Idiot*, though, that I want to follow his line of argument further in order to see the contradictions it entails.

It is easy to take these accounts as confirmations of existence through the confrontation with death ("If you want to feel alive, try being led before a firing squad. Characters in Dostoevsky are regularly tempted to confirm their existence by contemplating the passage between life and death," Welsh, p. 204)—as if the condemned man were *shocked* into the knowledge that he is mortal. The difficulties with this interpretation are various. We know that if the executed man achieves some significant knowledge at the moment he approaches death, then he must learn something that he did not know beforehand. If we say that he comes to know what he does because he is shocked into it, then we mean that his knowledge is the result of the change in his position, i.e., that before he faced death he was not in a position to know his mortality. This is a plausible explanation, although not, I think, the correct one. If we mean to say that by the change in his position he learns something that he could not have known beforehand, then the claim is clearly false: the condemned man did in fact know that he was going to die, and was told so explicitly—that was the point of sentencing him. If we think that he did not know his mortality until he was in a position to know it, moreover, then the Prince's account would have limited sense for his audience in the novel and for us as readers, for we are all in the position of the man before he was led to the gallows. If neither we nor his fictive audience is in a position to

[86]

know what the condemned man learns, then the Prince's account can only have the force of a threat or a warning, rather than express a possibility for living. An answer which I think is better suited to the sense of these accounts is this: if the prisoner comes to know something as he approaches the gallows, it is of course true that he did not know it beforehand, but not because he could not know it—rather, because he must have doubted it. The implication is that the position he is in before he faces death, just as the position we ordinarily find ourselves in, is one of skepticism: knowing (i.e., informed, or with strong reasons to suspect) that we will die, yet living effectively in doubt of it, or at any rate not awake to it.

This sounds like a rather complex argument to show that a conscious being, thinking about death, is normally skeptical, but it is supported rather strongly, and rather directly, by Dostoevsky's text. As the Prince remarks to the female members of the Yepanchin household on the occasion of his second account of the execution, the prisoner himself showed all the conventional signs of skeptical doubt:

He has been in prison, waiting for his execution for a week at least; he had been counting on the usual red-tape, on the paper with his sentence having to be forwarded somewhere and coming back only after a week . . . But for some reason the procedure was cut short. He began arguing that the paper with his sentence would not be ready for a week . . . I cannot help thinking that while he was being driven through the town he must have thought on the way, "I've still a long, long time; there are still three streets more to live. As soon as I pass through this, there will be that one, and then that one with the bakery on the right—oh, it'll be ages before we get to the bakery!" (p. 91)

Why is it, then, that he finally comes to recognize the fact of his mortality? What allows him to come to such self-knowledge before the axe falls? Hegel's answer is that skepticism is abandoned because of the contradictions which plague it. Consider the case of the prisoner on his way to the execution block, doubting the fact that he will ever get there. His ability to doubt the fact that he will die may well be stronger than any proof we could offer to the contrary; one can tell him, and can show him the overwhelming statistical evidence, but there is no a priori logic which could prove his death as a (logical) necessity; he will ask us to show him just why it must be certain that he will die, and we find that we cannot. The Prince himself seems obsessed with the idea of determining the certainty of death; indeed, he seems almost to crave this knowledge:

> to think that he [the condemned man] goes on to the last fraction of a second when his head already lies on the block and he waits, and he—*knows*, and suddenly he hears the iron come slithering down over his head! He must certainly hear that! If I were lying there, I'd listen for it on purpose and I'd hear it. There is only perhaps one tenth of a second left, but one would certainly hear it. (pp. 92–93)

Dostoevsky is leading up to the conclusion that the only logical proof of death is one that is absurd, for the only time when the condemned man's death is absolutely certain (certain in the sense that it could be logically or empirically determined) is after he is dead, and this knowledge would be completely hollow, of no use to the person making the claim and of no force against a skeptic on the way to his death: "imagine, there are still some people who maintain that when the head is cut off, it knows for a second perhaps that it has been cut off—what a thought! And what if it knows it for five seconds?'" (p. 93).

As the Prince blends his thoughts with those of the condemned man on the way to the execution block, he brings to light contradictions which resemble the ones that Hegel described—an independent self-consciousness which is led to deny the reality external to it and to deny its relationship to that reality (the world which ultimately constrains his thoughts, which determines the conditions of death, for instance). The skeptic's actions and his thoughts are contradictory, moreover, because only an absurd proof could give him the knowledge that he seeks. In this sense, the near-death encounter offers no direct solution whatsoever to the condemned man's skepticism; in fact, the Prince recounts another episode which could be taken as further fuel for the skeptic's position. The two mentions of the execution at Lyons are punctuated by his recollection of the case of a reprieved prisoner, an episode which Dostoevsky based on personal experience: "'He [the prisoner] was to be shot for a political crime. Twenty minutes later his reprieve was read out to him, another penalty being substituted. Yet the interval between the two sentences—twenty minutes or, at least, a quarter of an hour—he passed with the absolute certainty that in a few minutes he would be dead," p. 86). My claim is not that the near-death experience shocks the man out of his skepticism (for then what would we say to him in the case of a reprieve?); it is that his denial of impending death—his skepticism—is contradictory and, finally, untenable.

In Hegel's scheme of things, the independent self-consciousness, seeking to preserve its freedom, resolves contradictions as a part of the general workings of the rational Spirit; this is a process of reflection and sublimation. But *The Idiot* suggests that the contradictions of skepticism cannot be resolved by reflection, and that no tour de force of reasoning can work the skeptic out of his predicament, for his predicament was itself due, in good measure, to rational reflection. Instead, *The Idiot* turns the question of existence into a question of self-identity, posing a rather different question, and suggesting a new mode of knowledge to satisfy it. *Knowing that* one is becomes a matter of *being who* one is, and that is not validated by an appeal to reason or by reflective meditation. As the case of the man executed at Lyons shows, this knowledge requires "alienation," not reflection, the ability to see oneself from without, as foolish, or ridiculous; given the public aspect of the execution, the condemned man sees himself as the world sees him:

The next three or four hours were spent on the usual things: the priest, the breakfast at which he was given wine, coffee, and boiled beef. (Isn't that a mockery? Just think how cruel it is, and yet, on the other hand, these innocent people do it out of pure kindness of heart and convinced that it's an act of humanity.) Then he was dressed for the execution (do you know what the dressing of a condemned criminal is like?), and at last they took him through the town to the scaffold. . . . All round him there were crowds of people yelling, shouting, ten thousand faces, ten thousand eyes—and all this had to be endured, and worst of all, the thought: "There are ten thousand of them, and none of them is going to be executed, but I am going to be executed!" (p. 91)

[89]

The impasse of rational knowing, and the distinction between having information about human finitude and realizing our own mortality, which underlies this "alienation," are among Kierkegaard's major themes in the *Concluding Unscientific Postscript*. He points out how immensely difficult it is to give sense to the statement that we "know" that we will die:

I know concerning this what people in general know about it; I know that I shall die if I take a dose of sulphuric acid, and also if I drown myself, or go to sleep in an atmosphere of coal gas, and so forth. . . . I know that death may result from so ridiculous and trivial a circumstance that even the most serious-minded of men cannot help laughing at death; I know that it is possible to escape what appears to be certain death, and so forth.

—all or most of which a skeptic might also say. "Nonetheless, in spite of this almost extraordinary knowledge or facility in knowledge, I can by no means regard death as something I have understood" (pp. 147–48). The answer that Kierkegaard gives, which I think fits *The Idiot,* is that we must learn to change the basis of our relationship to the fact of our death (as to all the other really important questions Kierkegaard raises, such as "What does it mean to get married?" or "What does it mean to thank God for the good He bestows upon me?" or "What does it mean to be immortal?"). When the independent consciousness considers death "in general," it fails to consider what the individual's death might mean to him, which is a fault similar to the one Hegel described as the skeptic's denial of his *relationship* to reality ("For a man in general, for an absent-minded individual like Soldin or a systematic philosopher, to think death in general is indeed no act or deed; it is only something in general," *Postscript,* p. 151). But the individual must attend to the meaning of death, of his death, not to the *idea* of death (this is what Kierkegaard means by becoming "subjective"). He must place himself in relationship to death itself, to "think death," and not simply *about* death: "If the task of life is to become subjective, then the thought of death is not, for the individual subject, something in general, but is verily a deed." This means incorporating our awareness of death into life, not simply to know it as a bit of information, but to become awakened to it.

The difference between a knowledge of human mortality and an awakening to it is a prominent theme of the Prince's accounts of near-death and execution in *The Idiot*, and it is this awakening to death which allows the condemned prisoners to achieve deep self-knowledge. The Prince underscores the personal illumination, the intense self-awareness of these moments; the knowledge of the human condition is complete and it is lucid. In this context, the condemned man finally comes to abrogate his skepticism ("His head, his face is as white as paper, the priest is holding up the cross, the man greedily puts out his blue lips and looks and—*knows everything*," p. 93). What the Prince is speaking of is a total enlightenment, an absolute lucidity, which reflects on the mortal condition. In the case of the reprieved man, for instance,

He remembered everything with the most extraordinary distinctness, and he used to say that he would never forget anything he had been through during those minutes. . . . He told me that those five minutes were like an eternity to him, riches beyond the dream of avarice; he felt that during those five minutes he would live through so many lives that it was quite unnecessary for him to think of the last moment. (pp. 86–87)

It makes no difference, for the knowledge which he gains, that his death is allayed. It is not that the prisoner is convinced that he will die, or that he takes the brush with death as a warning; there is nothing of the *memento mori* in the Prince's accounts. Rather, the reprieved man is awakened to the meaning of his life: "What if I had not had to die! What if I could return to life—oh, what an eternity! And all that would be mine! I should turn every minute into an age, I should lose nothing. I should count every minute separately and waste none!'" (pp. 87–88).

The importance of this relationship between the knowledge of death and the meaning of life for the condemned man's self-knowledge could be put this way: the condemned man does not so much "know" that he will die as he is awakened to life, and this in turn illuminates him: "'He remembered staring with awful intensity at that roof and the sunbeams flashing from it; he could not tear his eyes off those rays of light: those rays seemed to him to be his new nature, and he felt that in three minutes he would somehow merge

[91]

with them'" (p. 87). At the second retelling of the Lyons execution, the Prince is struck by the resemblance of a painting he saw
at Basel to the condemned man's face at the moment before
execution:

"Just now when you asked me for a subject for a picture it occurred to me
to tell you to paint the face of a condemned man a minute before the fall of
the guillotine blade, when he is still standing on the scaffold and before
he lies down on the plank" . . . "It's exactly one minute before death," the
prince began quite readily, carried away by his memories and apparently
forgetting everything else in an instant—"the moment he has mounted
the ladder and stepped on the scaffold. Just then he glanced in my direction. I looked at his face and understood everything. But how am I to tell
you about it?" (pp. 90–91)

It is said by philosophy, and the Prince repeats it, that at the
moment of death body and soul split apart ("'this moment your soul
will fly out of your body, and that you will be a human being no
longer,'" p. 47). If that is so, then it is as if this face were a
transparent window on the soul at the moment of death, as if the
body were no longer capable of concealment. The picture the
Prince is thinking of, he tells Adelaida, must render the expression
of someone who, at one moment, has gathered his entire life before
him, someone who has made his existence present to him, and
himself to it: "'you see, you must show everything that happened
before—everything, everything. He has been in prison, waiting for
his execution for a week at least,'" (p. 91).

The awakening of which the Prince tells is strikingly similar to
his own experience during the epileptic fits that he occasionally
suffers,

an intense heightening of awareness—if this condition had to be expressed in one word—of awareness and at the same time of the most direct
sensation of one's own existence to the most intense degree. If in that
second—that is to say, at the last conscious moment before the fit—he
had time to say to himself, consciously and clearly, "Yes, I could give my
whole life for this moment," then this moment by itself was, of course,
worth the whole of life. (II, 5; p. 259)

The Prince's remarks are not meant as an encouragement to seek out the mystical or irrational ("he did not insist on the dialectical part of his argument: stupor, darkness, idiocy stood before him as the plain consequences of those 'highest moments.' Seriously, of course, he would not have argued the point. There was, no doubt, some flaw in his argument—that is, in his appraisal of that minute—but the reality of the sensation troubled him all the same"). His comments are a general guide to our estimation of the moments of intense self-knowledge which the condemned prisoners also experience. The value of his knowledge lies not in the experience itself, but in the willingness for it, or openness to it, for which we must provide in our lives. The task is then to live a life which might be worth trading for such a moment of self-illumination, which is to say, a life destined for self-knowledge, becoming who we are.

The Prince's comments also explain why our knowledge of the fact that we are, as Heidegger says, headed "towards death" ought not to be taken as ground to conclude that life is absurd and suicide justifiable. Dostoevsky gives the counterexample of the figure of Ippolit, whose suicide attempt fails miserably. One of the group at the Yepanchin's, Keller, notices something flash in Ippolit's hand, "and at the same moment saw a little pocket pistol was close to his temple. Keller rushed to seize his hand, but at that very moment Ippolit pulled the trigger. There was the sound of a sharp metallic click, but no report followed. . . . They had all heard the click of the trigger and saw a man who was alive, not even scratched" (III, 7; pp. 457–58). The circumstances of his case are particularly ironic, because his doctors have diagnosed him as terminally ill and with only a short time to live ("'today is the last time I shall be out in the air among people, and in a fortnight I shall most certainly be under the ground,'" he says at the Yepanchin's, II, 9; p. 322). Ippolit takes the diagnosis of his illness and the news of his imminent death as a piece of information, as telling something special about him, when the fact of human mortality is commonplace and unremarkable; for this reason, the knowledge does nothing to reveal what is unique about him, nothing to help him gain self-knowledge or personal illumination. The example is a foil to any argument that would claim that the imminent approach of death will, in itself, shock us into the sense of the fact that we exist; Dostoevsky shows that people may know that they will die and still be dead to their lives; what is required beyond the knowledge is an openness to it, a willingness for the anxiety of knowing who we are.

What the suicide wants from his act is the preservation of his freedom and a confirmation of his capacity for action ("suicide is perhaps the only thing I have still time to begin and end of my own free will. Well, perhaps I want the last possibility of *action*. A protest is sometimes no small matter," III, 7; pp. 453–54), yet he must deny the endurance of the world beyond him. We may in fact be fated to last in the world for longer than we bargained, but what it means to be awake to our identity as mortal beings in the world is to realize that the world into which we are "thrown" (Heidegger's phrase) is not the product of our will, and that we must therefore relinquish our claims on it (cf. Ippolit's comments: "'I still possess the power to die, though the days I give back are numbered. I'm afraid it is no great power; it is no great rebellion either,'" p. 453). As one commentator on Hegel's *Phenomenology of the Spirit* said, a major difficulty with the Skeptical moment of consciousness is that "Genuine freedom is too hard to take; it involves self-reliance and responsibility—for a world!"[8] Where both the executed man and the reprieved prisoner in *The Idiot* can lay claim to their existence and to a world (to their world), the suicide cannot. The suicidal approach to death begets a nihilistic approach to life and substitutes false freedom and responsibility for the authentic values. What Ippolit does not learn is what Kierkegaard called the "secret of life, that everyone must sew for himself."[9]

All this is not to say that the abandonment of Skepticism on account of its contradictions will resolve the incongruities of the world. It means instead that we will take action in the face of paradox, and engage in what Kierkegaard calls the "teleological suspension of the ethical"—an abrogation of the ethics that reason teaches. This may indeed mean that we will appear foolish in the eyes of the world, but anything less than these "authentic movements of faith" would be doubt and not conviction, which is to say, skepticism. Kierkegaard's example of foolish faithfulness, which he takes up at length in *Fear and Trembling*, is Abraham: "Abraham believed and did not doubt, he believed in the preposterous" (p. 35); the story is implicitly recalled in the Prince's account of the reprieved prisoner.

The Biblical story of Abraham and Isaac is, on Kierkegaard's account, an illustration of the bounds of reason and a demonstration of faith, which begins "precisely where thinking leaves off" (p. 64). It asks us to see that faith and philosophy are of different orders ("Philosophy cannot and should not give faith, but it should understand itself and know what it has to offer and take away nothing," p. 44). The story is an example of the exercise of freedom in the face of paradox. Like Dostoevsky's reprieved prisoner, Abraham only finds out that his worst expectations are not borne out *after* he is convinced that his actions will have mortal consequences. The point of the story, and of Dostoevsky's and Kierkegaard's texts, is that we must learn to act in the awareness that our death is not for us to arbitrate, even though our lives must be for us to lose. We must be willing to act as foolish Abrahams, "to let our actions go out of our hands" (cf. Don Quixote), to be open for the anxiety this entails. Like Abraham at the instant of the Lord's reprieve, the condemned man who is brought to recognize his mortality is able to claim his life as his own, even if he is not instrumentally responsible for his death. The independence which he achieves is a personal autonomy, a freedom from the support of false confidences in life.

In the passages of The Idiot which I have been discussing, Dostoevsky was profoundly influenced by Victor Hugo's Le Dernier jour d'un condamné (1829). But the insights into the nexus of human mortality and self-knowledge which have become the prominent subjects of later fiction are those which Dostoevsky developed. The fiction of Kafka and Camus, which I want to consider briefly here, deals with the link between the fact of our death and our knowledge of it; as in Dostoevsky, this relationship turns out to be crucial in determining personal identity. The Dostoevskian influence is nearly explicit in The Trial and The Stranger, and those texts confirm the formulation of topics I have so far given in connection with The Idiot. One might well describe Kafka's chalky, anonymous characters in terms of neurosis and paranoia, their maladjustment to the world as a product of the world's bizarreness or inhospitality to them. But their "alienation" is not only psychological; it is, in a Kierkegaardian sense, at the root of a process by which they win personal identity. The major difference between Dostoevsky, Kierkegaard, and the more modern authors, though—as Kafka illustrates so well—is that foolish actions are no longer guided by a faith in transcendental reality; as we will see in *The Stranger,* Camus finds it especially difficult to give sense to questions about the meaning of eternal life.

Kafka's parable "Abraham" evokes Kierkegaard and Don Quixote, but his several Abrahams are ridiculous creatures. One of them finds it inconceivable to abrogate logic by a leap of faith ("If he had done everything, and yet was to be raised still higher, then something had to be taken away from him, at least in appearance: this would be logical and no leap"[10]). Another of his Abrahams is likened to a waiter, prompt in his service ("One who wanted to perform the sacrifice altogether in the right way and had a correct sense in general of the whole affair") but who is unable to believe that *he* was the one summoned by the Lord ("he, an ugly old man, and the dirty youngster that was his child"). What this Abraham fears is that he will appear ridiculous to himself, that on the way to Mount Moriah he will see himself as Don Quixote and not as Abraham, and that he will mock himself ("He is afraid that after starting out as Abraham with his son he could change on the way into Don Quixote. The world would have been enraged at Abraham could it have beheld him at the time, but this one is afraid that the world would laugh itself to death at the sight of him. However, it is not the ridiculousness as such that he is afraid of—though he is, of course—afraid of that too and, above all, of his joining in the laughter—but in the main he is afraid that this ridiculousness will make him even older and uglier," pp. 44–45).

Alexander Welsh took this parable as an example of practical joking. The observation is incisive, but I would underscore the point of the joke and what it teaches: that we must be willing for the world to witness us in all our foolishness, willing for ridicule and anxiety.

It is as if, at the end of the year, when the best student was solemnly about to receive a prize, the worst student rose in the expectant stillness and came forward from his dirty desk in the last row because he had made a mistake in hearing, and the whole class burst out laughing. And perhaps he had made no mistake at all, his name really was called, it having been the teacher's intention to make the rewarding of the best student at the same time a punishment for the worst one. (p. 45)

Despite the vast difference in tone, Kafka's version of the Abraham story is congruent with Kierkegaard's. Kafka's Abraham suffers ridicule at the hands of the world, which is what Kierkegaard meant to say was involved in the process of winning personal identity; this suffering is the source of the anxiety and "alienation" by which the self is won.

In *The Trial*, the Kierkegaardian bias is strongly colored by reminiscences of Dostoevsky. The fate of Joseph K., which culminates in his execution in the final pages of the book, follows a form that is familiar from *The Idiot*. K. is convicted and is submitted to the ordeals of a "logical" inquest, but it becomes clear that the substantive meaning of his conviction is null, that there has been no crime, and that the trial machine is hollow. His conviction occurs, as the famous passage puts it, "one fine morning," and for no reason, and might have happened any time ("Someone must have traduced Joseph K., for without having done anything wrong he was arrested one fine morning"[11]). Kafka's point, I think, is that there is nothing new or remarkable that a trial, as such, could discover about Joseph K.; he must discover it for himself ("'it is only a trial if I recognize it as such,'" he says at one point; p. 51). What the trial allows for is his awakening to his own life, to the identity which is already his, but which he may not have discovered: "to meet an unknown accusation [as he is asked to do by the trial], not to mention other possible charges arising out of it, the whole of one's life would have to be recalled to mind, down to the smallest actions and accidents, clearly formulated and examined from every angle" (p. 161).

In *The Trial*, as in *The Idiot*, there is a special relationship between self-knowledge and our knowledge of human mortality. Like

Dostoevsky, Kafka shows that death, whether decreed by special sentence or not, tells only what is common about us; taken as a fact, as a piece of information, it reveals nothing special; it is up to each one of us to understand this fact and to fashion a personal identity in its light. Near the end of *The Trial*, K.'s self-knowledge is closely linked with his physical, almost animal presence before his executioners (the episode recalls Dimitri Karamazov's arrest in *The Brothers Karamazov*, III, 3). K. is physically shamed, but this shame, an emotion which attaches to the body, points up his human, mortal condition. As his executioners engage in meaningless rituals and formalities, K. stands naked before them; his reactions are almost instinctual: "One of them finally came up to K. and removed his coat, his waistcoat, and finally his shirt. K. shivered involuntarily, whereupon the man gave him a light, reassuring pat on the back" (p. 284); his posture is "contorted and unnatural-looking" (p. 285), as if in expression of its animal nature.

Finally, in a famous scene, K.'s executioners pass the knife back and forth between them and expect him to take it up, to make himself an accomplice of the trial ("Once more the odious courtesies began, the first handed the knife across K. to the second, who handed it across K. back again to the first. K. now perceived clearly that he was supposed to seize the knife himself, as it traveled from hand to hand above him, plunge it into his own breast. But he did not do so, he merely turned his head, which was still free to move, and gazed around him," p. 285). There's a circle of irony and paradox which radiates from this refusal. It is, no doubt, a failure ("He could not completely rise to the occasion, he could not relieve the officials of their tasks; the responsibility for this last failure lay with him who had not left him the remnant of strength necessary for the deed"), but it is a failure of the same order as Ippolit's aborted suicide. To take the knife would mean suicide, and that would be senseless, since K. is certain to die in any case. The simple fact that he has been sentenced to death should in no way diminish his will to live ("Logic is doubtless unshakable, but it cannot withstand a man who wants to go on living," p. 286). In the same way that Ippolit provides us with a basis for understanding what it means to accept responsibility for human mortality, and for a human world, K.'s inability to take the knife bespeaks a radically humanistic sensibility. K. resists taking the knife because the trial is teaching him something about life.

The very final paragraphs of *The Trial* bring together K.'s self-awareness and his public mockery, the anxiety which the world exacts as the price of that self-knowledge. K. sees a flicker of light and notices a human figure, "faint and insubstantial at that distance and that height, [who] leaned abruptly far forward and stretched both arms still further. Who was it? A friend? A good man? Someone who sympathized? Someone who wanted to help? Was it one person only? Or was it mankind? Was help at hand? Were there arguments in his favor that had been overlooked? Of course there must be." There is no help at hand, and K. dies an ignominious death, but his ability to recognize this man, or mankind, as a *semblable* and *frère*, represents an important piece of learning. The trial has taught him something, even if this is only what it means to be in the human condition; earlier, he had said that "I always wanted to snatch at the world with twenty hands, and not for a very laudable motive, either. That was wrong, and am I to show now that not even a year's trial has taught me anything? Am I to leave this world as a man who has no common sense?" (pp. 282–83). If anything, K. gains "common sense," a sense for what is common about him. In comparison to what he knows at the beginning of the book—that his conviction must in some way single him out—this represents significant knowledge. K. looks on as he dies and he sees himself shamed; he is "alienated" from himself in the sense that Kierkegaard intends: "With failing eyes, K. could still see the two of them immediately before him, cheek against cheek, watching the final act. 'Like a dog!' he said, it was as if the shame of it must outlive him" (p. 286). K. knows that his actions have larger consequences than he might expect and he knows, moreover, what a suicide refuses to acknowledge: that the world which outlasts us will register our fate. His self-understanding at the end of the book is the fulfillment of the motive which he stated very near the start: "to understand his situation clearly" (p. 7).

Aside from *The Trial*, perhaps the most significant literary comment on Dostoevsky's sense of human mortality and the identity derived therefrom is *The Stranger.* Mersault is convicted of a crime and suffers the absolute and seemingly bizarre logic of an inquest, just as Kafka's K. Camus's lifelong interest in Dostoevsky is colored by his philosophical engagement with Nietzsche, though, and *The Stranger* considers the possibilities and implications of nihilism more deeply than either *The Idiot* or *The Trial:* "'It's common knowledge that life isn't worth living anyhow,'" Mersault says at one point after his conviction; "'And, on a wide view, I could see that it makes little difference whether one dies at the age of thirty or threescore and ten.'"[12] The proposition could be taken as a warrant for suicide, or as the basis for the kind of senseless rebellion that Dostoevsky's Ippolit attempts. But in *The Stranger,* the condemned man's condition eventually becomes the source of a positive perception of our mortal nature.

The direct communication between the Prince's accounts in *The Idiot* and *The Stranger,* and the issue which shifts Mersault's budding nihilism toward a positive conception of existence, is not so much the matter of the condemned man's death as the matter of his *knowing* it. What torments Mersault is the idea that his death is absolutely *certain:* "after taking much thought, calmly, I came to the conclusion that what was wrong about the guillotine was that the condemned man had no chance at all, absolutely none. In fact, the patient's death had been ordained irrevocably. It was a foregone conclusion" (p. 139). Even though Mersault "knows" that his death is certain, he is loath to acknowledge the fact. "What was wanted, to my mind, was to give the criminal a chance, if only a dog's chance; say, one chance in a thousand. There might be some drug, or combination of drugs, which would kill the patient (I thought of him as 'the patient') nine hundred and ninety times in a thousand. That he should know this was, of course, essential." He becomes obsessed by the problem of "circumventing the machine," of denying the inevitable: "I blame myself for not having given more attention to public executions. . . . I might have found escape stories. Surely they would have told me that in one case, anyhow, the wheels had stopped; that once, if only once, in that inexorable march of events, chance or luck had played a happy part. Just once!'" (pp. 136–37).

The extreme difficulty with the idea of a reprieve, though, is that it is contradictory. It would require a denial of what is precisely most common and human about us—our mortality—a phenomenon which Mersault expresses in terms which give one to think of Cervantes' man of glass, viz., as a vanishing of the human: "'I am always wondering if there have been cases of condemned prisoners escaping through the police cordon, vanishing in the nick of time before the guillotine falls" (p. 136). What Mersault comes to see, then, is that any view *except* the one that says that we will certainly die is untenable and, I would add, skeptical: "'Once you're up against it,'" Mersault says, "'the precise manner of your death has obviously small importance. Therefore—but it was hard not to lose the thread of the argument leading up to that "therefore"—I should be prepared to face the dismissal of my appeal'" (p. 143). Mersault's change of attitude, so manifest and effortful in this passage, turns him away from nihilism and toward the acceptance of his death. When he finally says that "the man under sentence had to cooperate mentally, it was in his interest that all should go off without a hitch" (pp. 139–40), he does not mean to encourage suicide but rather to say that we must take a part in shaping the course which will lead to our death.

When Mersault is first in prison, his thoughts roam freely ("There was one thing in those early days that was really irksome: my habit of thinking like a free man," p. 95). Writing about Dostoevsky in a similar context, Robert Louis Jackson said that "the convict's life represents an effort, largely mental, to vault over the wall that surrounds him;" "if only for one moment, the convict feels free."[13] His free thoughts are a denial of reality; Mersault for instance is skeptical about the condition he is in, and shows it much the way that Hegel described: "For instance, I would suddenly be seized with a desire to go down to the beach for a swim" (p. 95), which is of course impossible for him. Eventually he recognizes the contradiction that such thoughts entail, and he abandons them: "merely to have imagined the sound of ripples at my feet, the smooth feel of water on my body as I struck out, and the wonderful sensation of relief it gave brought home still more cruelly the narrowness of my cell. . . . Afterward, I had prisoner's thoughts." The same contradictions which lead Mersault to accept the fact of his being "towards death" lead him to reject the priest's questions about the possibility of eternal life. When the priest asks him if he thinks "that when you die you die outright" (p. 147), Mersault can only say that the idea is the expression of a wish. On one view, that wish is trivial ("Everybody had that wish at times. But that had no more importance than wishing to be rich, or to swim very fast, or to have a better shaped mouth. It was in the same order of things"; p. 150). On another view, that wish represents an unfathomable proposition, a wish which is unfulfillable unless we conceive of a vanishing of the human: "'How did I picture life after the grave?'", the priest wants to know; Mersault's idea of life after death is the only idea which he *could* be expected to have of it, "'A life in which I can remember this life on earth. That's all I want of it. And in the same breath I told him that I'd had enough of his company.'" Mersault's reply to the priest suggests a deeply humanist ethos. He says that our project on earth, given the certainty of our death, must be to live a life that might be worth remembering. The encounter recalls Kierkegaard's observation in the *Concluding Unscientific Postscript*: that the question of *immortality*, like death, is one whose meaning we do not know in any complete sense, that immortality is something which we only think *about*. What Camus adds to Kierkegaard's insight is that the idea of our immortality is something which we *can* only think about, not claim or fully appropriate.

For Mersault to accept the priest's inference, to conceive of a life beyond the grave, or some kind of permanent reprieve, would mean for him to deny the very fact which he has come to face, viz., that he exists and is mortal. Mersault sees his death-sentence as a guide to the meaning of his existence: he worries that the priest's faith in the afterlife may become a substitute for living on earth and that the idea of a more enduring life may lead him to postpone his responsibilities to this one while he is here: "[the priest] seemed so cocksure, you see. And yet none of his certainties was worth one strand of a woman's hair. Living as he was, like a corpse, he couldn't even be sure of being alive" (p. 151). In contrast to the priest's false faith and illusory certainties—on account of which he lives "like a corpse"—Mersault gains assurance of himself and his human condition; he learns, in Kierkegaard's terms, to think death "as a deed," and not simply as an idea. He turns the fact of his inevitable death into a source of self-knowledge: "I was sure of myself, sure about everything, far surer than he; sure of my present life and of the death that was coming. That, no doubt, was all I had; but at least that certainty was something I could get my teeth into—just as it had got its teeth into me."

As in *The Trial*, the legal proceedings and death-sentence in the second part of *The Stranger* are, substantively, hollow; as in *The Idiot*, they provide no new information about Mersault, nothing which he could not already have known. And yet his conviction is the key to his personal identity; this becomes a central issue of his trial: "I was questioned several times immediately after my arrest. But they were all formal examinations, *as to my identity* and so forth" (p. 77, italics added); later, he remarks that "for the nth time I was asked to give particulars of my identity and, though heartily sick of this formality, I realized that it was natural enough; after all, it would be shocking for the court to be trying the wrong man" (p. 108). Mersault's apparently innocent question, spoken out of exasperation ("But, damn it, who's on trial in this court, I'd like to know?" p. 124) cannot simply be answered by naming "Mersault" any more than his death-sentence tells him what it means *for him* to be human; the Prosecutor might expect so, but he would also expect that a person can be defined by inspecting his "soul":

The prosecutor was considering what he called my "soul." He said he'd studied it closely—and he had found a blank, "literally nothing, gentlemen of the jury." Really, he said, I had no soul, there was nothing human about me, not one of those moral qualities which normal men possess had any place in my mentality. "No doubt," he added, "we should not reproach him with this. We cannot blame a man for lacking what it was never in his power to acquire." (p. 127)

The conclusion to be drawn from the Prosecutor's inquest into the "human" and from the trial's inquest into Mersault's identity is that there is nowhere to look for such qualities in a person, because they are not for others to find: they must be discovered by, and for, oneself.

It is this process of self-discovery which Camus expresses by a metaphor of personal awakening, the coming of the "dawn": "I'd been waiting for this moment, for that dawn, tomorrow's or another day's, which was to justify me" (p. 152). What Mersault understands—the knowledge which "justifies" him, reveals his happiness to him (which are nearly the same thing)—is that this "dawning" may necessarily be accompanied by anxiety. We are revealed to ourselves, as Kierkegaard said, only in alienation: "gazing up at the dark sky spangled with its signs and stars, for the first time, for the first, I laid my heart open to the benign indifference of the universe. To feel it so like myself, indeed, so brotherly, made me realize that I'd been happy, and that I was happy still. For all to be accomplished, for me to feel less lonely, all that remained to hope was that on the day of my execution there should be a huge crowd of spectators and that they should greet me with howls of execration" (p. 154). At the end of *The Stranger*, as at the conclusion of *The Trial*, and in the near-death encounters related in *The Idiot*, the simple fact of human mortality becomes a source of alienation and self-understanding.[14] The meaning of existence does not come as rational knowledge, which would be hollow, but as a revelation, an awakening: "They always come for one at dawn" (p. 141). Mersault's words echo a passage in Dostoevsky spoken by Dimitri Karamazov, which I will discuss further in the following pages: "I would have killed myself before all this, without waiting for the dawn. I know that myself now. I couldn't have learned so much in twenty years as I've found out in this accursed night" (*The Brothers Karamazov*, III, 3). The task is not simply to know that there is an end in human existence, but to find it for oneself, to recognize when the dawn has come in you.

In anticipation of my next topic, I want to conclude with the observation that in *The Stranger*, as in *The Trial*, and as in the Prince's accounts of the execution at Lyons in *The Idiot*, the conviction and death-sentence which are officially handed down give only a factual statement of the disposition of the case at hand. If death is to be a source of authentic learning or wisdom, each man must, in addition, acknowledge his mortality and convict himself of it. This is how the man executed at Lyons converts the factual information about his death into a personal revelation, and it is how Mersault finds the "dawn" in him. In answering the Court's questions at the inquest, Mersault supplies enough information to have himself found guilty; when they ask him why he killed the Arab, for instance, he replies "because of the sun." But he finds that this is not yet his own conviction, that he cannot claim these words as his own ("I spoke too quickly and ran my words into each other. I was only too conscious that it sounded nonsensical, and, in fact, I heard people tittering," p. 130). At this point his words are, literally, spoken by someone else ("I pricked my ears; it was when I heard him saying: 'It is true I killed a man.' He went on in the same strain, saying 'I' when he referred to me"). He is at first shocked when he hears his voice: "I heard something that I hadn't heard for months. It was the sound of a voice, my own voice, there was no mistaking it. And I recognized it as the voice that for many a day of late had been sounding in my ears" (p. 110). What Mersault accomplishes during the course of his imprisonment is to claim his words as his own and to appropriate their force, and hence the meaning of his life, for himself. This involves the transition from his legal conviction to his personal conviction of his human nature and identity. It is this transition, which turns on the dual sense of "conviction," which I will take up in my following discussion of Dostoevsky. What the priest tells Mersault is a good introduction to the topic: "first one must repent, and become like a child, with a simple, trustful heart, open to conviction" (p. 85).

CRIME AND CONVICTION

IN THIS SECTION, I want to move back from my excursus into *The Stranger* and *The Trial* to three of Dostoevsky's major novels—*Crime and Punishment*, *The Brothers Karamazov*, and *The Idiot*. As Proust is said once to have remarked, virtually the whole of Dostoevsky's fiction could be described by the single title "The Story of a Crime," but these novels bring out a special, philosophical sense of the logic of crime and conviction. Each is anchored by a crime, and ends in a legal conviction, but the "convictions" which they yield are also forms of knowledge, answers to skepticism deeper than reason could provide. Dostoevsky's characters learn that their actions have consequences in the world, and that the world is unfailingly there to bear witness to them. If this were not the case, if their actions left no traces, if there were a "perfect crime," then they could resist this conviction and deny their actions, or remain in doubt about the existence of the world. But eventually these characters come to seek out conviction, and so to clear free of the skepticism Dostoevsky shows them to harbor.

A turn from knowledge to conviction, which marks the point at which skepticism is abrogated and where reasons cease to avail, was already evident in our discussion of the *Quixote*. When Don Quixote and Sancho butt-up against the world, as when Sancho is blanketed at the inn, or when Don Quixote is given a strappadoing, any doubt that the world exists and is real is difficult to sustain; and the world presents itself with such force that their knowledge of it overwhelms any mere rational claim that it is real. That the external world exists is, at a point like this, beyond the scope of reason to determine or refute. The pattern we see in Dostoevsky is closely related. His characters act as skeptics and attempt to deny their actions in the world. In this way they overcome the skepticism which Hegel saw as endemic to independent self-consciousness: they come to live as responsible agents in relationship to a world. But whereas in Cervantes the characters are convicted *by* the world, in Dostoevsky they are convicted *of* it; that is to say, it is not the world alone which brings them to abrogate skepticism but they themselves, who choose to recognize their dependence on the world—the fact that it has claims on them, that they are of *it*, rather than the other way around, as the skeptic thinks.

Let us begin with *Crime and Punishment*. It is usual for critics to say that there is a contrast, or a dialectic of contrasts, between Raskolnikov's actual crime and his ideas of it—the theories, dreams, and wild ruminations relative to the murders. Indeed, Porfiry the inspector himself says at one point that "'We're dealing with bookish dreams here, with a heart exacerbated by theories;'"[1] yet we see that the crime has tangible effects in the world. Part I of the novel is constructed like a great arc built of this dialectic: it begins with Raskolnikov's self-absorption and reveries and ends with the murder of the old pawnbroker and her sister Lisaveta. Set within this major arc are two or three smaller structures of similar contrasts: Raskolnikov's test visit to the pawnbroker (I,1), and his dream of the beating of the old mare, (I,5); his material preparation for the crime (readying the hatchet and the sling), and his worries about leaving clues and traces behind (I, 6). The commission of the crime does not resolve this dialectic; Raskolnikov ends Part I with "scraps and fragments of thoughts" swarming in his head, and he is unable to settle them: "he could not concentrate on a single one of them even for a short time, much as he tried to" (I,1; p. 106).

John Bayley said that virtually all of Dostoevsky's characters are "involved in a dream, in a dramatic relation with their own self-consciousness."[2] Robert Louis Jackson described this pattern in *Crime and Punishment* as the "dialectic of consciousness in Raskolnikov."[3] This characterization recalls the moment of independent self-consciousness which Hegel called Skepticism in the *Phenomenology of Spirit* and suggests that the contrast between Raskolnikov's crime and his ideas about it are a product of a consciousness acting to maintain its freedom through a denial of the world. From the very beginning of the novel, in fact, Raskolnikov resembles the Hegelian Skeptical Consciousness by his inward retreat ("He had been so absorbed in himself and had led so cloistered a life that he was afraid of meeting anybody," I, 1; p. 19). We know that the dialectic can be traced specifically to Raskolnikov's *consciousness*, rather than to the crime, because it begins before the murders ever occur. From the start, we see Raskolnikov's melancholic broodings and dark ruminations, his Hamletian "habit of indulging in soliloquies" (p. 20).

Although Robert Louis Jackson does not explicitly say so, he seems to have Hegel in mind when he describes the final resolution of this dialectic, and the marked change which we see in Raskolnikov, in the Epilogue. Raskolnikov demonstrates, in his words, "a qualitatively different state of consciousness from the chaos of mind he experienced right after the murder. These two moments of consciousness are in almost symmetrical opposition. The movement or shift from one to the other constitutes the movement in Raskolnikov's consciousness from hate (unfreedom) to love (freedom)" (p. 90). This might be clarified by saying that Raskolnikov progresses from one *kind* of freedom (a false freedom, one that is based on vanity and self-love) to another, authentic freedom founded on suffering and altruistic love. The crucial point of interpretation, though, is not so much how we construe these two moments of consciousness as how we view the relationship between them and how we account for Raskolnikov's advance. The only outward fact which distinguishes these two moments, and the apparent cause of the shift, is the fact that Raskolnikov comes to confess his crime and to convict himself of it. What changes is his manner of *relationship* to the crime. My purpose here will be to show more fully that Raskolnikov's conviction—in both senses of the word, legal and philosophical—entails something more than simple knowledge of what he has done; Raskolnikov brings himself to a point where "life had taken the place of logic" (Epilogue, 2; p. 588) because he finds a meaningful relationship to the crime: he comes to see himself as its author and he defines himself as being *of* the world in which his actions have effects.

In his notebooks for *Crime and Punishment*, Dostoevsky said that the "chief anatomy of the novel" was to be based on a "clash with reality and the logical outcome in the law of nature and duty."[4] Dostoevsky's notebooks are filled with statements of "major ideas" and themes of "first importance," many of them misleading, but in this case his description fits closely with the facts. The organizing "clash with reality" in *Crime and Punishment* begins in Part I and continues until the Epilogue. It is initiated by a skeptical denial of the world, and it is terminated by Raskolnikov's self-conviction. On the one hand we see that Raskolnikov is tormented by "delusions, imaginary terrors, phantom visions" (II, 7; p. 208), that he is preoccupied with the need to eradicate the material traces of his crime (II,2), that he insists the investigators have no hard facts to prove his guilt (III, 6); he "murders" the old pawnbroker again, but only in a dream, and awakens with the skeptical remark "'Am I still dreaming or not?'" (III, 6; p. 295) which he repeats nearly verbatim as Part IV of the novel begins ("'Surely this is not a continuation of my dream?'" IV, 1; p. 296). On the other hand, each of these denials of reality is countered by evidence that the world is there and is real. In response to the growing awareness that his actions have material consequences, for instance, Raskolnikov must try to remove the traces of his crime in Part II. After the death of Marmeladov, Raskolnikov vows to reject his delusions and his dreams; he seems to conquer his skeptical madness, and to affirm reality as such: "'Enough!' he said solemnly and resolutely. 'No more delusions, no more imaginary terrors, no more phantom visions! There is such a thing as life! Life is real! Haven't I lived just now? My life hasn't come to an end with the death of the old woman!'" (II, 7; p. 208).

As these contrasts show, the basic outline of *Crime and Punishment* is antiskeptical. The novel follows a pattern which we know from *Don Quixote*, viz., the "clash with reality" that Don Quixote finds in nearly every one of his adventures. What is troubling about this novel, though, is that Raskolnikov's "dialectic of consciousness," his denials of the world and of his crime, should persist for so long. It turns out that none of the "clashes with reality" listed above is by itself sufficient to move Raskolnikov to confess his crime, and there are times when he allows surrounding circumstances to per-petuate his denials. When he returns to the pawnbroker's flat he finds that the floors have been scrubbed clean and that the blood-stains are gone (II, 6); when Porfiry tries to convict him (VI, 2), there is no material evidence to be found. Raskolnikov himself is loath to act upon the resolve he expresses at the close of Part II ("'No more delusions. . . !'").

It would be reasonable to say that a clash with reality is not by itself enough to move Raskolnikov to confess because his change of consciousness is closely bound up with his relationship to Sonia, not only to the external world. His progression from inauthentic freedom, vanity, and a denial of the world to authentic freedom and to suffering at the hands of the world turns on the altruistic love which Sonia awakens in him. Sonia initiates a process in Raskolnikov remarkably close to what Kierkegaard would call "alienation." She allows him to recognize others *as others,* not as extensions of himself—as in Part V, where he seems to see Lisaveta's face in Sonia's face. What we need to explain, then, is why Raskolnikov's "alienation" comes when it does, and why, in parti-cular, it is so long delayed. As late as Part V, after he has already met Sonia, Raskolnikov still does not recognize *why* he has com-mitted the crime; he is reluctant, or unable, to claim responsibility for his actions. His confession to Sonia in V, 2 is followed by an elaboration of his own "theory" of the crime; he says that he com-mitted the crime in order to show that he was an "extraordinary man," not one of the "ordinary souls." Yet in the Epilogue he admits that his actions contradict his own theory, that a truly extraordi-nary individual would not have needed a test to prove his greatness ("Oh, how happy he would have been if he really could have re-garded himself as guilty of a crime! He would have put up with everything, even with his shame and disgrace. But he judged him-self severely, and his obdurate conscience could find no specially terrible fault in his past, except perhaps the fault of committing a simple *blunder,* which could have happened to anyone. What he was ashamed of was that he, Raskolnikov, should have perished so utterly, so hopelessly, and so stupidly . . . 'I was not successful and therefore I had no right to permit myself such a step,'" Epilogue, 2;

p. 551). Raskolnikov's reluctance to confess his crime, even after he has met Sonia, casts some doubt on the depth of her influence on him. Indeed, if confession is something to which only *he* can bring himself, then how could we expect Sonia to implant it in him?

The termination of Raskolnikov's "dialectic of consciousness," in which his theories, delusions, and doubts give way to self-conviction, is brought about by a change in attitude on Raskolnikov's part, by his willingness to admit his crime. The importance of his admission becomes clear if we look at the problem of conviction in a legalistic sense and, for a moment, consider the book as a detective novel. *Crime and Punishment* fits the title which Proust suggested for all of Dostoevsky's fiction—"The Story of a Crime"—because it is shaped around the discovery of a murderer. Razumikhin and Porfiry are, at various times, taken up with this project. But on reflection this is a rather odd detective story: there is no suspense or mystery involved; the reader is never in doubt about who the murderer is. What matters in this novel is not so much to discover the criminal but to have him discover himself. The only sense in which the identity of the murderer is a mystery is that until Raskolnikov acknowledges his crime, and admits his responsibility for it, his actions are a mystery to him and he, as their agent, does not fully understand who he is. Michael Holquist described him as his own detective, a "detective of his old self's motive, in order to create a new identity, a new life for himself. If he can understand *why* his old self committed the crime he will know the self whodunit [sic]; and insofar as he understands whodunit, he will know who he is."[5] As Holquist's analysis suggests, Raskolnikov transcends both skeptical doubt *and* reason by confessing his crime: since Raskolnikov is the crime's agent, he knows all there is (factually) to know about it. What he lacks is not any additional knowledge, as the skeptic demands, but acknowledgment of his responsibility for his actions, his private—and also public—admission of guilt.

As we move from the detective plot of the novel to the Epilogue, the importance of self-understanding over factual knowledge becomes crucial. Holquist described this relationship in terms of two different narrative shapes and two correspondingly different orders of meaning and interpretation: the detective plot describes a one-dimensional, linear shape, a structure which we expect can be completed by logical extension or by the summation of accumulated facts; but the Epilogue is what he calls a "wisdom tale," a story which asks for no additional facts but instead demands a changed relationship to what we already "know." The detective work in *Crime and Punishment* itself points up the limitations of the former mode of narrative exposition and interpretive knowing. Porfiry the inspector wants facts and hard evidence for his case, but he finally sees that the only way for him to catch his man is to let the criminal convict himself ("'Ever watch a moth before a lighted candle? Well, he, too, will be circling round and round me like a moth round a candle. He'll get sick of his freedom. He'll start brooding. He'll get himself so thoroughly entangled that he won't be able to get out. He'll worry himself to death. And what's more, he'll provide me with a nice, easy mathematical problem like twice two—if I give him enough rope. And he'll keep on describing circles round me, smaller and smaller circles, till—bang! he'll fly straight into my mouth and I'll swallow him!'" IV, 5; p. 355). The role of the court in Raskolnikov's conviction is almost nil: "the criminal, far from trying to justify [exculpate] himself, seemed to be anxious to incriminate himself more and more" (Epilogue, 1; p. 545).

If Raskolnikov's conviction turns on his ability to acknowledge his crime, then this suggests that he had acted irresponsibly—unwilling, or unable, to claim the act as his own. He enters the pawnbroker's flat unnoticed, screened from the scene of his crime by a passing cart. His indecisiveness and hesitation are in fact notorious; from the very start of the novel we see that he is "unable to make up his mind." Robert Louis Jackson said that "Raskolnikov will never decide to commit the crime. He will never consciously, actively, with his whole moral being choose to kill—or, the reverse, choose not to kill" (p. 202). Raskolnikov is not lacking in resolve to commit the crime, though, because it does not take resolve to commit the crime; what takes resolve and moral fibre is to admit what he has done, and to accept the consequences of his action. This is what Philip Rhav indicated when he said that Raskolnikov passes from an inauthentic to an authentic relationship to his crime; Raskolnikov comes to see that he is the crime's *author*:

Raskolnikov stands in an inauthentic relationship to his crime . . . The crime does not truly belong to him, and that is the reason he affects us as being almost ludicrously inadequate to the deed, as when he faints in the police station the day right after the murder, even though there is as yet no suspicion attached to him, and calls attention to himself in other ways too. In spite of all his protestations to the contrary, he is prostrate with guilt and the yearning for punishment. It is not that he lacks the strength to kill and bear responsibility for it to the end, but that he killed for himself alone, deranged by unconscious urges and over-conscious theories.[6]

As we have already begun to see, and as I will comment further, it is clear that Raskolnikov's "over-conscious" theories may block his recognition of responsibility; as part of his "dialectic of consciousness," they are central to Raskolnikov's denial of reality. Where I would disagree with Rhav is in the relative weight and importance of Raskolnikov's "unconscious urges." It is perhaps natural to read *Crime and Punishment* as a psychological novel, and to attribute Raskolnikov's actions to forces beyond his control. Albert Guerard, to take a representative case, said that the book is "an exercise in abnormal psychology," and that "the severity of Raskolnikov's anxieties and repressions results in much compulsive behavior and even periods of amnesia"; he calls *Crime and Punishment* "a supreme novelistic record of stress."[7] Dostoevsky himself wrote in a letter that he was planning the book as the "psychological account of a crime."[8] My objection to this approach, despite Dostoevsky's remark, is that it *relieves* Raskolnikov of responsibility for his crime, works against the movement of the plot toward his conviction, and is, along with other "explanations" of the crime, explicitly critiqued in the final version of the text.

The psychological account of Raskolnikov's crime stands among a series of views on it which are brought forth in the book. On textual evidence alone we might attribute the crime to social, economic, or biological causes; indeed, there are critics and sociologists (e.g., Edward Sagarin, in *Raskolnikov and Others*, 1981) who read the book in criminological terms. Dostoevsky himself said, in the letter quoted above, that his subject was "not at all eccentric," i.e., that Raskolnikov's crime was a reflection of actual social conditions:

Last year in Moscow I was told (this is actually true) about a certain student expelled from the University after the incident with the Moscow students, that he decided to break into a post office and kill the postman. In our papers there are still many traces of this unusual informity of notions which is materializing into terrible deeds. (That seminarian who killed a girl in a barn after an agreement with her, and whom they arrested an hour later at lunch, and so forth.) In a word, I feel convinced that my subject is justified in part by contemporary life!

The psychological, sociological, biological, and economic accounts of the crime are all tempting explanations of it because they seem to respond so well to the texture of the novel, with its detailed descriptions which seem to recreate the entire range of conditions bearing on this Russian student. My view is that they are nonetheless insufficient explanations of the crime because they do not explain it, but rather explain it away. They seem to fit the facts but they are unable to show Raskolnikov what he needs most to see: that he is the crime's agent, the one to be held responsible for it. His own article on crime, for instance, says that all crimes are accompanied by illness, and in fact Raskolnikov falls ill when he commits the murders; but this does not mean that his illness drove him to it. The explanation amounts to an excuse, and it helps him to avoid responsibility. Razumikhin gives a socioeconomic explanation of the crime; he accounts for it in terms of the general moral lassitude of society ("'I hardly need mention the fact that crime has increased during the last five years among the lower classes; nor need I mention the large number of cases of robbery and arson all over the country; but what does seem very strange to me is that the number of crimes committed by members of the upper classes has also increased correspondingly, as it were . . . So now if this woman moneylender is murdered by one of her clients, I am ready to bet anything you like that he, too, belonged to the higher strata of society, for peasants do not pawn gold articles. How, then, do we explain this loosening of moral standards among the civilized section of our society?'" II, 5; pp. 169–70). Razumikhin is of course wrong in his analysis—or, better put, wrong*headed*—and the alternative conclusions, which he rejects, are equally misguided

[114]

("'crime is a protest against bad and abnormal social conditions and nothing more. No other causes are admitted. Nothing! . . . [The socialists] reduce everything to one common cause—environment. Environment is the root of all evil—and nothing else! A favourite phrase. And the direct consequence of it is that if society is organized on normal lines, all crimes will vanish at once, for there will be nothing to protest against, and all men will become righteous in the twinkling of an eye,'" III, 5; pp. 272–73). Porfiry continues exactly in this vein when he says that a crime can be explained in terms of the environment ("'a forty-year-old man violates a ten-year-old girl—was it environment that drove him to do it?' 'Well, strictly speaking, it probably was environment,' Porfiry said with surprising gravity. 'A crime committed against a little girl may be explained by environment,'" pp. 273–74). One sociological explanation or another is bound to fit the circumstances of the crime and the criminal, but they are all unsatisfying because they dissolve the bond of responsibility between the agent and the crime. Actions are excused, accountability is absorbed by the conditions of society at large.

Crime and Punishment shows that to understand these things about an action—what would explain it and what would excuse it—is to understand what it would mean to act responsibly. The sociological, psychological, and economic "explanations" of Raskolnikov's crime obscure the meaning of human agency because they excuse him from responsibility. Porfiry frankly admits at one point that his detective methods are of lamentably little use ("'These profound psychological methods of ours are, to be sure, exceedingly absurd,'" IV, 5; p. 353); they are unable to convict the criminal. Raskolnikov is the only one who can supply a convincing explanation of the crime; he is the only one who can convict himself. W. D. Snodgrass said that Raskolnikov committed the murder in order "to achieve punishment,"[9] but it is conviction, more than punishment, that Raskolnikov seeks.

We know from a letter of 1859 that Dostoevsky had originally envisioned *Crime and Punishment* as a confessional novel. Even after he abandoned the idea of a monologue format, he continued to speak of his hero's "compulsion" to give himself up—"compelled so that even if he perish in penal servitude, nonetheless he might once again be united to men."[10] Raskolnikov's admission of responsibility hinges on his willingness to acknowledge that his actions have consequences in the world, and on his willingness to confess his actions publicly. It is only after he kisses the earth in Haymarket Square, late in Part VI, that his self-conviction is possible. This is not to ignore the lingering doubts about his moral regeneration; but confession does not guarantee permanent conversion; it is not insurance against sin. What the public confession and punishment simply show is that Raskolnikov's ideas about the crime, what he says and what he does, are now one, whereas before they were divided in what critics call his "dialectic of consciousness." As I will discuss in relation to *The Idiot*, this unity is the basis of authentic conviction: meaning what one says *means* that one's words must not only have a private but also a public sense; it means in fact joining these two senses together. That Raskolnikov's conviction turns on a public act thus recalls a theme that we first saw in connection with Cervantes: that knowledge sufficient to respond to skepticism is common, public, not private, just as Raskolnikov's conviction here is.

Still, the book leaves us with doubts about how, and how deeply, Raskolnikov is brought to self-conviction. He vacillates after his confession, and there are moments, as late as the Epilogue, where he is decidedly unrepentant ("And if fate had only sent him repentance—burning repentance that is accompanied by terrible agony which makes one long for the noose or the river! Oh, how happy he would have been if he could have felt such repentance! Agony and tears—why, that, too, was life! But he did not repent of his crime," Epilogue, 2; p. 552). Raskolnikov confesses, but how can we judge the sincerity of his heart or know when his words are fully meant? How can we, who are outside him, tell when his public conviction is authentic and sincere? That is to say that public self-conviction is not itself enough. Earlier in the novel we meet a false convict, Nikolay, and there is nothing he could say which would make him guilty of the crime: why then take Raskolnikov's word? As he reaches for the New Testament that Sonia has left, he asks "'Is it possible that her convictions can be mine, too, now? Her feelings, her yearnings, at least . . .'" (p. 558). How can we possibly know, much less assume for ourselves, the convictions in another's heart?

Crime and Punishment shows clearly enough that the only valid conviction is self-conviction, but Dostoevsky hints at the greater problem of how to recognize conviction in others. The inference he makes is deeply troubling, and I will return to it in my discussion of skepticism and the problem of others: that personal conviction is at odds with human community, that our knowledge of ourselves and our knowledge of others are ultimately unalike. While Raskolnikov lies in the hospital during Lent and Easter, he dreams of a plague, a sickness of the spirit in which men become zealous preachers of their personal ideas and beliefs; the problem is that "They did not understand each other. Each of them believed that the truth only resided in him, and was miserable looking at the others, and smote his breast, wept, wrung his hands. They did not know whom to put on trial or how to pass judgment; they could not agree what was good or what was evil" (p. 555). In his letter, Dostoevsky said that he hoped Raskolnikov would be united to other men in prison, but Raskolnikov's dream is a nearly explicit contradiction of those hopes. Raskolnikov ends not only convicted but also alienated, in much the sense that Kierkegaard meant: he knows himself, and he also knows that he is separate and distinct from others in the world.

The special sense of conviction which informs *Crime and Punishment* is central to Dimitri Karamazov's conviction in *The Brothers Karamazov*, but there are at least two major differences between the novels. The first is a difference of form and presentation. In *Crime and Punishment*, the murder of the old pawnbroker and her sister Lisaveta, which Raskolnikov is slow to acknowledge, is always clear to the reader. We know all the facts about the murder that there are to know, even if, like the police inspector Porfiry, we are powerless to convict Raskolnikov until he convicts himself. But in *The Brothers Karamazov*, the murder of Fyodor Pavlovich is withheld from our view. At the very moment of the murder, there is a hiatus in the narrative, reminiscent of the interruption in *Don Quixote* I, 8. We know the crime only in re-presentation, by indirect evidence, hearsay, and report. Even from before the crime, we are piqued to search for a solution—there is the narrator's intriguing remark that "'on the day before the event, Mitya had not a farthing. . . .' I note this fact; later on it will become apparent why I do so."[11] Afterwards, there is the police captain's inquiry (Book IX) and, finally, the detailed review of evidence presented at Dimitri's trial. All the tracks and traces of the crime lead to him: "Fyodor Pavlovich's silk dressing gown, stained with blood, the fatal brass pestle with which the supposed murder had been committed; Mitya's shirt, with a bloodstained sleeve; his coat, stained with blood in patches behind the pocket in which he had put his handkerchief; the handkerchief itself, stiff with blood and by now quite yellow; the pistol loaded by Mitya at Perkhotin's with a view to suicide, and taken from him only on the sly at Mokroe by Trifon Borisovich; the envelope in which the three thousand rubles had been put ready for Grushenka; the narrow pink ribbon with which it had been tied, and many other articles" (XII, 1; p. 626). Dimitri's rivalry with his father over Grushenka provides a clear motive for the crime, and we know that Dimitri had tried to kill Fyodor Pavlovich earlier; he vowed to fulfill his purpose in the future ("'If I haven't killed him, I'll come again and kill him. You can't protect him!'" I, 3; p. 127). At the moment of the crime, just before the narration breaks off, Dimitri voices deep hatred for his father; he admits that he is entirely capable of parricide ("'I'm afraid he'll suddenly be so loathsome to me at that moment, with that face of his. I hate his Adam's apple, his nose, his eyes, his shameless grin. I feel a personal repulsion. That's what I'm afraid of, that's what may be too much for me,'" III, 8; p. 370). In addition, there is the incriminating letter to Katerina Ivanovna which is brought forth at the trial ("'I shall kill myself, but first of all that cur. I shall tear three thousand [rubles] from him and fling it to you. Though I've been a scoundrel to you, I am not a thief! You can expect three thousand. That cur keeps it under his mattress, in pink ribbon. I am not a thief, but I'll murder my thief. Katya, don't look disdainful. Dimitri is not a thief, but a murderer! He had murdered his father and ruined himself to hold his ground, rather than endure your pride'" IV, 11; p. 586). Ivan, for one, takes the letter as "conclusive proof" that Dimitri has murdered his father.

Unlike *Crime and Punishment*, though, where the evidence points

to the true agent of the crime, the amassed evidence which convicts Dimitri Karamazov is false; there is a "miscarriage of justice."
This is the second major difference between *Crime and Punishment*
and *The Brothers Karamazov*. The evidence in *Crime and Punishment*
is not, by itself, sufficient to convict Raskolnikov, who must convict himself, but nonetheless it tells the truth. The problem which
The Brothers Karamazov raises is whether conviction can hold *in*
spite of the evidence. We know, from Dimitri's own words following
the break in the narrative, that he did not kill his father: "'God was
watching me then,'" he says (III, 4; p. 370). For reasons beyond his
ken he was restrained from murder: "Whether it was someone's
tears, or my mother prayed to god, or a good Angel kissed me at that
instant, I don't know. But the devil was conquered" (III, 9; p. 466).
Alyosha recognizes that his brother is innocent even though he has
nothing more than the look on his face from which to tell ("'I saw
from his face he wasn't lying,'" IV, 12; p. 643); on the same evidence, he is convinced that Smerdyakov, the half-brother who has
confessed to the crime, is in fact guilty. The Court looks at the
evidence which points to Dimitri, and refuses to hear Smerdyakov.

But on closer inspection, Dimitri's conviction is not this simple;
there are closer parallels to *Crime and Punishment* than may at first
be apparent. (By way of anticipation of what I will say about Prince
Myshkin in *The Idiot*, there are reasons to fault Alyosha's judgment
of his brother.) During the long weeks preceding his trial, Dimitri
shows great fortitude and remarkable powers of reflection. Following the pattern we know from *The Idiot*, *The Trial*, and *The Stranger*,
he finds in prison that life is meaningful, that the simplest truth of
existence is cause for ecstasy: "What a thirst for existence and
consciousness has sprung up in me within these peeling walls . . . I
think I could stand anything, any suffering, only to be able to say
and to repeat to myself every moment, 'I exist'" (X, 4; pp. 560–61).
His moments of reflection represent a significant advancement of
personal knowledge for him; he experiences a human renaissance
when faced with his inevitable conviction: "'Brother,'" he says to
Alyosha, "'these last two months I've found in myself a new man. A
new man has risen up in me. He was hidden in me, but would never
have come to the surface if it hadn't been for this blow from
heaven'" (p. 560). In prison, he accepts suffering; he speaks the

[119]

words of Father Zosima: "'We are all responsible for all . . . I go for all, because someone must go for all. I didn't kill father, but I've got to go. I accept it.'"

Dimitri could well avail himself of the same "explanations" (i.e., "excuses") that Raskolnikov gave; there are theories which would relieve him of responsibility for the crime. Rakitin would prove him the victim of "environment"; the doctor would prove him mad; there are the "Claude Bernards" of the world who would show that "it's all chemistry." But Dimitri says to Alyosha "'All these philosophers are the death of me. Damn them.'" As the proceedings of the trial make clear, his refusal of responsibility would imply a denial of reality; the counsel for the defense for instance tries to prove that there was no robbery, no crime, and no murder at all. But Dimitri rejects this sophistical reasoning out of hand:

"What am I to say, gentlemen of the jury? The hour of judgment has come for me, I feel the hand of God upon me! The end has come to an erring man! But before God, I repeat to you, I am innocent of my father's blood! For the last time I repeat, it wasn't I who killed him! I erred, but I loved what is good. Every instant I strove to reform, but I lived like a wild beast. I thank the prosecutor, he told me many things about myself that I did not know; but it's not true that I killed my father, the prosecutor is mistaken. I thank my counsel, too. I cried listening to him; but it's not true that I killed my father, and he needn't have supposed it. And don't believe the doctors. I am perfectly sane, only my heart is empty." (XII, 14; p. 713)

Dimitri will plead his innocence, but he will not deny the world, and this refusal means that he must be willing to be held accountable for it; that is the sense of his conviction. He holds himself responsible not so much for the crime itself, of which he was not the instrumental cause, as for the world, and the state it is in. Thus he is one of the characters of whom I said earlier that they are convicted *of* the world: accepting responsibility for the world, especially where he is guilty of no crime, means that the world cannot be of him, that it cannot be a product of his ideas, delusions, or dreams, but rather that he is of it, accountable to and for it.

Dimitri Karamazov's trial is informed by Plato's account of the trial of Socrates in the *Apology* and of his death in the *Phaedo*. Like

Dimitri, Socrates refused to defend himself by the shameless effrontery and sophistical arguments common in the courts of law. This refusal is his defense, and it is his conviction as well ("'I much prefer to die by such a defense than to live by the other sort'"). Socrates maintained his innocence to the end, openly and resolutely refusing to give sentence against himself ("'being convinced that I have wronged no man, I certainly will not wrong myself; I will not give sentence against myself, and say that I am worthy of something bad, I will not estimate anything bad for myself'"). Because he resists defenses of mere convenience, his conviction is moral and ethical, not merely legal.

The comparison with Socrates is not meant to say that Dimitri is a martyr to the cause of human understanding; he is no saint. His self-conviction is mixed with signs of weakness, as in his plans for escape; he vacillates, often in a single breath ("'But I do condemn myself!' cried Mitya. 'I shall escape, that was settled apart from you; could Mitya Karamazov do anything but run away? But I shall condemn myself, and I will pray for my sin forever,'" Epilogue, p. 724). Alyosha helps him with plans for escape because he is convinced that Dimitri has made a permanent advance; but Dimitri's conviction is partial, his conversion temporary. His comportment at the trial gives evidence of moral backsliding; he enters the courtroom looking "terribly dandyish in a brand-new frock coat" (IV, 12; p. 627). His final plea is simply that he be "spared"; he is not ready to bear the suffering of all mankind. As Richard B. Sewall said, Dimitri experiences a "momentary insight": "[Dimitri] ends as neither martyr nor religious hero nor (in the old commanding sense) tragic hero. What he has found on his pulses has not the power to sustain; it is only a momentary insight, indicating what might have been but, tragically, is not to be."[12] Alyosha is convinced that his brother has made a significant spiritual advance, and agrees to help him escape; but there is no evidence that Alyosha is right. As at the close of Crime and Punishment, there are doubts that this conviction is permanent; we do not know, because we cannot judge another's heart.

Dimitri's conviction serves the same function, is the same source of self-understanding, and poses the same questions of personal knowledge, as Raskolnikov's in *Crime and Punishment*. One apparent difference is that Raskolnikov committed a crime, while Dimitri did not, but that, it turns out, does not matter; taken together, this suggests that conviction is something independent of the facts: in Raskolnikov's case, no amount of evidence, no closer scrutiny, could hold him responsible for his crime; and in *The Brothers Karamazov*, Dimitri's conviction is valuable despite the fact that the evidence against him is false.

This perplexing state of affairs can be taken as evidence that Dostoevsky holds ethics as separate from epistemology, and conviction as having an ethical dimension that simple knowledge does not. This does not mean that ethics and epistemology might not both belong to some general value-structure, such as "responsiveness to the world" (on the contrary, that is what Father Zosima preaches), but their specific shapes and conditions will be unalike. In particular, we can see that conviction adds a crucial component in what we describe as "knowledge." We hold that we know something when our belief is a true belief (corresponds to the "facts") *and* when we can give the right reason for it: knowledge is justified belief.[13] Dostoevsky concentrates on the second of these terms, viz., on our responsibility for our beliefs, even—as in Dimitri's case—in *contradiction* to the facts.

This ethical sense of conviction, its essential difference from knowledge of facts, is central to Father Zosima's perplexing claim that we are "all responsible for all." Where we hold ourselves responsible, with conviction, we must be willing to measure our actions apart from any strict correspondence to the facts. Ivan, the quintessential rationalist, had asked Alyosha to account for the apparently senseless suffering of the world; he challenged his brother to explain the suffering of innocent children:

"With my pitiful, earthly, Euclidean understanding, all I know is that there is suffering and that there are none guilty; . . . What comfort is it to me to know that there are none guilty and that cause follows effect simply and directly, and that I know it—I must have retribution, or I will destroy myself. And not retribution in some remote infinite time and space, but here on earth, and that I could see myself." (II, 5; pp. 224–25)

Ivan expects a direct and visible relationship between suffering and its cause; he wants the assignation of moral responsibility to be determined by Newtonian laws; but he fails to see that ethical action conforms to different rules, that we are responsible to (and for) the world, regardless of the "facts." Father Zosima's words, which Dimitri later speaks, are an implicit rejection of Ivan's tenets. Ivan sees the suffering in the world, and he finds it senseless, and causeless, because he fails to place himself in relationship to it. Dimitri, by contrast, recognizes his involvement with the suffering that he sees, and ignores the fact that he is not instrumentally its cause: "Suddenly [Dimitri] began talking [to Alyosha] about a 'babe'—that is, about some child. 'Why is the babe so poor?', he said. 'It's for that babe I am going to Siberia now. I am not a murderer, but I must go to Siberia'" (IV, 11; p. 538). In this way Dimitri, and not Ivan, demonstrates a responsiveness to the world, and a responsibility for it, that no skeptic could accept.

Dimitri recognizes the basic principles of Christian community, viz., that being together in this world, we must be responsible to, and for, our neighbors. His acceptance of suffering is a powerful reply to Ivan, who is mystified at the implications of Christian love ("'I could never understand how one can love one's neighbors. It's just one's neighbors, to my mind, that one can't love, though one might love those at a distance,'" II, 5; p. 217). As Father Zosima says, these are times in which the pursuit of individualism (i.e., of privacy) has placed human community in peril; the age is an age of isolation and spiritlessness, terms which recall the diagnoses that Hegel and Kierkegaard gave:

"The isolation that prevails everywhere, above all in our age—it has not fully developed, it has not reached its limit yet. For everyone strives to keep his individuality as apart as possible, wishes to secure the greatest possible fullness of life for himself; but meantime all his efforts result not in attaining fullness of life but self-destruction, for instead of self-realization he ends by arriving at complete isolation. All mankind in our age have split up into units, they all keep apart, each in his own groove. . . . For he is accustomed to rely upon himself alone and to cut himself off from the whole. . . . Everywhere in these days men have, in their mockery, ceased to understand that the true security is to be found in social solidarity rather than in isolated individual effort. But this terrible individualism must inevitably have an end, and all will suddenly understand how unnaturally they are separated from one another." (p. 283)

Zosima's principles of general responsibility can be taken as an excuse, as exempting us from individual response. But, as Dimitri's interpretation shows, they are meant to urge us to seek out our neighbor in specific human relationships, to respond to him here and now: "'There, in the mines, underground, I may find a human heart in another convict and murderer side by side, and I may make friends with him, for even there one may live and love and suffer. One may resurrect and receive a frozen heart in that convict, one may wait upon him for years, and at last bring forth an angel, resurrect a hero! There are so many of them, and we are all responsible for them" (IV, 11; p. 560). Dimitri Karamazov looks forward to a reintegration of the human community, the same integration which Dostoevsky foresaw, in his letter, for Raskolnikov at the end of *Crime and Punishment*. But we do not know, perhaps because Dostoevsky means to say that we *cannot* know, whether either of these characters achieves this goal; in exile, the chances seem slim.

Throughout his career, Dostoevsky was moved by a deeply Christian ethos. *The Brothers Karamazov* sets that ethic of love in sharp contrast to the claims of reason and its ethics. As Dimitri Chizhevsky wrote in a probing study of the "double" in Dostoevsky, "Ethical rationalism understands only love for man in general, while the 'neighbor' is strange and distant. It is, however, precisely the concrete individuality of the 'neighbor' that should be the object of ethical action. The ethical rationalist is incapable of loving a concrete man, i.e., the idea of man hides the living man for him."[14] There is nothing inherently wrong with preaching love for Mankind; the problem with ethical rationalism is that it leads to the avoidance of love for concrete beings. What Dostoevsky rejects about it is not so much the ethos as the premise of reason on which it is founded.

The morality of rationalism is consequent, first, on the skeptical belief that the world of "appearances" is false. If the world in which we live is "false," then ethical action may be postponed; there is no need to respond to individuals in actual circumstances. (This was the sense of Kierkegaard's rebuke of Hegel and, parenthetically, of Kant, in the *Concluding Unscientific Postscript:* "The ethical reality of the individual is the *only* reality," p. 291; my emphasis.) If we declare that the world is false, if we deny it as the skeptic does, then we can deny morality as well; as Nietzsche said, to a rather different end, "to the extent that morality is itself a part of this world, morality is false."[15] The difference between Dostoevsky and Nietzsche is that where Nietzsche's irrationalism leads him to the transvaluation of all values, Dostoevsky would replace ethical rationalism by the values of Christian love, by *caritas;* where Nietzsche moves from the "will to truth" to the "will to power," Dostoevsky would urge the morality of self-commanding knowledge and conviction. When Dimitri Karamazov rejects the sophistries of the counsel for the defense, he rejects an ethos founded on reason. His response fulfills a pronouncement made by Father Zosima earlier in the novel: "'[The upper classes], following science, want to base justice on reason alone, but not with Christ, as before, and they have already proclaimed that there is no crime, that there is no sin. And that's consistent, for if you have no God what is the meaning of crime? In Europe the people are already rising up against the rich with violence . . . ,'" III, 7; p. 294).

The second premise of ethical rationalism shows its effects in the spiritual malaise and human isolation that Father Zosima notes as characteristic of the times; it is expressed most directly in Ivan's philosophy. When Ivan rejects Christian love and the possibility of general responsibility, his objection is that it is impossible to *know,* much less share, the suffering of other men. On Ivan's account, we would have to look on others with a transcendental eye, as spies of God, in order to know their suffering. The ethical rationalist wants to form judgments from the cool distance of reason, but he finds, especially with regard to his responsiveness to other men, that he cannot: "'To my thinking, Christ-like love for men is a miracle impossible on earth. He was God. But we are not gods. Suppose I, for instance, suffer intensely. Another can never know how much I suffer, because he is another and not I'" (II, 5; p. 218). Dimitri Karamazov's acceptance of responsibility, his willingness for ethical action, outside the bounds of reason, represents a reply to Ivan's skepticism much as Don Quixote might have given; as we have already seen, Don Quixote is convicted at the hands of the world because he lets his actions go out of his hands, and he is a model of ethical action because his project of justice resists the detachment of reason, instead engaging the virtues in the practice of a role.

In *Crime and Punishment* and *The Brothers Karamazov*, Dostoevsky allows us privileged insight into his characters' inner lives; we are privy to Raskolnikov's dialectic of consciousness, and we overhear some of Dimitri's darkest thoughts as he contemplates parricide. Apparently, Dostoevsky gives his readers a window on his characters' personal beliefs; he seems to place us in a position to judge them in just the way that the course of events seems to contravene. The significant fact is that both Dimitri and Raskolnikov (and, in *The Idiot*, Prince Myshkin) end their lives in exile and that there they become dark to us. The question which Ivan raises about knowing other persons cannot, in other words, so simply be put to rest. Dimitri's conviction may or may not be permanent; as outsiders to him, we do not know the fortune of his heart.

The cases of ethical conviction we have seen so far in *Crime and Punishment* and *The Brothers Karamazov* argue that our relationship to the world of things and persons must entail an active and authentic responsiveness. This relationship cannot be adequately determined by thoughts, theories and ideas (as in Raskolnikov's case) or, (as in Dimitri Karamazov's case) by simple "correspondence to the facts." As Raskolnikov's "dialectic of consciousness" is terminated, as Dimitri rejects the sophistries in his defense, these characters come to grips with reality in its concrete forms. They demonstrate a capacity for meaningful action because they interest themselves in the world. They respond successfully to what Kierkegaard posed as the central problem of human existence. "Existence," he said, "constitutes the highest interest of the existing individual, and his interest in his existence constitutes his reality" (*Postscript*, p. 279). "The difficulty that inheres in existence," though, "is one that never receives an explanation. Because abstract thought is *sub specie aeterni* it ignores the concrete and the temporal, the existential process, the predicament of the existing individual arising from his being a synthesis of the temporal and the external situated in existence" (p. 267). The "abstract thinker," the professional skeptic or epistemologist, wants to found existence on pure cognition (e.g., as in Descartes's *cogito* argument); but in so doing he denies existence; he fails to fashion an actual response to the world ("What reality is cannot be expressed in the language of abstraction. Reality is an *interesse*," p. 279). The individual is most meaningfully justified by ethical action, not by the contemplation of possibility ("The real subject is not the cognitive subject, since in knowing he moves in the sphere of the possible; the real subject is the ethically existing subject," p. 281). The ethically existing subject proves himself as Don Quixote, by conviction in the world. He demonstrates an interest in actuality, does not evade his responsibility to this world by a retreat into abstract thought.

Like *Crime and Punishment* and *The Brothers Karamazov*, *The Idiot* is informed by the ethical sense of conviction, but in *The Idiot* the need for conviction shows up primarily by its lack. Like those novels, the action of *The Idiot* is anchored by a crime. From the moment in Part I when Prince Myshkin and Ganya speak of Rogozhin and Nastasya Filippovna ("'I can't marry anyone,' said the prince. 'I'm a sick man.' 'And would Rogozhin marry her? What do you think?' 'Well, there's no difficulty about marrying a person: one could do it any time. He might marry her tomorrow and, perhaps, murder her a week later,'" I, 3; p. 62), the action is carried toward the murder in the concluding part. Rogozhin, the guilty one, is legally convicted, but he shows none of the self-conviction that we have seen in Dostoevsky's other characters. He resists the advances which Raskolnikov and Dimitri Karamazov are able to make: he accepts explanations (excuses) for his crime, and makes no objection to the sophistries spoken in his defense: "During his trial Rogozhin did not attempt to speak. He did not contradict his eloquent and clever counsel, who proved clearly and logically that the crime was the result of the brain fever, which had set in long before the crime was committed, as a consequence of the great distress of the accused" (IV, 12; p. 658).

As in *The Brothers Karamazov*, the murder in *The Idiot* is withheld from our view; we know it only after the fact. In a remarkable passage of concrete description, Rogozhin and Prince Myshkin keep watch over Natasya Filippovna's corpse. She lies in bed, covered from head to foot with a white sheet; the lifeless calm of the scene is broken only by a fly: "The prince looked, and he felt that the longer he looked the more still and death-like the room became. Suddenly a fly, awakened from its sleep, started buzzing, and after flying over the bed, settled at the top of it. The prince gave a start" (IV, 11; p. 652). The fly is one of Dostoevsky's favored notations, a sign of the minimal presence of life. It appears also in *Crime and Punishment*, at the conclusion of Raskolnikov's dream: "A fly, wakened, suddenly knocked violently against a window-pane in its flight, and began to buzz plaintively" (III, 6; p. 294).

The power of the death-bed scene, and its remarkable descriptive force, stands in stark contrast to the haunting indeterminancy surrounding the crime. As conceived by Rogozhin, the murder is to be the "perfect crime." But as his actions reveal, his unwillingness to face conviction bespeaks an avoidance of love on his part. At the wedding of Nastasya and the Prince, Rogozhin absconds with the bride. In their flight, he covers her with a cloak, a suitable disguise; it points up his will to deny Nastasya, to remove her from his sight. Until the Prince comes upon them in silence, with Rogozhin guarding the corpse, his investigations in Petersburg reveal "not a trace" of his bride (IV, 11; p. 646). It is catastrophically ironic that Rogozhin's love for Nastasya should issue in her death, but it is equally telling that the Prince should also be unable to consummate his love for her. Neither one is able to respond to her as a human "actuality"; she is, for both of them, reduced to what Kierkegaard would call a mere "possibility."

Rogozhin is not the only character in *The Idiot* who contemplates a "perfect crime." The society that Dostoevsky depicts is full of potential killers, even if Rogozhin is the only one who acts. Ippolit, for instance, says that he may commit a dozen murders and go unconvicted (III, 7); but his own attempt at suicide fails. He knows he is a man under medical "sentence of death" (III, 5; p. 432), but he does not transform the knowledge of his limits into meaningful action; as his written "Explanation" (a form of excuse) so clearly points up, he is lacking in conviction. He has despaired of life ("'it is not worth living for a few weeks,'" p. 430), but he is jealous of those he counts among the "living" ("'He is alive, so everything's in his power!'" p. 431). The irony of his case is that he can look at himself and judge his own deficiencies and yet be powerless to change: he recognizes the difference between his judgments and his actions, between what he says and what he does; he sees that people are bound to take him for a "'madman . . . who quite naturally believes that everyone except him esteems life far too lightly, is in the habit of wasting it too cheaply and using it too lazily and too unscrupulously, so that none of them is worthy of it!'" (p. 432); he admits that he has been deceiving himself ("'I have been telling myself fairytales. I have filled whole nights with them. I can remember them all now . . . I do not want to tell a lie: reality has been trying to catch me, too, in a trap during the last six months,'" III, 6; pp. 432–33). Yet none of this stalls his suicide attempt. That attempt is a failure because Ippolit's self-judgments are not grounded in conviction. He excuses himself from living a responsible, interested life.

It is unclear just why Ippolit is incapable of self-conviction. A dream he recounts shows well enough that there would be significant risks involved; any willingness to encounter the world as an actuality may bring us physical harm. In the dream he tells, a great Newfoundland dog comes across a scorpion and is taken aback at the sight of it, as if out of supernatural fear; and when the dog finally catches the creature in his mouth, it is severely stung: "The shell cracked between her teeth; the tails and legs of the creature, which hung out of the dog's mouth, moved about with terrible rapidity. Suddenly Norma yelped piteously: the reptile had succeeded in stinging her tongue after all. She opened her mouth wide with pain, whining and yelping" (III, 5; p. 429). The sting is painfully real. The dog's encounter is a sign that the world cannot be wished away, denied, or explained as the work of supernatural forces. It yields a first-hand knowledge of reality that some of the

[129]

characters in this book never obtain. Ippolit, for instance, never finds even the ambiguous confirmation of his existence that suicide might bring. Rebellion, he says, is of no great force (III, 7).

There is a manifest will, among the characters of *The Idiot*, to test reality by physical means, but these attempts are foiled by a staunch refusal to accept the world, by an unwillingness to risk conviction at its hands. The expressions of the spirit—love, *caritas*, self-sacrifice—consistently fail to take physical shape. Aglaya for instance boasts that Ganya has burnt his hand "'to show that he loved me more than his life'" (p. 471), but her story is a fabrication, apparently conceived to impress the Prince. She discusses the possibility of knowing another's heart, but the irony of the conversation with Myshkin is that the Prince's love, the feelings of *his* heart, are unresponsive to her passionate needs. He may say that he loves her, but he is unable to prove his love in tangible ways; he is physically infirm and spiritually overdetermined. He may "love" Nastasya Filippovna as well, but he will not commit himself to either one. His dual attraction is free of conflict for as long as his love is an abstraction, an idea, a mere possibility, uncommitted to the actuality of other living individuals. As Radomsky chides him near the end of the book, "'Aglaya loved like a woman, like a human being, and not like—a disembodied spirit! Do you know what I think, my poor Prince? Most likely you've never loved either of them!'" (IV, 9; p. 627). Murray Krieger said, in this regard, that Prince Myshkin suffers from a "curse of saintliness."[16] This curse shows up in his avoidance of love, and it implicates him in the murder of Nastasya Filippovna—not because of what he has done but because of what he has failed to do. His crime is not, on balance, so different from Rogozhin's: the Prince's denial of love is simply a more "perfect" instance of the will to escape conviction, perhaps a "perfect crime."

The Prince is conceived as a half-saint, a near-perfect soul, closely watchful of his moral purity. He is, as Dostoevsky put it in terms that echo Goethe's *Wilhelm Meister* and Hegel's *Phenomenology of Spirit*, a "beautiful soul," one who would maintain his inward spirituality by a retreat from the world. In Hegel's scheme, the "beautiful soul" resembles the Skeptical Consciousness, with the important difference that it is engaged in a struggle with others, not simply with the material world. The beautiful soul has a deep moral awareness, and a profound sense of duty; it is, in Hegel's words, a spirit which "is certain of itself and which deals with the world as a moral being because its self-consciousness knows duty as the absolute essence" (*Phenomenology of Spirit*, pp. 364–65). Yet it is incapable of bringing this sense of moral obligation to bear fruit in a world composed of actual beings. It is confronted with ethical needs, but it cannot fashion a suitable response. The beautiful soul

lacks the power to externalize itself, the power to make itself into a Thing, and to endure [mere] being. It lives in dread of besmirching the splendour of its inner being by action and existence; and, in order to preserve the purity of its heart, it flees from contact with the actual world, and persists in its self-willed impotence to renounce its self which is reduced to the extreme of ultimate abstraction, and to give itself a substantial existence, or to transform its thought into being and put its trust in the absolute difference [between thought and being] (pp. 399–400).

The "beautiful soul" is reluctant, or unable, to commit itself. It judges but is incapable of self-conviction, hence its judgments, its expressions of moral obligation, are feckless and alienating. Thus after Ippolit's suicide attempt, which the Prince condemns, Aglaya can tell him "'it's very callous to think like that and judge a man's soul as you judge Ippolit'" (III, 8; p. 465).

As Murray Krieger said, the Prince is implicated in the final catastrophe of *The Idiot*, and in the minor calamities which precede the death of Nastasya Filippovna, precisely *because* he is the judge of others. "What is so destructive in him is the sense others must get from his infinite meekness that they are being judged. Of course, Myshkin knows the sin of pride that is involved in judging and so carefully refrains, condemning himself instead. But this very inversion of the process constitutes a form of judgment too for the guilty, in many ways a more painful one than conventional judgment" ("The Curse of Saintliness," p. 48). Because of its judgments, the "beautiful soul" appears to others as hypocritical and potentially evil; as Aglaya says to Myshkin when he exposes Ippolit's likely

[131]

motives for suicide. "'You have no tenderness [compassion]: only truth, and that's why you're unfair'" (III, 8; p. 465).

The problem with the beautiful soul is that it is certain of itself and of its judgments, but ignorant of others' lives. In order adequately and responsibly to judge another individual, we should understand that person from within, know everything about them, in order to respond to them as lived actualities. "'Why is it we can never know *everything* about another person, when we ought to, when the other person is to blame!'" the Prince says in exasperation near the end of the novel. "' . . . I'm afraid I don't know what I'm saying—I'm all muddled!'" (IV, 9; p. 627). Kierkegaard expressed this same dilemma when he said, in reference to *Matthew* 7:1 ("Judge not that ye be not judged"): "One human cannot judge another ethically, because he cannot understand him except as a possibility. When therefore anyone attempts to judge another, the expression for his impotence is that he merely judges them" (*Postscript*, p. 286).

If Dostoevsky seems closer to Kierkegaard than to Hegel in his implicit critique of the "beautiful soul," this is because the Prince recognizes that his sense of moral duty, as expressed in his judgments, is insignificant without actions; words without deeds neither convince nor convict (he says this much of Aglaya: "He could not understand how so disdainful, stern, and beautiful a girl could be such a child, a child who perhaps really didn't understand *all the words*," III, 8; p. 469). Hegel said that "consciousness declares its *conviction*; it is in this conviction alone that the action is a duty; also it is valid solely through the conviction being declared" (*Phenomenology of Spirit*, p. 396), but Dostoevsky shows rather the contrary to be the case: that the mere declaration of duty, the simple expression of obligation in words, is insufficient grounds for conviction. Raskolnikov in *Crime and Punishment*, for instance, can speak the words of self-conviction (e.g., as he half-seriously confesses his crime in the police station, or earlier, as he says teasingly to Zamyotov, "'And what if it was I who murdered the old woman and Lisaveta?'" I, 13; p. 184); but these words do not hold unless they are followed through in deeds. Raskolnikov's moral conscience is alive, his sense of duty is urgent at times, but these are meaningless if he does not admit his crime publicly and accept suffering and punishment. What is needed for conviction, and what the "beautiful soul" lacks, is not just the expression of conviction in words, but what Kierkegaard in *Fear and Trembling* calls the "authentic movements of faith." Words must lead to actions, what we say must be validated in what we do. That is the sense of Prince Myshkin's sudden realization in the final pages of *The Idiot* that "at that moment, and for some time past, he had been saying not what he had been meaning to say and had been doing what he should not have been doing" (IV, 11; p. 656). The problem is that he recognizes this too late. The destruction of the women he loves is virtually complete, and there are no significant amends that the Prince can now make; with Nastasya Filippovna dead, and Aglaya about to marry a Polish Count, the moment for conviction is past.

The explanation I have given of Prince Myshkin's lack of conviction parallels the contrast between Hegel and Kierkegaard on the question of our knowledge of others. An outline of this difference here will help prepare for the work of the following pages, and it will preface my concluding section on skepticism and the knowledge of others. Hegel is convinced that the difference between self and other can ultimately be mediated, overcome by an act of mutual recognition or interpersonal acknowledgment; as Mark C. Taylor said, "As a result of their interrelationship, each subject gradually acknowledges the tenability of the viewpoint of the other, and thereby comes to recognize *itself* in the other. The judging self admits the insufficiency of words without deeds, and the judged self accepts the inevitable plurality of its acts. This self-awareness, which is mediated by relation to other, involves both the confession of the self's guilt and the forgiveness of the opposing self."[17] But in *The Idiot* this mediation never takes place. The Prince remains distant and aloof. For this reason *The Idiot* imports wisdom that parallels Kierkegaard's views of ethical selfhood more closely than Hegel's. For Kierkegaard, the end-state of ethical selfhood simply *is* alienation; there is no final mediation of opposites, no bridge or synthesis of self and other. This mediation never obtains, self and other remain apart, because there is no way to know the other from within; abstract thought, the language of faith and morals, are in particular insufficient to the task: "With respect to every reality external to myself, I can get hold of it only through thinking it. In order to get hold of it really, I should have to be able to make myself into the other, the acting individual, and make the foreign reality my own reality, which is impossible. For if I make the foreign reality my own, this does not mean that I become the other through knowing his reality, but it means that I acquire a new reality, which belongs to me as opposed to him . . . . This implies that there is no immediate relationship, ethically, between subject and subject" (*Postscript*, p. 285). Kierkegaard's description of the relations of self and other provide an apt image for the relations among characters in certain of the novels at hand; one thinks of Don Quixote and Sancho, who work changes on one another, but who nevertheless end apart. And one thinks of Prince Myshkin, who admits the insufficiency of words without deeds, but who remains unconvicted and who ends once again in exile, in Dr. Schneider's Swiss clinic. Kierkegaard says that we are on a solitary sojourn along the stages of life's way. These novelists accept the fact of that solitude, but as I hope also to show, they give us good reason to think that solitude can at least be shared.

OUTSIDERS

IN *Crime and Punishment, The Idiot,* and *The Brothers Karamazov,* we have seen that conviction is a form of knowledge that turns on self-understanding and public acknowledgment, but that doubts still remain about the depth of Raskolnikov's, Dimitri's, and Prince Myshkin's convictions. To an important degree, these conclusions are contradictory. What does it mean to say that conviction depends both on self-knowledge and the public acknowledgment of it if we say that there are doubts about those convictions, i.e., that they are uncertain to us on the outside? If this objection holds, then the problem of skepticism toward others is left intact, and that means accepting the disparity of the problems of self-knowledge and the knowledge of other minds. We do not doubt, for example, that Dimitri Karamazov knows the fortunes of his own heart, only that we might. To see the failure of our knowledge of others as *consequent* on this disparity, and hence on our outsideness to them, is premised on the assumption that self-knowledge, knowledge from within, is a privileged kind of knowing; but there are reasons to question the primacy of the insider's position, reasons which might also explain why Dostoevsky's heroes end in exile, as outsiders to their human others. If we accept, for instance, that the insider's claim of self-knowledge, "I am I," is a tautology, and hence empty, then knowing who I am might better be told by knowing something about me, say a description of my identity, or by knowing that I am *an* I, one among others—something which an outsider might be in a better position to know about me than I. And if this is so, then I, as an outsider to an other (i.e., to an other I) might be in a better position to know the identity of that other than he.[1]

The objection can of course be raised that this line of reasoning does nothing more than transform the problems of self-knowledge and the knowledge of others into versions of one another, with no significant advance. What we would need in order to be known *by* an other (not just another I), as what we would need in order to *know* an other (as an other, not as an extension of this I) is some formulation of the problem of knowing persons which might resist this collapse, or some term beside the other and the I. In Hegel's philosophy, as in the philosophy of Sartre, this term is supplied by a mediating third; for Kierkegaard there is no mediation, which is why our knowledge of ourselves is, on his account of it, given in alienation. In more classical epistemology and its responses to skepticism, it is supplied by a radical Outsider, by someone outside to me and to all other minds.

My work in this section will be to investigate just what that image might mean and to suggest certain ways in which Dostoevsky's Prince Myshkin is an expression of it. One could take this work as providing an account of half of the Prince's nature—his saintly half. What is remarkable in the case of the Prince, though, is that his saintliness blocks his capacity to respond to just what it is we most want to know about other persons—their human existence or "actuality" (Kierkegaard's word), their humanity. While the Prince is an Outsider in the epistemological sense, he is also an Outsider in the metaphysical sense, separate from others, as if the one were the price of the other. Whether this price is worth paying will depend, of course, on who you are, and what you imagine knowledge to be. Some have taken this price as their reward, envisioning perfect knowledge in the form of a liberation from the human (Cervantes' Licenciado, who thinks he is made from glass, is one example at hand), or an escape from the human conditions of knowing. If one takes the Outsider as a god, as Descartes for instance would, then the escape from the human is no price at all, nor is it a reward; nor will it any longer be *human* knowing that we are envisioning, by which I mean that whatever this Outsider knows will not be an answer to the problem of "other minds," i.e., our (human) knowledge of other minds. But if we expect the Outsider to be human, then we are demanding something *inhuman* of him. Taken together, these difficulties may help explain on the one hand the image of the God-man, Christ, and on the other Dostoevsky's half-saintly Prince—the one who succeeds in knowing others, and who proves His knowledge by a demonstration of His limiting (human) condition, and the other whose failures of knowledge are tied to his partial freedom from human limits.

The notion of an Outsider as someone whose position might be best for knowing the existence of others begins, philosophically, as a continuation of material object skepticism and the problems raised earlier regarding criteria and the nature of ideas in connection with Cervantes and Descartes. Recall that Descartes warned that "the principal error and the commonest which we may meet with in them, consists in my judging that the ideas which are in me are conformable to the things which are outside me."[2] Presumably I cannot tell whether my ideas conform to the things of the world or not, but an Outsider might be able to stand obliquely to the ideas which are "in my mind" and make such a comparison. Similarly, if two individuals cannot agree which of their ideas best conforms to the things of the world, if they cannot agree for instance whether a certain thing is a barber's basin or a helmet, then someone wholly apart from that community of minds might be able to tell. Would such an absolute Outsider, someone external to my mind *and* to other minds, be able to settle skeptical questions with regard to knowledge of others?

In extending the problems and possible solutions of material object skepticism to our knowledge of other minds, we need to say first exactly what it is we hold in doubt about others and what it is we want to know of them. In the case of material object skepticism, we do not doubt that we see anything at all, but we resist the ordinary identification of things, holding out, as it were, in case they might not be what they appear to be. In the case of skepticism with regard to others, our doubt might be expressed by the worry, or the fantasy, that the other bodies we see are not inhabited by other minds. This is one of the sources behind Descartes's image of the human body as a machine, "built and composed of nerves, muscles, veins, blood and skin, that even though there were no mind in it at all, it would not cease to have the same motions as at present" (*Meditation IV*, p. 195). Suppose that there were a body, human in every respect except that it were attached to no mind; suppose that it were built, as Descartes says, like a well-made (i.e., perfect) clock, and that it responded to stimuli in every way that mind-driven bodies do. How could we tell this body from one that is *entirely* like mine, i.e., attached to a mind like mine as well?

In response to problems of this order, Descartes thinks of an Outsider, someone who could tell these things, as a being himself free from the human condition and hence free from the conditions (or constraints) of human knowing. In order to tell whether he is a solitary I or whether he is one among other minds Descartes invokes the idea of God as "independent, all-knowing, all-powerful" (*Meditation* III, p. 165). He says that while it would be easy to conceive that "the ideas which represent to me other men or animals, or angels . . . might be formed by an admixture of other ideas which I have of myself, of corporeal things, and of God, *even though there were apart from me neither men nor animals, nor angels in the world*" (p. 164, italics added), the idea of God, of this Outsider, "cannot have proceeded from myself" (p. 165). This is of course meant as an argument for the existence of God, but the argument matters because it enables Descartes to deduce such things as the certainty of his own existence, from which he can then argue the existence of the material world and others in it.

There are well-known difficulties with the Cartesian strategy. Some would claim for example that deducing the existence of God and the existence of a single I does nothing for the problem of our skepticism toward others except make it imaginable. I do not think that is itself the problem here, at least not in that formulation. My worry about it stems from a different cavil. Suppose, for instance, that this Outsider were not benevolent as Descartes imagines him to be but were instead devious and deceiving, bent on fooling him about the existence of the world, and of those in it. (Suppose we take the world not as the work of God, but of the devil.) This is in fact what Descartes imagines when he conjures up his idea of an evil demon, also a genius in matters of knowing, smart enough to deceive him about every aspect of every thing in the world, and equally as malicious as God is good. (In certain philosophical formulations of the problem of skepticism, this evil demon is played by the mad super-scientist, manipulating brains in a vat, producing the image of a world and bodies in it.) What, or who, is to say that the Outsider is not the demon?

Looking at some recent writing on this question, I find in Jacques Derrida's critique of Michel Foucault, for instance,[3] the complaint that Descartes is dogmatic in his choice to privilege God over the demon or, if not dogmatic, then repressive of what the demon might mean—not mere sensory error about the world, but rather delusion; not just a mistake about something in the world, or even about the existence of the world, but the mad idea that I, *and* others like me, might not exist at all. Certainly this is a legitimate complaint. What it means for my purposes is that the Cartesian Outsider is not as radically Outside as he is set up to be. Since he cannot subvert the *cogito*, which founds all existence on thought, he is limited in the tasks which he can perform. Consider, as Stanley Cavell does at one point in *The Claim of Reason*, the vast difference in the powers of judgment we will allow an Outsider in the case of material object skepticism and an Outsider in the case of our knowledge of others or ourselves. What would happen if, on the advice of an Outsider, we were to learn that someone's extraordinary identifications of the things of the world were correct, and that ours were in error? (That, I said, was a possibility that Cervantes left open.) We would say that we were wrong or mistaken. But what would we say in comparing my (human) sensations to those of another if, on the advice of an Outsider, we were told that another's pains or feelings were genuine, and mine not? Either we would not allow our Outsider to say such a thing (which is Descartes's solution), or we would say that we were mad (the aversion from which is the source of Derrida's complaint). What we need, it seems, is an Outsider who is also *in* us (and the courage to face the prospect of self-subversion), one who might be capable of knowing mine and other minds from *within* a human mind. Framed in this way, our wanting to know other minds is like wanting an escape from the human and then wanting to bring the human back. Here, I will discuss this contradictory demand as it takes shape in Prince Myshkin, but I would also point ahead to my concluding pages on Emma Bovary, where I say how she comes to terms with this same wish.

Dostoevsky does not, like Descartes, look to God as confirmation of the fact that we are not alone in the world, that we are among other minds; the Prince's fits of epileptic madness suggest that he may have been open to certain lines of skepticism that Descartes was not. Dostoevsky portrays a society which has lost its image of God, one which has asked mere mortals to bear the burdens of knowing other minds. This too may seem more daring and honest than Descartes, insofar as the knowledge we require of other minds is that they be known *by* other minds. But the conclusion from this is that this human wish to know others is somehow inhuman: taking on for ourselves the Outsider's burdens, we live, in our knowledge of others, or in its failure, as outsiders to them. This does not say that we *cannot* know the existence of others, which is what the skeptic threatens, but that the conditions of this knowledge, whatever else they may be, will prove our outsideness to others. The fact of this outsideness is the groundwork of the tragic action of *The Idiot.*

We have known, roughly since Nietzsche's *Antichrist,* that the image of outsideness is central to Dostoevsky's vision of the Prince and his geminate condition. Myshkin is, literally, an "idiot," which Nietzsche derives from its ancient Greek etymon meaning a "private person."[4] He comes as one bearing truth and light to a world ruled by the Apocalypse's dark horse. Like Don Quixote, he is defeated at the hands of the world, and he is isolated in it as well (Dostoevsky spoke of him as a Quixote in the serious vein). The Prince traces his feelings of outsideness to his days in Switzerland under Dr. Schneider's care: "'The thing that affected me the most was the thought that everything was *foreign.* I realized that. The fact that it was foreign depressed me terribly'" (I, 5; p. 82). Later in the book, after the episode with Ippolit, he recalls his stay in Switzerland; he thinks back on the vast oneness of nature and his haunting estrangement from it:

He remembered now how he had stretched out his arms toward that bright and limitless expanse of blue and had wept. What tormented him was that he was a complete stranger to all of this. What banquet was it, what grand everlasting festival, to which he had long felt drawn, always—ever since he was a child, and which he could never join? . . . Everything has its path, and everything knows its path; it departs with a song and it comes back with a song; only he knows nothing, understands nothing, neither men nor sounds, a stranger to everything and an outcast." (III, 7; p. 462)

When the Prince returns to Russia, those who meet him recognize him instantly as different. He is the last of the line of the Myshkins, he has no education, and he is an invalid of sorts;[5] he associates with children, and lives obliquely to the society into which he comes. Yet he has a remarkable will to understand people. He is valued for his perspicacity, for his inward vision, and is widely consulted for his opinions. He stands in a position to see others because he stands as an outsider to them. He is able to judge them; as a half-saint, he can tell what specific difference the human in their nature makes. But he must pay for his privileged position with oppression, boredom, and solitude. "'Now I'm going to see *people*,'" he says, "'with people perhaps I'll be bored and oppressed.'"[6]

The Russian critic Konstantin Mochulsky saw the Prince as someone who is himself all but free from human nature and its flaws. The Prince, he said, "opposes himself not only to adults, but also to people in general: he is not fully a man and therefore among people he feels oppressed; he passionately yearns to enter human life and cannot" (*Dostoevsky*, p. 375). Mochulsky explains this half-inhuman nature in terms of the Prince's outsideness to history— that is to say, his outsideness to human history: "The prince is a being of another aeon—before the Fall: he has a different destiny." This explanation seems to me particularly significant: the Prince, as Outsider, is figured as pre-Lapsarian man, man before the Fall. The human history which began at that supposed moment is of course the history of our ignorance, of our deprivation from perfect knowledge, the beginning of our conditioned knowing. But rather than seek to escape those conditions, the Prince yearns, and fails, to achieve a human destiny. Dostoevsky himself remarked on the extreme difficulty of finding an appropriate shape in which to couch his hero: "I am obliged to construct an image. Will it develop under my pen?"[7] This worry shows up in the novel, almost verbatim, in connection with Ippolit's dream and his obsession by phantomlike forms: "Can anything appear in a vivid image which has no image?" (III, 6; p. 448).

Mochulsky said that "The fact of [Myshkin's] not being fully incarnated is connected with his asexuality [because sex is part of the human destiny, which is not shared, for instance, by the angels]: 'Because of my inherent disease, I have no knowledge at all of women . . . I can't marry anyone.' It seems that he does not tread upon the earth, but hovers over it like a bloodless spirit in ineffectual pity for sinful men. . . . Sinless himself, he does not understand that sin requires redemption and that the cross of Golgotha is inscribed into the history of the world." The Prince is a paradox of being—at once human, yet free from human nature. But whereas this condition is taken as a blessing for those few others in history who have been so privileged—Christ, the Virgin Mary—it is a curse for the Prince, his "curse of saintliness," as Murray Krieger said: it is at the root of his failure to love at close-range, rather than simply to pity and judge from a distance, as he does. The Prince's spirituality, oddly enough, blocks his ability to be Christ to others.

Dostoevsky said that only one individual could bear the demand that he be our God, and for that individual godliness was proved by the body, by His also being Christ: "On earth there is only one positively beautiful person—Christ, so that the appearance of this immeasurable, infinitely beautiful person is, of course, an infinite miracle in itself. (The entire gospel of John is in this sense: it finds the whole miracle of the *incarnation* alone, in the manifestation of the beautiful alone.)"[8] In *The Idiot*, what is lacking among people is their ability to be Christ to one another. They fail in this because they fail, as Wittgenstein puts it, to see the human body as the best picture of the human soul. They ignore that our knowledge of others must entail our acknowledgment of their incarnation. In the second part of this section, I will take up concerns which closely match these in my discussion of the crucified Christ represented by the Holbein painting. To anticipate the emergent contrast, it could be said that here, the ignorance of the other's body would be parallel to a failure to see Christ as the embodied God; there, it is proof of godliness which is found to be unaskable of the body—or askable only on pain of a denial of Christ.

The Prince comes as if "sent from God" (II, 12; p. 355). He is, like Christ, an image of "truth bursting into a world of falsehood" (Mochulsky's words, p. 370). Society, as he finds it, is the ground of estrangement, not community. He meets a collection of human natures with no idea of God and which is thus immune to the truths which any Outsider could tell it. (Cervantes' Knight, and the man of glass, have similar experiences, albeit for different reasons.) The world which Myshkin enters is filled with passionate rivalries. It turns on the fierce forces of individualism, and is in fact wholly composed of outsiders. The insight is something like Rousseau's in the *Social Contract*. Whereas Rousseau finds that human bondage is implicit in man's freedom to shape his own manner of association (i.e., that "Man was born free, and everywhere he is in chains"), Dostoevsky finds that our sociability, our possibility for community and what we have made of it, implicates us as outsiders to one another. We are, as in Rousseau, outsiders to one another *in* society; and we have made others our outsiders because we have made them our gods, but not our Christs.

The loss of the idea of God is, in a broad way, at the bottom of the human blindness, the failures to recognize and actively acknowledge others, which we see in the general sweep of the action in *The Idiot* ("'lots of people don't believe nowadays. . . . in Russia we have more unbelievers than in other countries,'" Rogozhin tells the Prince, II, 4; p. 251); it is at the root of serious delusions about the natural world and about human nature. Failing to recognize God as distant and as different, as absolutely Outside, people fail to see reality as it is, and themselves as inside it, as neighbor to each other: "People, who have lost God, have forfeited reality," Mochulsky said, "they live amidst phantoms and fictions" (p. 270). Forfeiting the idea of God, one is bound to take others as ghosts or as phantoms, and to think that the world is inhabited by nonhuman beings. With no clear idea of God, of a being Outside us, who then could tell what is human from what is not?

The image of the other as ghostly and phantomlike is one sign of our alienation in the world; it is consequent not only on our loss of the idea of what it might mean to know others as human but also on the loss of the hope that we might be known *by* other humans. Ippolit, the consumptive, tells in the "Explanation" how Rogozhin, who entered his room in silence, in tacit denial of him, seemed ghostlike to him: "'Rogozhin leaned against the table and began to stare at me in silence. So passed two or three minutes, and I remember that I was very much hurt by his silence. Why wouldn't he speak?'" (III, 6; p. 448). Ippolit claims that he was certain that he had seen Rogozhin, and that he did not believe in ghosts ("'That it really was Rogozhin and not a phantom or a hallucination I had no doubt whatever at first. Indeed, the idea of doubting it never occurred to me'"; "'Neither during my illness nor before it have I ever seen a ghost; but I always felt, even as a boy and even now—that is, quite recently—that if I ever saw a ghost, I should die on the spot though I don't believe in ghosts,'" p. 449). But after remaining for twenty minutes in the presence of Rogozhin, with no acknowledgment from him, the horrible idea does occur to Ippolit: "'. . . what if it isn't Rogozhin but just a phantom?'" Earlier in the narrative, Ippolit explained that he was able to recognize Rogozhin, but now that Rogozhin appears not to know him, he sees him as a ghost: "'At that very moment, as though guessing that I was afraid, Rogozhin moved away the hand on which he was leaning, straightened out, and began opening his mouth as though he were going to laugh; . . . but as I had vowed not to start talking first, I stayed in bed, particularly as I was still undecided whether it was Rogozhin or not.'"

The worry that he might not be able to tell Rogozhin from a ghost, the fear that there might be some nonhuman being in his place, is more than just a blow to his intellectual pride, more than just a response to a failure of knowledge on his part. Ippolit is horrified at the vision of Rogozhin as a ghost because he fears that he may be *unknowable* by other humans. Thus Ippolit sees something monstrous in the human, something demonic and radically alien in it, something like the inability of the human to recognize itself. This is the source of Ippolit's fright. In a related passage, he describes this sense of the demonic and alien in the image of a tarantula, which he says he saw in a dream: "'I saw, in a sort of strange and impossible form, that infinite power, that dark, deaf-and-dumb creature. I remember that someone seemed to lead me by the hand, with a lighted candle, and show me some huge and horrible tarantula'" (p. 448). On his own account, the demonic and the inhuman which he finds in human nature carry an enormous power—a power which must be *greater* than the power to know the human. This power is, on his own account, at the root of his temptation to suicide: "'It was this curious incident which I have described at such length that was the cause of my making up my mind *definitively*. It was, therefore, not logic, not a logical conviction, but disgust that helped me to arrive at my final decision. It is impossible to go on living when life assumes such grotesque and humiliating forms. That apparition humiliated me. I cannot submit to a dark power which assumes the form of a tarantula'" (p. 450).

Throughout the novel, Rogozhin is figured as central in a quest for a recognition of the human which results, as in the murder of Nastasya Filippovna, in the discovery of our outsideness to one another. It is a quest, and a failure, which deeply involve the Prince as well. From nearly the start, Rogozhin and the Prince are set up as parallel figures; they exchange crosses (II, 4), and the Prince muses that they are "like brothers." Yet even they who are this close fail to know one another; Rogozhin fails to embrace his adopted brother, and the Prince asks, probingly, "did he know Rogozhin?" (II, 5; p. 261). As Myshkin says at one point, Rogozhin is dark and mysterious to him. He reveals the limits of the Prince's ability to assess people:

"It is difficult to make out the new people one meets in a new country." He did, however, begin to believe passionately in the Russian soul. Oh, during those six months he had been through a great deal—a great deal that was quite new to him, a great deal that he had never suspected, nor heard, nor expected! But a stranger's soul is a dark mystery—a mystery to many. He had been friends with Rogozhin for a long time, they had been intimate friends, they had been "like brothers."

Now he claims he does not know Rogozhin.

As we know from Ivan's comment in *The Brothers Karamazov*, the failure of knowledge should be no surprise to someone convinced of the idea of a generalized "Russian soul." The same failure is made apparent, and for much the same reason, in the maddening letter which Nastasya writes to Aglaya:

Can anyone love everyone, all men, all one's neighbors? I have often asked myself that question. Of course not, and indeed, it would be un-natural. In abstract love of humanity one almost always loves oneself. But that's impossible for us, and you are a different matter: how could you not love anyone when you cannot compare yourself to anyone, when you are above every insult, every personal resentment? (III, 10; p. 494)

Taken in tandem with the principal action of the book—the Prince's failure to find conviction in his love for Nastasya Filippovna—these passages suggest that he aims too high in looking for other souls, thinking that they might be revealed in some individual or collec-tive "spirit," when really he ought to look lower, as they are only knowable in and through their bodies. The best instance for know-ing the existence of others is the specific instance, not the gener-alized case; the best condition for knowing them is the embodied condition. The paradox, though—which we already know from Cervantes' man of glass, and which is reconfirmed for us in the striking death scene at the end of *The Idiot*—is that the body, in which each of us is sealed, is also the sign of the limits of our knowledge of others, the sign of our metaphysical outsideness to them.

The troubling relationship between Rogozhin and the Prince is intensified by special, haunting, references to the eyes:

He had been extremely anxious to see "those eyes," so as to be absolutely sure that he would most certainly meet them *there*, at that house. That was a spasmodic wish of his, so why be so crushed and amazed now that he had seen them? As though he had not expected it! Yes, those were the *same* eyes (and there could be no doubt that they were the same) as those which had flashed fire at him in the crowd this morning when he got out of the Moscow train at the Nikolayevsk station; they were the same (absolutely the same!) he had caught looking at him from behind that afternoon as he was sitting down at Rogozhin's. Rogozhin had denied it: he had asked with a wry, chilling smile, "Whose eyes were they?" And quite recently, at the station when he was getting into the train to go to Pavlovsk to see Aglaya and suddenly caught sight of those eyes again, for the third time that day, the prince had a strong impulse to go up to Rogozhin and say to him, "Whose eyes were they?" (II, 5; pp. 264–65)

The Prince can be standing in the physical presence of Rogozhin, and yet be unable to recognize him, unable to *know* him. At one point he remarks that he stood in Rogozhin's presence "like an accuser and a judge—in full view." What he finds is perhaps what he would rather deny: that Rogozhin, who is so much like a "brother" to him, is radically "other," and poses a violent, subversive threat. The Prince's searing insight into the darkness of Rogozhin's heart sparks the first of his epileptic fits since his release from Dr. Schneider's care:

Those two eyes—*the same two eyes*—suddenly met his own. The man who was hiding in the niche, had also taken a step forward. For a second they stood face to face and almost touching each other. Suddenly the prince seized him by the shoulders, turned him round towards the staircase, nearer to the light: he wanted to see his face clearly.

Rogozhin's eyes glittered and a frenzied smile contorted his face. He raised his right hand and something flashed in it. The Prince did not try to stop him. All he remembered was that he seemed to have shouted:

"Parfyon, I don't believe it!"

Then suddenly some gulf seemed to open up before him: a blinding *inner* light flooded his soul. The moment lasted perhaps half a second, yet he clearly and consciously remembered the beginning, the first sound of the dreadful scream, which burst from his chest of its own accord and which he could have done nothing to suppress. Then his consciousness was completely extinguished and complete darkness set in. (II, 5; pp. 267–68)

The alienating power of the eyes, the impenetrable human otherness signaled by the human glance, becomes a major theme of Existentialist literature, much of which follows Dostoevsky's example. In *The Idiot* our outsideness to others, as registered in the eyes, reinforces the calamitous action of the book, the Prince's failure of acknowledgment and denial of love. When Myshkin reviews Nastasya's letters to Aglaya, he reads comments which take up his own concerns about the capacity of the Russian soul; perhaps Aglaya, who knows how to love "like a human" and not like a "disembodied spirit," knows that the problem of other minds, of telling what is human from what is not, finds its best case in the individual instance, which demands from us a human response. Certainly, the Prince does not. After reviewing the letters, he sees Nastasya, who seems like an apparition.

His heart was pounding, his thoughts in a tangle, and everything round him seemed like a dream. And suddenly, just as before when he had twice awakened at the same apparition in his dream, the very same apparition again appeared before him. The same woman came out of the park and stood before him, as though expecting him to be there. He gave a start and stopped dead; she seized his hand and squeezed it tightly. "No, it is not an apparition!" (III, 10; p. 497)

The reference in this passage is to a nightmare, in which the Prince is tormented by his inability to recognize a woman: he seems to see her face, and senses that he wants to draw near, but finds himself immobilized, incapable of the task. The dream is a foreshadowing of his final failure of love. Together, the nightmare and the scene in the park suggest a central theme of this book: that our knowledge of human others must be conditioned by a human response. As Dostoevsky sees it, though, this is just where we are most liable to discover the limits of our knowledge of others, and our status as outsiders to them.

How are we to take the Prince's failure, as an Outsider, to know the humanity of those persons he meets? One could say, self-evidently I suppose, that if an Outsider's knowledge fails, then the "ideal" case for knowing has failed. But I think it can be seen that that failure will bode worse for the skeptic's opponent than for the skeptic himself. Lacking any perfect position on which to base or verify our knowledge, one has recourse to ordinary, everyday cases, to what the skeptic describes as "best" cases, instances or positions of knowledge which are accessible to us all, not just to specialists or to those with privileged access to the Truth. But in *The Idiot* we see that the Prince is likewise reluctant to accept the challenge of knowledge in such "best" (i.e., everyday) cases. In part, he shares the fate of a society which has lost its idea of God, an absolute Outsider, and in which men have failed to take on for themselves the responsibilities and requirements of knowledge in "best" cases. Yet perhaps still searching or hoping for some Outsider, a redeemer or a savior, they have asked one another to assume the power of the Outsider, and hence have made themselves outsiders to one another. Put in other words, they fail to acknowledge what a "best case" requires: that our knowledge of others, if it is to succeed at all, must succeed in the individual case, with regard to actual, existing, human others. In *The Idiot* Dostoevsky brings forth a powerful image of this human denial, the crucified Christ. In the concluding pages of this section, I hope to complete the discussion of that particular line of skepticism which informs the epistemologist's image of the body as a machine composed of inner "states" by a more detailed discussion of Dostoevsky's use of this image.

In Rogozhin's house there hangs a remarkable copy of Holbein's "Christ Taken Down from the Cross." The painting is a brutally vivid depiction of the suffering Christ; the body and face are contorted in pain, wholly bereft of the beautiful aura which characterizes more conventional renderings. The Prince is struck by the painting on one visit to Rogozhin's (II, 4) and recalls that he had seen the original abroad; Ippolit comments on it at length in the course of his "Explanation":

In Rogozhin's picture there was no trace of beauty. It was a faithful representation of the dead body of a man who has undergone unbearable torments before the crucifixion, been wounded, tortured, beaten by the guards, beaten by the people, when he carried the cross and fell under its weight, and, at last, has suffered the agony of crucifixion, lasting for six hours (according to my calculation, at least). It is true, it is the face of a man who has only *just* been taken from the cross—that is, still retaining a great deal of warmth and life; rigor mortis had not yet set in, so that there is still a look of suffering on the face of the dead man, as though he were

[149]

still feeling it (that has been well caught by the artist); on the other hand, the face has not been spared in the least; it is nature itself, and, indeed, any man's corpse would look like that after such suffering. . . . In the picture the face is terribly smashed with blows, swollen, covered with terrible, swollen, and bloodstained bruises, the eyes open and squinting; the large, open whites of the eyes have a sort of dead and glassy glint. (III, 7; pp. 446–47)

Ippolit takes the painting, congruent with Church teachings, as "material proof" of the sufferings of Christ ("'I know that the Christian Church laid it down in the first few centuries of its existence that Christ really did suffer and that the Passion was not symbolical. His body on the cross was therefore fully and entirely subject to the laws of nature'"). But there are serious problems with what Ippolit says. There is every likelihood that the physical suffering of Christ may be taken as grounds to doubt His Godliness. To accept His suffering as real and not merely as symbolic may lead one to repeat the challenges of the skeptics who asked why Christ, if he were God, did not then come down from the cross. To see the body of the God-man as destroyed by natural forces may prompt doubts about His ability to overcome nature, and hence raise doubts about His claims to divinity ("'as one looks at the dead body of this tortured man, one cannot help asking oneself the peculiar and interesting question: if such a corpse . . . was seen by all His disciples, by his future chief apostles, by the woman who followed Him and stood by the cross, by all who believed in Him and worshipped Him, then how could they possibly have believed, as they looked at the corpse, that that martyr would rise again?'"). The more general difficulty with what Ippolit says, which shows up in his continuing remarks about the opposition of God and nature, are the assumptions that underlie the expectations of the doubting Thomas—not simply the demand for material proof of the spiritual life—which is thought of as impossible—but the notion that these two are radically different, that there is something like an unseen, inner spirit, which drives the body (a "pilot in a ship," in Descartes's image), a soul or mind to which the body is tethered.

Ippolit, who takes the Holbein as a shockingly literal depiction of the suffering of Christ, sees the crucifixion as nature's destruction of a "great and priceless Being." He looks on nature as "some huge engine of the latest design," and takes God and nature, the worlds of matter and spirit, as opposing one another. The notion of such an opposition follows from the assumptions which underlie the skeptic's demands for material proof of the spiritual life. Nietzsche explained this phenomenon in *The Antichrist* as a fruit of the Platonic tradition, and its late religions, in which the True is the Ideal, and the world of matter, of the body, is false, a "fallen" world. In place of a lived religion, he claims that Christianity has substituted a vast phantasmagoria of "imaginary" causes and effects (sin, redemption, grace), "imaginary beings" (God, spirits, souls), an "imaginary psychology" (pangs of conscience, temptation by the devil, repentance), and an "imaginary teleology" (the Last Judgment and the Kingdom of God). These ideas of morality and religion have lost contact with and have obscured reality because—like Ippolit's comments on the Holbein—they are founded on the assumption of a split between the material and the spiritual worlds: "Once the concept of 'nature' had been invented as the opposite of 'god,' 'natural' had to become a synonym of 'reprehensible': this whole world of fiction is rooted in a *hatred* of the natural (of reality!)."9

This Nietzschean gloss on Ippolit's skeptical concerns is corroborated later in the novel when the Prince remarks that Catholicism is an "unchristian religion." He says that it preaches a "distorted Christ, a Christ calumniated and defamed by it, the opposite of Christ"; as a consequence, "vast numbers of the common people are beginning to lose their faith—at first from darkness and lies, and now from fanaticism, hatred of the Church and Christianity" (II, 4; p. 250). The Prince sees the institutional Church as a continuation of the Holy Roman Empire; it has gone astray because of a fundamental misconception of its temporal powers ("'The Pope seized the earth, an earthly throne, and took up the sword; and since then everything has gone the same way, except that they've added lies, fraud, deceit, fanaticism, superstition, wickedness,'" IV, 7; p. 585). The problem is not that it is difficult to find the right temporal forms, the correct symbols, to express our ultimate concern, but that we have divorced the "temporal" from the "spiritual" in the first place, and have come to rely on symbols at all.

Earlier in the novel, Rogozhin had commented to the Prince that the Holbein was having similar effects: "'some people may lose their faith by looking at that picture'" (II, 4; p. 250). This anticipates his comment, which I adduced earlier in support of the claim that this society had lost its *idea* of God, that "'lots of people don't believe nowadays . . . in Russia we have more unbelievers than in other countries.'" The Holbein can cause a loss of faith because it is too "perfect" a depiction of Christ's suffering. If people lose their faith because of it, that is because they have come to think of the body as proof of the spirit, which implies taking the spirit as unknowable. To rely on the body to this end is no more desirable than the actions of the Prince, whose spiritual overdetermination results in his reluctance to acknowledge the body at all. To think of body and soul as distinct, and the one as proof of the other, is bound to lead one to think of them as in opposition (as in Ippolit's commentary), or to devotion to an unchristian religion (as Nietzsche, and the Prince, conceive the Church), a religion which has failed to recognize Christ.

The question of the failure to recognize Christ is posed in relation to a *painting* of the crucified Christ because the problem itself lies in the desire to read the body as a "representation" of the soul. What is wrong with understanding the inner life of others as constituted by inner "states" is the same thing that is wrong with understanding the suffering of Christ as almost perfectly imaged in the Holbein: the notion that the body is a representation of the spirit at all. If we take the human animal as composed of inner "states" that are withheld from our view, we are bound to behave as doubting Thomases and demand material proof of every facet of the inner life; but in so doing, in thinking of the body as somehow "hiding" the essential, inner human nature, we effectively deny that nature. The problem is not whether that nature is more, or less, perfectly represented in the body, or whether the evidence which the body gives is correct, but the very idea of the body as a container of something unseen. If the inner life is unseen, perhaps that is because it is not "inner" at all.

The idea of a container recalls a parable about a pot and a picture of a pot which Wittgenstein tells in the *Philosophical Investigations.*

At one point, Wittgenstein says "Of course, if water boils in a pot, steam comes out of the pot and also pictured steam comes out of the pictured pot. But what if one insisted on saying that there must also be something boiling in the picture of the pot?"[10] The general thrust of the *Investigations* at this point is to show the nonsense involved in talking about human beings as if their inner (spiritual) lives were composed of nonmaterial "objects" fully located in their bodies ("Isn't it absurd to say of a *body* that it has pain?—And why does one feel an absurdity in that? In what sense is it true that my hand does not feel pain, but I in my hand? . . . if someone has a pain in his hand, then the hand does not say so (unless it writes it) and one does not comfort the hand, but the sufferer: one looks into his face"[11]). The point of the illustration about the boiling pot, at this juncture in Wittgenstein's discussion, is to suggest that the division between "inner" and "outer," between body and soul, is one of the "pictures" which holds us captive. We are as wrong-headed to take the body as the best "picture" of the human soul (if by that we mean to say that there is a soul somewhere behind it) as we are to look for water boiling in the picture of the pot.

What are the consequences of these views? Applied to the public reaction to the Holbein *Christ* in *The Idiot*, Wittgenstein's parable suggests that those who are struck by the *Christ* lose their faith, and thus become like skeptics, because they expect the painting, or the body on analogy to the painting, to conceal some invisible spiritual life. Holding such "beliefs" (which are more like superstitions, or what Wittgenstein would call "bewitchments"), one can only be a doubting Thomas, constantly in search of material proof of the spiritual, proof from the body of the soul, clues to the "inner" in the "outer." Our conceptual picture of matter and spirit, or body and soul, as thus related, and hence divided, is itself at fault. In *The Idiot*, it lays the groundwork for a tragic plot—the failure to know the other as such, or to use Kierkegaard's terms once again, the failure to know him as an actual, existing individual, rather than as an abstract possibility.

The parable of the boiling pot serves to explain *The Idiot* in part because the characters in the novel behave roughly as Wittgen-stein's interlocutor, in search of the hidden life of others (e.g., when the interlocutor says "'Yes, but there is *something* there all the same accompanying my cry of pain. And it is on account of that that I utter it. And this something is what is important—and frightful,'" §296). But beyond this, the parable is appropriate because the problem of our knowledge of others in Dostoevsky's novel is also figured in terms of a picture—specifically, in terms of a painting, the Holbein *Christ*. Through it, Dostoevsky is at pains to show that private experience is not "pictured" in the outward expressions of the body because a person's face, his behavior, the "evidence" which the body gives, simply *is* the state he is in. Anything else is a fiction of our manufacture, a dangerous fiction, because it leads us to look past the other, as he confronts us, in pursuit of a nonexistent "inner life," and saves us from having to reckon with the fact of our outsideness to him. It may be objected that this is a conclusion reached on "behaviorist" grounds (one of Wittgenstein's interlocutors in fact says to him in the *Investigations*, "'Are you not really a behaviorist in disguise? Aren't you at bottom really saying that everything except human behavior is a fiction?'" p. 307); but we don't call someone who refuses to look inside the pictured pot for boiling water a "behaviorist." If this is the case, then we must learn to read others not like picture-signs which carry an "inner" meaning, but rather more like icons, as *already* meaning all they can.

In *The Idiot*, we see a society in which the failure to know others is rooted in the same assumptions which come into play in the interpretation of the Holbein *Christ*. People take one another as having "inner" lives which are hidden from view and unknowable. The consequence of such assumptions, as Dostoevsky's recurring imagery suggests, is that we take others as having a phantomlike existence, their inward feelings as unseen, ghostly parts of them; in such a world, others become, in their essential nature, ghosts and phantoms to us. If we are unable to know the inner life of another— whether because we take that life as hidden, or because we see that there is nothing there for us to know—the full weight of response falls on our willingness to acknowledge the body. Yet this is precisely where Prince Myshkin fails; he is unwilling, or unable, to recognize that his ability to know others, to love them, requires his commitment to their physical, "fallen" natures, a commitment which must also be of his body.

The failure of Prince Myshkin in his love for Nastasya Filippovna is anticipated from the first time he sees her—indeed, from the first time he sees her picture. When he is shown her portrait at the Yepanchin's, he is immediately struck by her beauty. But he finds the face a "mystery," as hiding some secret experience which he would like to know ("He seemed anxious to solve some mystery that was hidden in that face and that had struck him before. . . . 'Because, you see, there is so much suffering in that face,'" I, 7; pp. 107-8). The Prince takes the face as a riddle, something to be deciphered, "evidence" of Nastasya's inward life. His comments are preceded by the episode at the Yepanchin's where he is asked to "interpret" the faces of the women there; he tries to guess the personality of each from the evidence of her outward appearance:

You asked me about your faces and what I noticed in them. I'll tell you with pleasure. You, Miss Adelaida, have a happy face, the most sympathetic face of the three. Besides your being very good looking, one can't help saying to oneself when one looks at you, 'She has the face of a kind sister.' You approach one simply and gaily, but you are quick to know a man's heart. That's what I think of your face. You, Miss Alexandra, have also a very sweet and beautiful face, but perhaps you have some secret sorrow. You have, I'm sure, the kindest heart—but you are not gay. There's something special about your face which reminds me of Holbein's Madonna in Dresden. Well, so much for your face. Am I good at guessing? You yourselves said I was. But your face, Mrs. Yepanchin,' he said, turning suddenly to Mrs. Yepanchin, 'your face tells me—and I am not conjecturing but I say so with absolute confidence—that you are a perfect child in everything, in everything good and in everything bad, in spite of your age.'" (I, 6; pp. 103-4)

Taken in conjunction with the catastrophic action of the novel, these passages suggest that the Prince's ability to "read into" others, however uncanny, is insignificant if he fails to love them. He can presume to know Nastasya and Aglaya from the look on their faces: he can decipher the feelings of the heart in the expression of a portrait, and still be unable to fashion an active response, a meaningful love. If the example of the Holbein *Christ* is any guide—and the Prince's phrase about Nastasya's portrait, "'there is so much suffering in that face,'" suggests that it is—this failure may well root in his capacity for "insight." It is *because* the Prince takes the face as the outward sign of a mysteriously hidden "inner life" that he is led to deny the humanity of the other. Our response to the other, as Prince Myshkin's failure suggests, must take the shape of human love; that is a form of knowledge that requires a human response, one that will not look past the other's embodiment, nor past the fact that the body is also a sign of our outsideness to others, hence of the limits of love.

III.
FLAUBERT

THE FEMALE QUIXOTE:
AESTHETICS AND SEDUCTION

"What she must learn is to go through all the movements of infinity, to sway, to lull herself in her moods, to confuse poetry and reality, truth and romance, to be tossed about in the infinite."

—Kierkegaard, *Either/Or*

KIERKEGAARD is generally credited with having been the first to foresee a relationship between *Don Quixote* and *Madame Bovary*. In a footnote to the first part of *Either/Or*, Kierkegaard's "A" says that it is "altogether remarkable that the whole of European literature lacks a feminine counterpart to *Don Quixote*."[1] He asks, rhetorically, if the time for such a figure is not at hand: "may not the continent of sentimentality yet be discovered?" These remarks were prompted by Eugène Scribe's *The First Love*, a play of 1832, but actually the first "female Quixote" had been invented nearly a century before, in a novel of that title by Charlotte Lennox (*The Female Quixote*, 1752). That book is a burlesque of French heroic romances of the seventeenth century in which the heroine, Arabella, also figures as the principal character in a serious love story, a "romance" in the amorous sense. In Scribe and in Lennox, respectively, the theatrical contrivance and the admixture of burlesque humor block any significant development of the characters' "sentimentality." It was not until Flaubert's *Madame Bovary* that the full meaning of what Kierkegaard called "sentimentality" became apparent, and that literature was able to develop this "continent" in any depth. If the results were not to be mawkish or saccharine, the task demanded an author with a considerable talent for irony; Harry Levin explained it this way: "To set forth what Kierkegaard had spied out, to invade the continent of sentimentality, to create a female Quixote—mock romantic where Cervantes had been mock-heroic—

[159]

was a man's job. . . . The act of detachment had to be incisive and virile, the gesture of a crusty bachelor interrupting the banns to point out the impediments."[2]

Irony is equally important in Cervantes and Flaubert, although it is of special note in Madame Bovary and I shall talk about it further in connection with Flaubert's narrative technique. But to begin I want to look more closely at what Kierkegaard might have meant by "sentimentality"; an incomplete reading of the term, I think, leads Harry Levin to overlook Flaubert's ironic sympathies for the described events of Madame Bovary. In Levin's interpretation, "sentimental" means something like "emotional." He writes, for instance, that "In sharpest distinction to Don Quixote, whose vagaries were intellectual, Emma Bovary's are emotional. Hence they are counterweighted by no earthbound Sancho Panza, but by the intellectually pretentious M. Homais" (p. 249). The comment about Emma's emotions is doubtless true, but the context of Kierkegaard's remark points up a striking similarity between Don Quixote and Emma Bovary in an opposite way: in approaching the world, both shun intellectuality, especially as it is manifested in reason. When Kierkegaard speaks of "sentimentality" he also means to take the word in its literal sense, as having to do with the senses; alternatively, he would call the cultivation of sentimentality "aestheticism," and it is in their devotion to the aesthetic way of life that, allowing for obvious differences between them (e.g., Don Quixote's commitment to a moral project), Don Quixote and Emma Bovary resemble "A" of Kierkegaard's Either/Or. Part of my work here will be to explain how these two facets of sentimentality—the emotions and the senses—are in tension and work against the aesthete's satisfaction. Like Kierkegaard's "A," Emma Bovary seeks to know the world, to appropriate it to herself, primarily by means of the senses, not the mind. Yet this project destroys her, largely because of her reflective emotionality. Emma's cultivation of sensorial immediacy is a potentially powerful response to skepticism, which tells of the deceit of the senses; yet in her failure she discovers her seduction by the world. To be sure, her aesthetic project requires no less heroism than does Don Quixote's pursuit of the virtues of knight-errantry; in recoil from skepticism, Emma refuses to shrink from the world. She has what Nietzsche would call the courage of her passions—we might say, of her convictions—and so discovers the irreducibility of her sensuous response.

Either/Or is a book of complex design. In it, Kierkegaard presents the collected papers of two writers, "A" and "B," as they have been assembled by a third, Victor Eremita. The personality and way of life that Kierkegaard suggests in the papers of "A" are those of an inward, "sentimental" man, one who lives his life at the aesthetic (as opposed to the ethical or religious) level. In his lyrical aphorisms (the "Diapsalmata"), in his observations on Mozart's *Don Giovanni*, in his review of Scribe's play where we find the key footnote on the female Quixote, and in a diary which he transcribes (the "Diary of the Seducer"), "A" shows himself to be a paragon of self-interest, "inward" in the sense that he exists for himself and not for others. As Kierkegaard described him later in the *Concluding Unscientific Postscript*, "A" is "a young, richly gifted, partly hopeful human being, experimenting with himself and with his life."[3] The figures that interest him—Don Juan, the Seducer—and the music that attracts him suggest that he is in search of an unmediated relationship to the world about him—an immediacy which, it should be noted, Kierkegaard in his irony lets us see as not fully attainable, or desirable. At the same time, "A" is given to great waves of emotion; his feelings are deeply swayed by his imagination of the objects of his desire. He is driven by an active inward life which, if largely unknown to Don Quixote, figures prominently in the makeup of Emma Bovary; he seeks sensual immediacy, but his aesthetic project is governed and impeded by a wide range of passions, emotions, and reflective feelings. There is a rift within him between the (immediate) aesthetic and the more reflective life which, in turn, guides his search for pleasure, fashions his conception of it, and finally foils his ability to achieve satisfaction: hence his constant and seemingly self-induced suffering, his broodings, his melancholy emotions.

The "inward" aspect of the aesthete's life mediates his sensorial experience and thus works against the immediacy that he seeks. It is in the sense of mediation that the notion of "inwardness" passes over into Kierkegaard's description of Don Quixote in the *Postscript* (he calls him "the prototype for a subjective madness, in which the passion of inwardness embraces a particular finite fixed idea," p. 175), and from there into Lukács's *Theory of the Novel*. Don Quixote's relationship to the world is not mediated by the emotional life as it is for "A" or for Emma Bovary, yet his practice of knight-errantry, his engagment of its virtues, depends on the books he reads; he knows the chivalric way of life as it is re-presented and *already* mediated. When Kierkegaard's notions come up in Lukács (e.g., where Lukács says that the novel tells of the "adventure of interiority," or where he cites Browning's *Paracelsus*, "'I go to prove my soul'") he implies that in the novel there is always a disparity between immediate and inward, mediate experience. The notion is basic to the *Theory of the Novel* as an "historico-philosophical" accounting of a literary form; in the form and the content of literary creation, Lukács says, there is "always a symptom of the rift between 'inside' and 'outside,' a sign of the essential difference between the self and the world, the incongruence of soul and deed."[4]

Pursuit of the aesthetic way of life is an attempt to regain, through sensorial immediacy, this lost proximity of self and world. It is an alternative to philosophy, the attempt to approximate man to the world by reason, which, one can infer from Lukács's words, is itself a symptom of the rift. *Aisthésis* (Greek) is a way of sensing things, of placing them in our presence, and must be distinguished from the will to know them speculatively. Thus it is resistant to skepticism, the philosophy which begins from doubt. As Kierkegaard said, the "speculative point of view" is characterized by one trait: "it has no presuppositions. It proceeds from nothing; it assumes nothing as given, it begs no postulates" (*Postscript*, p. 49). It is the skeptical philosophy of Johannes Climacus: *de omnibus dubitandum est*. Kierkegaard's "A" and Flaubert's Emma put speculation aside as an impossible task, as irreconcilable with their aesthetic goals; it never occurs to Don Quixote, whose actions admit no possibility of doubt, whose chivalric behavior does indeed proceed from certain postulates, from a series of "givens" (i.e., those chivalric heroes after whom he fashions his role). As Kierkegaard would see it, these characters are capable of a way of existing which is incompatible with "speculation" ("If thus for example speculative philosophy, instead of objectively expounding *de omnibus dubitandum*, had made an attempt to represent such a doubter in his essential inwardness, so that one could see to the smallest detail how he made shift to do it—had it done this, that is, had it begun upon it, it would have given it up, and perceived with shame that the great phrase which every spouter has sworn that he has realized, is not only an infinitely difficult task, but an impossibility for an existing individual," *Postscript*, p. 228).

Discussing Cervantes and Dostoevsky in previous chapters, I gave reasons for rejecting the notion of an "inner life" as developed by rationalist (more generally, speculative) philosophy: in Cervantes' case because the notion of role, which defines a character's identity and shapes his actions, stands apart from and even against the traditions of thought that posit ideas as "inner objects" and human experience as composed of "inner states"; and in Dostoevsky's case because such a conception of human nature is shown to lead us to deny the human beings that we confront in what Sartre would call "situations." I want to clarify here however that the notion of Don Quixote's pursuit of knight-errantry as mediated by the books he reads does not impute to him the idea of experience as an "inner state." "Inwardness" as Kierkegaard intends it is not the same as the rationalist notion of "inner states," although they have similar names. Moreover, the two ideas are not mutually exclusive. In Dostoevsky, for instance, we saw that there is no reason to question the fact that the characters have "inner" (i.e., psychological, self-conscious) lives and also no reason to grant the fact of the characters' estrangements, their mediate relationships to and by one another, as in the case of Sonia and Raskolnikov.

In Flaubert, mediation takes the following form: it is not interpersonal, as in Dostoevsky, but rather internal; the inward emotions and self-reflective sentimentality intervene in the aesthetic experience to block any ultimate fulfillment of it. Emma is inherently unsatisfied, or rather, unsatisfiable ("Every smile concealed a yawn of boredom, every joy a curse, every pleasure its own disgust, and the sweetest kisses left upon your lips only the unattainable desire for a greater delight"⁵). Flaubert sees his characters as *condemned* to mediation; in fact, he sees the failure of the aesthetic project as inherent in the aesthete's will to immediacy. Hence his characters are fated to experience those symptoms of the "difference between the self and the world, the incongruence of soul and deed" which Lukács saw as endemic to the human condition as portrayed in the novel (*The Theory of the Novel*, p. 29). To look ahead to *Bouvard and Pécuchet*, Flaubert finds evidence of this incongruence—as Lukács himself does—in the work of "speculative" philosophy, which interposes itself between man and world; philosophy, Lukács said, "as a form of life or as that which determines the form and supplies the content of literary creation," was "symptomatic" of that fissure. In *The Temptation of Saint Anthony*, and in *Smarh*, it is the Devil who preaches Spinozistic philosophy, with its promising vision of God, Man, and Nature unified. Certainly, that vision would be enough to satisfy a Utopian wish, but its achievement through analysis is hardly acceptable; thus the Devil in *Smarh* also gives advice of the lessons of Spinozism: that all knowledge then can be reduced to doubt, lies, and nothingness.

In contrast to *The Temptation of Saint Anthony*, where knowledge is seen in the guise of temptation, Flaubert develops Emma's aestheticism in the shape of seduction, in blatant contrast to the "speculative" philosophy of the skeptic. The philosopher naturally resists seduction, and the customary seriousness of philosophical discourse reinforces this stance. But Flaubert finds that to avoid seduction is to resist the world and the (aesthetic) attractiveness that it has for us. To be willing for seduction by the world, on the other hand—as other characters we have seen are willing for conviction at its hands—is to risk defeat, but this is precisely where Flaubert discovers the possibilities of Emma's role. Toward the end of the novel, she frankly confronts the fact of her seduction, meaning also that she rises above deception, and hence above the threats of skepticism; she says of Léon, "'What does it matter if he betrays me! What do I care?'" (III, 6; p. 206). Having recognized that she is seduced enables her to take action, to be the seducer, and thus to gain mastery. When Rodolphe refuses her request for money she seizes the moment as an occasion of near heroic self-recognition:

"Now her plight, like an abyss, loomed before her. She was panting as if her heart would burst. Then in an ecstacy of heroism, that made her almost joyous, she ran down the hill . . ." (III, 8; p. 229).

Throughout *Madame Bovary* there are clear and abundant signs of Emma's fervid aestheticism, of her will for seduction. These traits were apparent to the earliest critics of the book; indeed, part of the scandal surrounding the work at publication can be attributed to the fact that Flaubert tempts his readers with the same sensuous pleasures that entice Emma Bovary. The frank sensuality of the novel was intended for "idle readers," spirits kindred to Emma, with an interest in passionate tales—the novels of Scott, the operas of Donizetti. Emma tells Léon, for instance, that she loves "'stories that rush breathlessly along, that frighten one. I detest commonplace heroes and moderate sentiments'" (II, 2; p. 59). She finds in the pursuit of pleasure an antidote to the indolence which gnaws at her quotidian existence, as it must have plagued the lives of readers of the book. Like Kierkegaard's "A" her swings of emotion are wide, ranging from frenzied excitement to lethargy. On one occasion her boredom is cured by a good dousing of perfumed water ("On certain days she chattered with feverish profusion, and this overexcitement was suddenly followed by a state of torpor, in which she remained without speaking, without moving. What then revived her was to pour a bottle of eau-de-cologne over her arms," I, 9; p. 48).

The wealth of sensuous incident in the novel is in large measure bait for the reader who will identify with Emma, as she has identified with the heroines of her books, unaware of the catastrophe toward which she will be drawn. The Flaubertian narrator can be dry and detached when necessary, as if to guarantee the author his ironic distance from the the final events of the novel and thus to preserve himself from seduction (it was this detachment that so struck Harry Levin). Yet there are long passages of prose in which Flaubert takes obvious pleasure in the sheer assemblage of aesthetic detail. The scene at Vaubyessard is perhaps the best example: the music and rhythms of the orchestra, the linens and brocade of the blouses, the food and table settings have seductive allure to which Emma, and the reader, fall prey:

Emma, on entering, felt herself wrapped round as by a warm breeze, a blending of the perfume of the flowers and of the fine linen, of the fumes of the roasts and the odour of the truffles. The candles in the candelabra threw their lights on the silver dish covers; the cut crystal, covered with a fine mist of steam, reflected pale rays of light; bouquets were placed in a row the whole length of the table; and in the large-bordered plates each napkin, arranged after the fashion of a bishop's mitre, held between its two gaping folds a small oval-shaped roll. The red claws of lobsters hung over the dishes; rich fruit in woven baskets was piled up on moss; the quails were dressed in their own plumage, smoke was rising; and in silk stockings, knee-breeches, white cravat, and frilled shirt, the steward, grave as a judge, passed between the shoulders of the guests, offering ready-carved dishes and, with a flick of the spoon, landed on one's plate the piece one had chosen. On the large porcelain stove inlaid with copper baguettes the statue of a woman, draped to the chin, gazed motionless on the crowded room.

.   .   .

Iced champagne was poured out. Emma shivered all over as she felt its cold in her mouth. She had never seen pomegranates nor tasted pineapples. Even the powdered sugar seemed to be whiter and finer than elsewhere. (I, 8; pp. 34–35)

What is remarkable about a passage like this, beyond the sheer luxury of the scene described, is the suggestion that the world presents itself to Emma of its own will. She seems to find that reality offers itself to her, that it surrenders with utter ease, as in the case of the meats on the platter that the waiter carries. This is in part because she is willing for seduction, and sees reality as inherently seductive; but it also means that she will look for seduction where there is none, romanticizing reality simply to maintain an interest in it. The affair at Vaubyessard for instance comes to assert itself over her lackluster and relatively boring former existence: "in the splendor of the present hour, her past life, so distinct until then, faded away completely, and she almost doubted having lived it" (p. 37).

The scene at Vaubyessard is of further importance to Flaubert's interpretation of the aesthetic stage of life because of the insistence on food and eating. There are, to be sure, immediate pleasures to be derived from food, but eating comes to underlie Emma's whole approach to the world; it becomes the customary mode by which she appropriates reality to herself. As critics have pointed out, she will also be undone in this way, dying by the ingestion of poison. Thus the scene at Vaubyessard, which might seem an example of unmitigated aestheticism on Flaubert's part, contains seeds of Emma's eventual demise. If she is seduced by the promise of aesthetic fulfillment, and is destroyed, she also seeks out seduction, and destroys herself.

Emma's passions are varied, and she finds it difficult, if not impossible, to give any order or direction to her wants; indeed, she is hard put to sustain any one interest for long stretches of time. Kierkegaard's "A" found a solution to the aesthete's dilemma in the alternation of pleasures, the dubious "rotation method," but Emma's difficulties appear more severe. At Lheureux's, for instance, the objects she sees for sale—the silk scarves which "rustle with a little noise, making the gold spangles of the material scintillate in the greenish twilight" (II, 5; p. 74)—would readily seduce her; yet she resists because she cannot be convinced long enough of her interest in or need for them. Lheureux will, of course, be one of her seducers ("'We shall understand one another by and by,'" he says to her, "'I have got a way with ladies'"[6]). Her end is in fact a consequence of debts she owes the merchants—literally, a fact of worldly claims upon her: these are ironic signs of a deep involvement in things, indications of an excess of interest, which ill befits the aesthete's more capricious goals.

The aesthete is driven by whim, by the will to gratuitous pleasures. That is why Emma can resist temptation on the grounds that she has no need for the objects which are offered her. It is thus that she can be wildly generous with the beggars who pass her by ("Emma was growing difficult, capricious. She ordered dishes for herself, then she did not touch them; one day drank only pure milk, and the next cups of tea by the dozen. Often she persisted in not going out, then, stifling, threw open the windows and put on light dresses. After she had well scolded her maid she gave her presents or sent her out to see neighbors. She sometimes threw beggars all the silver in her purse, although she was by no means tender-

hearted or easily accessible to the feelings of others," I, 9; p. 47).
There is something of the dandy in her, as there is in Kierkegaard's
"A." Her capricious actions recall an incident of which Judge
William of the second part of *Either/Or* reminds his nephew:

You once recounted to me that on one of your promenades you were
walking behind two old women. . . . They were two women from the
poorhouse. . . . While one woman was taking a pinch of snuff and offering it to the other she said, "If a body had five dollars." Perhaps she herself
was surprised at this daring wish, which echoed across the glaciers like a
prayer unanswered. You approached her, after having concealed a five
dollar bill in your sketch book before you took the decisive step, in order
that the situation might retain a befitting elasticity and that she might not
suspect something. You approached her with an almost subservient polite-
ness, as beseemed a ministering spirit; you gave her the five dollars and
vanished. You then enjoyed thinking of the impression this would make
upon her.[7]

The generosity here, as in Emma's case, is done for effect, for the
"impression it would make," rather than out of true interest in
others.

Taken together with *Madame Bovary*, the passage above is particularly instructive. It suggests that the aesthete's life can subsume
any sphere of human action or behavior. Emma for instance consistently draws religion under the sway of her aesthetic pursuits. When
she thinks of her youth, she recalls the springtime flowers on the
altar, the great candlesticks, the colonnaded tabernacle. "She
would have liked to be once more lost in the long line of white
veils, marked off here and there by the stiff black hoods of the good
sisters bending over their praying-chairs. At mass on Sundays,
when she looked up, she saw the gentle face of the Virgin amid the
blue smoke of the rising incense" (II, 6; p. 79). Later in the novel
when she falls ill, she is taken by the idea of becoming a saint. Her
notions of death and of the afterlife are shot through with the most
sensuous images and motifs of the Christian repertoire:

She let her head fall back, fancying she heard in space the music of
seraphic harps, and perceived in an azure sky, on a golden throne in the

[168]

midst of saints holding green palms, God the Father, resplendent with majesty. . . . This splendid vision dwelt in her memory as the most beautiful thing that it was possible to dream, so that now she strove to recall her sensation: it was still with her, albeit in a less overpowering manner . . . Amid the illusions of her hope, she saw a state of purity floating above the earth, mingling with heaven, to which she aspired [*où elle aspira d'être*]. She wanted to become a saint. She bought rosaries, and wore holy medals; she wished to have in her room, by the side of her bed, a reliquary set in emeralds that she might kiss it every evening. (II, 14; p. 154)

To the very end of the novel, Flaubert insists on the aesthetic possibilities of the religious: Emma receives the last rites, which both canonically and in Flaubert's special emphasis, is a sacrament of the body, a blessing of the senses:

First, upon the eyes, that had so coveted all worldly goods; then upon the nostrils, that had been so greedy of the warm breeze and the scents of love; then upon the hands that had taken delight in the texture of sensuality; and finally upon the soles of the feet, so swift when she had hastened to satisfy her desires, and that would now walk no more. (III, 8; p. 237)

These passages give some indication of Flaubert's duplicitous response to Emma's aesthetic way of life. As stylist-maker of these scenes, he must himself be involved with it, in part committed to it; the religious rites and their accompanying paraphernalia are portrayed as irresistible, even if the pursuit which they engender is in vain. Flaubert allows this aestheticism to run its course, mining the irony of its potential for self-destruction rather than condemning it from a standpoint of omniscience. The feast at Vaubyessard, for example, is given its grim reply when Emma swallows the poison, yet her "devotion" to the aesthete's varied pleasures is blessed when she receives the last sacrament. Flaubert describes the scene of her death as luxuriously as her earlier pleasures. This is a subtle technique of irony, powerful in its own right, and quite distinct from moralizing critique. The flaws in the aesthete's way of life are inherent to that life, and Flaubert allows them to flourish, admitting none of the skeptic's warnings to doubt the permanence of the things of this world and to turn our thoughts toward ultimate reality and truth. Hazel E. Barnes judged Flaubert's irony in the death-bed scene heavy-handed, especially where Emma bestows upon the crucifix "the fullest kiss of love that she had ever given,"[8] but surely its effect works in other directions. Flaubert's style colludes with his characters' interests and blocks the skeptic's moralizing dicta. Put in other words, his heroine is fated to be destroyed by the aesthetic way of life *and* to flourish in it.

Victor Brombert said that *Madame Bovary* is the "drama of reality."[9] The formal shape and inner movement of this drama are given in terms of Emma's disillusionment, concluding with the blind man's song and her final laugh at the destruction of her dreams of love and fulfillment. Gradually, she finds that her dreams are not powerful enough to alter the shape of the world; this is the wisdom that she gains in the course of her failure to satisfy her sensuous needs, and it is near tragic because it could be gained only in that failure. It brings an enlightenment of sorts, a lucidity not unlike that which comes to tragic heroes, free of any intellectualization. "Repeatedly, Emma 'wakes up' to the realization that her capacity to dream is powerless to change the world. To be sure, some of these awakenings—as when she suddenly discovers that her child has dirty ears—only confirm her slovenliness and her withdrawal to a selfish world of illusions" (*The Novels of Flaubert*, p. 85). Brombert's comment can be taken several ways. Certainly, Emma's dreams are dreams that destroy the dreamer; her refusal to cease in the pursuit of her fantasies only confirms, in her destruction, the inaccessibility of the world. In addition, her dreams mitigate her ability to love and hence destroy her capacity for a deep response to her husband or any one of her lovers. Yet she has the capacity, indeed the driving will, to *be* loved, the need to find the world's claim upon her. Thus she works toward her own demise, accumulating large debts (cf. Lheureux's comment to her: "'Did you think, my dear lady, that I was going to go on to the end of time providing you with merchandise and cash, just for the love of God?'" III, 6; p. 213). A character like Charles, so lacking in imagination, may be more capable of love than Emma (this is Barnes' crucial gloss of Sartre's reading of the novel); yet he has none of the willingness for seduction which draws Emma out of skepticism and to an encounter with the real.

The "aesthetic" is a mode of approaching the world through the senses, which I have identified in Emma Bovary in relation to Kierkegaard's "A," and which can also be seen in the figures of Don Juan and the Seducer whose diary so interests "A." Don Juan is of course a version of the seducer, yet there are differences between Kierkegaard's two figures that are worthy of note. Whereas Don Juan flaunts the sheer number of amorous conquests he makes, the Seducer is devoted to the idea of a single love; of the two, the Seducer is relatively more reflective: "The immediate Don Juan must seduce 1,003; the reflective need only seduce one, and what interests us is how he did it" (*Either/Or*, I, p. 107). This contrast invites a further comparison with *Madame Bovary* (the writing of the novel, we know, was closely bound up with a projected *Don Juan* of which only a fragment survives, "Une nuit de Don Juan"). Sartre's notes on *Madame Bovary* have caused some debate concerning the number and variety of Emma's loves; apparently she has many, but Sartre claims that she loved only Rodolphe, feeling but imaginary passion and lust for Léon. I would resolve the question rather differently, because I do not think Emma loved Rodolphe or Léon any more than she loved Charles, despite the fact that they awaken her passions while her husband does not. If Emma loves anything, she loves the *idea* of love, and it is just that which blocks the satisfaction of her immediate sensuous needs. She must constantly arrange for an amorous challenge to solve, or find another image of romantic love to imitate. This points up a second sense of the term "aesthetic," by which Emma resembles both Don Juan *and* the Seducer: the aesthetic refers to art, i.e., to what is artificial, arranged, or otherwise contrived; it shows up for instance in *Either/Or* in the planned "rotation method" of alternating pleasures, designed to insure the aesthete's constant engagement with his project. The aesthete does not find pleasure simply to be given for the asking; he must take part in arranging it, designing it and contriving to seek it out. The aesthete must paradoxically look to art, and to artifice, for his models of immediate satisfaction. Hence he discovers, as Louis Mackey said of the aesthetic stage in *Either/Or*, that "pure immediacy cannot be experienced as the content of actual life; it can only be savored as fantasy."[10] This is the source of what we would identify as Emma's quixotism, the multifarious ways in which she models her actions and seeks to contrive her pleasures on the basis of artistic examples; these forms of the imagination and fantasy mediate the aesthetic experience and, in so doing, attest to its evanescence. The basis for Emma's adulterous relationship with Rodolphe, for instance, is the *idea* of a transgression modeled on the romantic adventures which she has read:

"I have a lover! I have a lover!"

She repeated "I have a lover!" "I have a lover!" delighting at the idea as if a second puberty had come to her. So at last she was to know those joys of love, that fever of happiness of which she had despaired! She was entering upon a marvelous world where all would be passion, ecstasy, delirium. She felt herself surrounded by an endless rapture. A blue space surrounded her and ordinary existence appeared only intermittently between these heights, dark and far away beneath her.

Then she recalled the heroines of the books that she had read, and the lyric legion of these adulterous women began to sing in her memory with the voice of sisters that charmed her. She became herself, as it were, an actual part of these lyrical imaginings; at long last, as she saw herself among those lovers she had so envied, she fulfilled the love-dream of her youth. (II, 9; p. 117)

In *Madame Bovary*, Emma's strong will toward the immediate, sensuous appropriation of reality is consistently obstructed by mediations like these. Images formed of the heroines of the novels of Scott or Donizetti's Lucia are the sources of her ideas of romance, and block her ability to experience passion with any long-lasting joy. In Kierkegaard's analysis, this shows why the aesthetic always proves fleeting; it can never be experienced without mediation. In Emma's case aestheticism thus becomes the source of suffering, and this suffering a further denial of immediate experience. She cultivates this suffering, the inward reflection of her sensuous desires, and thus insures the failure: "the desires of the flesh, the longing for money, and the melancholy of passion all blended into one suffering, and instead of putting it out of her mind, she made her thoughts cling to it, urging herself to pain and seeking everywhere the opportunity to revive it" (II, 5; p. 77).

The truth of reality for the aesthete is given in the fact that such pursuits yield no immediate contact with the world. It is only in this

[172]

light that Flaubert can say of his passionate and overtly sensuous heroine that she was "passing through life scarcely touching it" (p. 76). For nearly every experience that is sought in immediacy, Flaubert includes one or more countervailing incidents that remove that experience from the ambit of the immediate and re-present it under the guise of reflection, memory, or the transformations of art. (This was precisely the use of aesthetic experience that Proust was to learn so well from Flaubert; the range of experience recounted in the *Recherche* is consigned to the final mediations of art and memory, as if in recognition of the fact that we are always already distanced from the world.)

Thus in *Madame Bovary* action and motif are guided by a logic of re-experience. All experience seems to be a second experience; even the most apparently direct presencings of the world are re-presencing. We find for instance that the clearest perceptions occur as a consequence of the work of memory, as a result of "that lengthening of perspective which memory gives to things" (p. 73). The ball at Vaubyessard is important not only in its first description but for all the occasions when it is called to mind again, the moments when the party is re-experienced through the prism of recollection. For Emma, remembered experience serves as a further spur to the aesthetic pursuit and to its failure, because the immediate experience is always in the past. The ball at Vaubyessard is recalled twice in the novel, first on a "dreary day" (II, 7), when Emma's interest in the reality at hand is low and when the depth of her ennui begins to show itself, when "Everything seemed shrouded in an atmosphere of bleakness that hung darkly over the outward aspect of things. . . . Her reverie was that of things gone forever, the exhaustion that seizes you after everything is done; the pain, in short, caused by the interruption of a familiar motion, the sudden halting of a long drawn out vibration" (p. 88). The second time, Emma's recollections are sparked by Rodolphe's perfumed hair. With an almost uncanny vision, she is able to look past, or through, Rodolphe and recall the Viscount who waltzed with her at Vaubyessard. Gazing at the "Hirondelle" she thinks also of Léon. Flaubert deftly superposes descriptive layers here, suggesting at once the presence of Rodolphe and the scent of powder, and the more distant yet far more impressive experiences with the Viscount and with Léon:

[Rodolphe's] arms were folded across his knees, and thus lifting his face at her from close by, he looked fixedly at her. She noticed in his eyes small golden lines radiating from the black pupils; she even smelt the perfume of the pomade that made his hair glossy. Then something gave way in her; she recalled the Viscount who had waltzed with her at Vaubyessard, and whose beard exhaled a similar scent of vanilla and lemon, and mechanically she half-closed her eyes the better to breathe it in. But in making this movement, as she leant back in her chair, she saw in the distance, right on the line of the horizon, the old diligence the "Hirondelle," that was slowly descending the hill of Leux, dragging after it a long trail of dust. It was in this yellow carriage that Léon had so often come back to her, and by this route down there that he had gone for ever. She fancied she saw him opposite at his window; then all grew confused; clouds gathered; it seemed to her that she was again turning in the waltz under the light of the lustres on the arm of the Viscount, and that Léon was not far away, that he was coming . . . and yet all the time she was conscious of Rodolphe's head by her side. The sweetness of this sensation revived her past desires, and like grains of sand under a gust of wind, they swirled around in the subtle breath of the perfume that diffused over her soul (II, 8; pp. 105–6).

It is the remembered character of experience, its instantaneous passage into the past, which is a foil to the aesthete's pursuit of sensual immediacy. The aesthete would live *aeterno modo*, in denial, or defiance, of time. (As Kierkegaard's "A" says, "Time flows, life is a stream, people say, and so on. I do not take notice. Time stands still, and I with it," *Either/Or*, I; p. 25.) In Mozart's *Don Giovanni* and in the original play by Tirso de Molina, the aesthete is set in constant motion, as if in flight from time; his pursuit of pleasure is as much an attempt to gain escape from the conditions of his own finitude as to achieve a presentness to the world; he understands, and would deny, that his nature as a temporal being deprives him of any lasting pleasures.

In *Madame Bovary*, Rodolphe's experiences with Emma are felt and experienced through the work of memory: they are marked by an essential pastness. The two exchange tokens of love, signs and images of affection, which point to the waning of vital passion. When Rodolphe reflects on Emma, she seemed to him to have receded into a far-off past, as if the resolution he had taken had suddenly placed an immeasurable distance between them. In order to recapture something of her presence, he fetched from the cupboard at the bedside an old Rheims cookie-box, in which he usually kept his love letters. An odour of dry dust and withered roses emanated from it. First he saw a handkerchief stained with pale drops. It was a handkerchief of hers. Once when they were walking her nose had bled; he had forgotten it. Near it, almost too large for the box, was Emma's miniature: her dress seemed pretentious to him, and her languishing look in the worst possible taste. Then, from looking at this image and recalling the memory of the original, Emma's features little by little grew confused in his remembrance, as if the living and the painted face, rubbing one against the other, had erased each other" (II, 13; p. 145).

The mediations of art, of time, and of memory which block the immediate aesthetic in *Madame Bovary* are so thorough and insistent that they suggest a further resemblance to Kierkegaard. Flaubert's novel, which, we have said, discovered the "continent of sentimentality," did so by revealing the general failure of the immediate aesthetic. We know from *Either/Or* and other writings that Kierkegaard envisioned the aesthetic stage of life to be superseded by the ethical and then by the religious stage, but we also know from that book, and from the *Postscript*, that he conceived of the immediate as indefensible and unfounded. This is grounds for a significant critique of the Hegelian "System," the *Logic*, of which the *Phenomenology* forms part. In Hegel's plan of things, the first moment of consciousness is that of immediacy, what he calls "sense-certainty": "The knowledge or knowing which is at the start or is immediately our object cannot be anything else but immediate knowledge itself, a knowledge of the immediate or of what simply *is*. . . . Because of its concrete content, sense-certainty immediately appears as the *richest* kind of knowledge, indeed a knowledge of infinite wealth for which no bounds can be known."[11] What Kierkegaard wonders, in response to Hegel, is how the System *begins* with the immediate, "*That is to say, does it begin with it immediately?* [sic] The answer to this question must be an unconditional negative," because "The beginning which begins with the immediate *is . . . itself reached by means of a process of reflection*" (*Postscript*, pp. 101–2; italics in original).

We have seen in Dostoevsky the instance of one particular moment of consciousness which resembles the skeptical moment in Hegel's *Phenomenology* and how that moment is abrogated because of the contradictions it contains; and we have also seen, in the case of Prince Myshkin, an example of the failure of a consciousness akin to another Hegelian moment, that of the "beautiful soul." In the case of *Madame Bovary*, there is in the first instance a parallel that can be drawn to Kierkegaard's critique of Hegel's notion of "immediacy." But beyond the discovery that there is no beginning, no "immediate" moment possible, we see that the ensuing development of consciousness, in its essential characteristics and relationships, is not given in terms of a progression toward ultimately self-integrating knowledge, as Hegel foresaw. Estrangement, irony, and finally "mediation" prevail in Flaubert, as they do in Kierkegaard. As we look ahead to *Sentimental Education*, it is good to keep Flaubert's affinity to Kierkegaard, and Kierkegaard's anti-Hegelianism, clearly in mind. Philosophers and critics such as Josiah Royce and M. H. Abrams have identified a similarity between Hegel's *Phenomenology* and conventional *Bildungsromane*,[12] but *Sentimental Education* is commonly recognized as a *Bildungsroman* in reverse; that is to say, it undercuts the trajectory toward the absolute, self-integrating moment of Spirit or reason knowing itself as such.

In *Madame Bovary*, Flaubert's rejection of the *possibility* of immediacy shows up not only in the final catastrophe to which the aesthetic project leads but also in the reflective sentimentality which guides Emma's amorous pursuits. Like the Seducer, who embodies the "reflective erotic," Emma is in love with the idea of love itself; at one point in his diary the Seducer writes "'Love is everything. For this reason, to one who loves, everything ceases to have significance in and of itself, and has it only in the interpretation that love puts upon it'" (*Either/Or*, I; p. 401). His delusion, like Emma's, is that he thinks that his "reflexivity" is a true image of love for another, when it is only a mirage, at best a form of self-love ("'People say that I am in love with myself; I don't wonder; for how could they notice that I am in love . . . with you? I am in love with myself, why? Because I am in love with you; for I love you truly, you alone, and everything which belongs to you, and so I love myself because this myself belongs to you, so if I cease to love you, I cease to love myself,'" p. 399). Both Emma and the figures of Part I of *Either/Or* succumb to this peculiar malaise of the romantic imagination, the love of the idea of love, which destroys their capacity for authentic love of others. Cervantes' Knight is equally devoted to his Dulcinea, and his devotion is modeled on what he reads in books, but Cervantes' treatment of his character's "romantic" excesses is burlesque, not ironic in the sentimental vein like Kierkegaard's and Flaubert's.

Unlike Don Quixote and Johannes the Seducer, Emma Bovary's devotion is not constant. In this respect she resembles Kierkegaard's "A." His advice in the "Rotation Method" is to avoid friendships for fear that they may be lasting; he is strictly opposed to marriage:

One must never enter into the relation of *marriage*. Husband and wife promise to love one another for eternity. This is all over fine, but it does not mean very much; for if their love comes to an end in time, it will surely be ended in eternity. If, instead of promising forever, the parties would say: until Easter, or until May-day comes, there might be some meaning in what they say. (*Either/Or*, I; p. 292)

The claim that in marriage husband and wife enter into a holy bond and become one is a "dark and mysterious saying" (p. 293), something which he finds beyond comprehension. Emma's difficulties are similar to the ones that "A" faces; she does not know the meaning of marriage ("'Why, for Heaven's sake, did I marry?'" I, 7; p. 31). In order to free herself from the constraints of a lasting relationship she avoids commitment to her lovers. When she accuses Léon of having designs on her with the intent of leaving her, she is outraged because she suspects that he will marry: "Ah! you too, you will leave me! You will marry! You will be like all the others. . . . You are all of you wretches'" (III, 5; p. 194). She finds nonetheless that even the adulterous affair is disappointing, that it is sick with the same cant that plagues marriage: "Emma found again in adultery all the platitudes of marriage. But how to get rid of him?" (III, 6; p. 211; cf. Nietzsche: "Even concubinage has been corrupted:—by marriage"[13]).

In order to be free to cultivate her own sentimentality, she must keep herself free from attachment to any one object; in order to sustain her ideas of love and fantasies of romance, her imaginings and passionate desires must remain largely unfixed. She avoids choice—hence the recurrent states of torpor and indolence which plague her (cf. Kierkegaard's "A": "I lie stretched out, inactive; the only thing I see is emptiness, the only thing I move about in is emptiness. I do not even suffer pain," *Either/Or*, I; p. 36). Emma's challenge is to turn her aestheticism, her experience of life as a mere possibility, into her existential experience of it, her experience of it as an actuality. She does this by cultivating and controling the pleasures of the senses: she swallows the poison apparently in order to avoid feeling any pain (a goal that is, to be sure, consistent with the aesthete's aims), and while her sensuous needs destroy her, she dominates them nonetheless; that is to say, she is in control of her own undoing.

I do not want to present the resemblances between Emma and Kierkegaard's male aesthetes at the expense of pointing up Emma's female nature. There is in fact something androgynous about Emma, which imputes to her a dual nature, as both seducer *and* seduced. There is a critical tradition going back at least to Baudelaire which detects something masculine in her otherwise female makeup. For Baudelaire, this lingering masculinity was symptomatic of Flaubert's inability fully to dissociate himself from his heroine. Emma Bovary thus becomes for him a model of the "ideal man," an embodiment of that "supreme and tyrannical faculty," the imagination, embodied in her creator, Flaubert.[14] Victor Brombert calls attention to the numerous instances in the novel where the narrator punctuates his descriptions of Emma's actions with the tag "comme un homme." For him, Emma's masculinity is the basis for role reversals in the novel: "A strange reversal of roles takes place," he says, "not only with her husband (it is he who, after the wedding night, looks like a deflowered virgin), but with her lover Léon, who plays the submissive part: 'It was he who was becoming her mistress rather than she his' (III, 5)" (*The Novels of Flaubert*, p. 89). This interpretation is particularly germane to my discussion because it will account for the resemblance between Emma and the male figures of *Either/Or*; it will help explain how Emma is both female and male, seducer and seduced.

This combination is familiar from Kierkegaard's Johannes the Seducer. Johannes prepares Cordelia for his love by cultivating the aesthetic possibilities within her. He would make of her an Emma Bovary *avant la lettre*, i.e., someone able to "go through all the movements of infinity, to sway, to lull herself in her moods, to confuse poetry and actuality, truth and romance, to be tossed about in the infinite" (*Either/Or*, I; p. 387). Finally he becomes convinced that he has succeeded in developing the "many-tongued reflection in her, that he has developed her aesthetically so far that she no longer listens humbly to one voice but is able to hear many voices at one time" (p. 305). But in the process he becomes seduced by his own designs. His thoughts become confused; he is carried off into the world of fantasy which his imaginative plans for seduction have generated, much in the way that Emma, in love with the idea of love, is seduced by that idea.

Emma is also seduced by Rodolphe, in a more literal way in the novel; Rodolphe plays Don Juan to her Elvira. He insists on the sheer number of amorous conquests he has made and, like the Libertine, he admits that they are all virtually the same to him:

"Do you love me?"
"Why, of course I love you," he answered.
"A great deal?"
"Certainly."
"You haven't loved any others?"
"Did you think you'd got a virgin?" he exclaimed laughing.

. . .

He had so often heard these things that they did not strike him as original. Emma was like all his mistresses; and the charm of novelty, gradually falling away like a garment, laid bare the eternal monotony of passion, that has always the same shape and the same language. He was unable to see, this man so full of experience, the variety of feelings hidden within the same expressions. (II, 12; pp. 137–8)

Rodolphe looks on Emma with the Libertine's strategic concerns in mind. His goal is to seduce her and, like Don Juan, then to free himself from her: "'poor little woman! She is gaping after love like a carp on the kitchen table after water. Three gallant words and she'd adore me, I'm sure of it. She'd be tender, charming. Yes; but how to get rid of her afterwards?'" (II, 7; p 93); his final comment is echoed nearly verbatim by Emma, speaking of Léon. Flaubert is explicit about Rodolphe's role as seducer; when he grows indifferent towards Emma, she recognizes that she has been seduced. Yet even though she fears subjugation by him she relishes his seductions: "She did not know if she regretted having yielded to him, or whether she did not wish, on the contrary, to love him even more. The humiliation of having given in turned into resentment, tempered by their voluptuous pleasures. It was not tenderness; it was like a continual seduction. He held her fully in his power; she almost feared him" (II, 10; p. 123). By the end of the novel, it is Emma whose passion wanes. She becomes bored with Léon. The once heated affair between them becomes cold and contrived: "They gradually began to talk more frequently of matters outside their love, and in the letters that Emma wrote him she spoke of flowers, poetry, the moon and the stars, naive resources of a waning passion striving to keep itself alive by all external aids" (III, 6; p. 205). This points up an inherent weakness in the aesthete's way of life: Emma cannot sustain her pursuit of immediacy, her own will for seduction, without the aid of her lovers and the supportive rites of love, that is, without in fact *being* seduced.

Because Emma resembles both Don Juan and the woman he seduces, she is a danger to herself. As Kierkegaard outlines in *Either/Or*, the seduced object is always a risk to the seducer. "A" writes for instance that Elvira is dangerous to Mozart's Don Giovanni once she has been seduced: "In the same sense, exactly in the same sense, Zerlina becomes dangerous to him when she is seduced. As soon as she is seduced, she is elevated to a higher sphere, to a consciousness that Don Juan does not have. Therefore, she is dangerous to him" (I, p. 96). In *Either/Or*, "A" sees Elvira's cloistered upbringing as crucial to the awakening of her passion ("It was no frivolous girl from boarding school, who had learned to love at school and to flirt at balls; the seduction of such a girl has no great significance. By contrast, Elvira has been brought up in the discipline of the cloister, but this has not been able to eradicate passion, but has taught her to suppress it, and thereby to make it more violent as soon as it is allowed to break forth," I, p. 189). Similarly, Emma's education and formative years drive her to seek an outlet for her passions by seduction. Brombert saw the pages on Emma's education as a "parable of the entire novel," in which she moves "from ennui to expectation, to escape, to confusion, back to ennui and to a yearning for nothingness" (*The Novels of Flaubert*, p. 55). In *Madame Bovary*, however, where Emma is both in need of seduction *and* where she is the aesthete, the seducer, her relationship to herself is unstable; her nature as the seducer who pursues seduction works toward her self-undoing, and is at the root of her demise.

"A" describes Mozart's Elvira as leading a "restless, wandering life, constantly occupied in pursuing Don Juan" (p. 194); like her, Emma devotes herself to the pursuit of seduction. In "A"'s analysis, Elvira is "as great a figure as Don Juan; for the power to seduce all women is the masculine expression which corresponds to the feminine one of being seduced once with her whole soul, and then of hating, or, if you will, of loving her seducer with an energy no wife ever had" (p. 195). In Emma Bovary, the masculine and feminine traits of the immediate aesthetic come together. She is both Don Juan and Elvira. Near the end of the book, when she approaches the notary for money and is propositioned in return—as clear a sign as any of her inherent seductibility—she refuses with the words "'You shamelessly take advantage of my distress, sir! I am to be pitied—not to be sold!'" (III, 7; p. 221). Thus she is in charge of her own will for seduction, and has taken a large step toward the moment when she will swallow the poison, thereby turning the aesthete's seductions back on herself. In this single character, Flaubert has worked out the contradictions of the aesthetic way of life. Emma's aestheticism is not superseded by any "higher" stage; there is no Judge William (whose papers Kierkegaard's "B" collects) to serve as an ethical corrective to her. In Flaubert's hands, the limitations and inherent failures of the aesthetic stage of life are played out within that stage alone; it is from this that Emma Bovary's greatness derives.

SOCIAL EPISTEMOLOGY:
THE MARRIAGE CONTRACT

"Why, for Heaven's sake, did I marry?"
—*Madame Bovary*

IN POINTING OUT the similarities which link Emma Bovary and Kierkegaard's "A," the aesthete of *Either/Or,* I have not yet commented on one significant difference between them. Because "A" seeks to hold himself free from any commitment of long duration, he resists entering into marriage. In the second part of Kierkegaard's book, Judge William, the "ethical individual," tries to convince "A" that marriage can incorporate the aesthetic way of life; he says that "romantic love can be united with and can persist in marriage" (II, p. 31). His nephew doubts him, and Emma Bovary would share those doubts. Her relationship with Charles suggests that she finds love and marriage incompatible. Hence she is in a more difficult and contradictory situation than "A": she is an aesthete living *in* the married state. Consequently, Emma is not only a female version of the male seducer, but an adulteress. Her will to maximize her personal pleasure involves the transgression of a contractual bond. Indeed, *Madame Bovary* was immediately recognized as potentially dangerous and offensive when it was first published in the *Revue de Paris.* Flaubert was accused and tried for having written a work that was threatening to bourgeois morals: his accuser saw the novel's heroine as a seductress unable to help herself, and the society in which she moves as unable to bring itself to condemn her.

In a recent study, Dominick LaCapra focused on the trial as a first "interpretation" of the social questions which the novel raises. Drawing on Derridean thought and on the earlier work of Sartre and Hans Robert Jauss, LaCapra describes this first reading of the novel in terms of the "decentering of the subject": "Most evident," he says, "is the issue of the 'bourgeois' individual who is supposed to have full moral and legal responsibility in his contractual relations with others," and, more broadly, "the problem of the autonomy of the individual subject, his relation to language and to social norms, and the extent to which his 'liability' is limited by forces not entirely within his control."[1] In *Adultery in the Novel: Contract and Transgression,* Tony Tanner explains Emma's adultery as the specific case of a society in crisis; she is unable to "define" herself in the context of meaningful or stable social relationships: "What is it that 'constitutes' Emma? She cannot find out, neither in marriage nor in adultery nor in any other experience nor in any terminology. The crisis of the meaning of marriage, which she experiences, is inextricably involved with, and indistinguishable from, a crisis in the language in and by which she is formed and rent."[2]

In this chapter, I will discuss *Madame Bovary* in light of the philosophical background to these issues, paying special attention to their formulation by Rousseau in the idea of the social contract and their development (and parody) by Kierkegaard in the second part of *Either/Or.* My claim is that the language community, which Tanner and LaCapra see as in crisis in this novel, is comparable to the social community, as founded by the social contract. This last caveat leads to some significant differences in our respective positions. I shall argue that the crises of language and society that we see in *Madame Bovary* are not as subversive or as deep as Tanner and LaCapra would suggest; they can be described specifically as crises of the "common," which is to say, as failures on the part of the characters to find and to say what they hold in common among them. A common language does of course exist; the characters do speak with one another. The trouble is that it is a language at the edge of emptiness; their social relationships are, consequently, debased.

Emma's adulterous relationships prompt what I shall call questions of "social epistemology": What is the nature of the bond which conjoins the individual to others in society? What factors legitimize that bond, and what might serve to break it? These are questions of *social* epistemology, as opposed, say, to scientific epis-

[184]

temology, because they cannot be answered by reference to the facts; further inspection of the evidence will not tell us what we need to know. What is necessary is a certain mode or inflection of knowledge, one which is determined by our relationship to the appropriate facts. Earlier, in connection with Dostoevsky, I described a similar structure of knowledge, which I then called an ethical dimension of it, as "conviction." Conviction does not just tell of the facts, but, like "social epistemology," of my relationship to and willingness for them, my recognition of their validity. When Emma asks, tellingly, "'Why, for Heaven's sake, did I marry?'" (I, 7; p. 31), she gives evidence that she may not know what would legitimize her convictions, what would tell her to which institutions she is obedient or with whom she is in community. Her questions raise concerns which no closer scrutiny of the facts could possibly answer.

Despite Emma's ignorance of these matters of social epistemology, however, we find in the novel the ever-present *possibility* for such knowledge. As an adulteress, for example, Emma seeks to place herself outside the community. If successful, such self-alienation would undermine the very basis for knowledge, but we find that she fails in her effort. The "common" has a stubborn durability which is dissolved neither by the failure to find what legitimizes it nor by any one person's will to avoid or ignore it. The point is central to my claims about the antiskeptical bias of the novel, especially insofar as it shows that all forms of knowledge are to an important degree social. The search for criteria as exemplified in the identifications that Don Quixote and Sancho give to the world, for instance, is a search for the common ground between them. In *Madame Bovary*, as in *Don Quixote*, there is an indestructible foundation of human knowledge because there is an unalienable basis for human community. It is this basis that shows up in the operation of criteria and it is this which leaves open the possibility of human understanding. To discover that the philosophical search for criteria is a search for the *basis* of human community, and to say, as we did for the *Quixote*, that criteria inhere in and operate through language, posits a common ground for "social," "epistemological," and "language" questions. All require reflection on one's relationship

[185]

to, or displacement from, a community, an inspection of what it means to be a member of a group—a polis, a family, a language- or criteria-sharing community. All the significant questions about Emma's marriage and adultery, such as the one she herself asks, can be framed in these terms.

Among the most important expressions of the centrality of community to matters of social epistemology have been given historically in the notion of the prior social contract. The idea is meant to explain certain facts which follow naturally from the remarks above: that if our agreements (e.g., our agreements in criteria) attest that we are bound to a group, then a contract must be in effect. The particular value of Rousseau's formulation of the idea of the *prior* contract is that we cannot seem ever to interrogate our social, epistemological, or language communities fully enough; we cannot, for instance, inquire into their beginnings, because they exist prior to us; and we cannot point to the moment at which we gave our consent to them, because that consent is more often than not tacitly given. What can it then tell us? In the presentation of the first book of the *Social Contract*, Rousseau says that he does not know how man, who was born free, and in a state of nature, has come to consent to the bonds of the civil state. The question he says he can settle is whether that state, for which man has forsaken the state of nature, is legitimate or not. The social contract, which describes the civil state, is thus not meant so much to define the state as to call into question the advantages it reputedly offers, and thus to test its legitimacy.

The idea of the contract in Rousseau, taken in this way—as meant to put the existing civil state into question by considering what conditions might legitimize it, and whether those conditions are being met—is the basis for social epistemology, not science, because those questions cannot be answered by knowing such things as when and where the contract was written, only by knowing what it requires of us to be in community with others, the responsibilities and obligations which we incur as a result. I underscore this formulation because this is just the aspect of the social contract that thinkers are apt to miss when they object, with Hume, that the contract was not "written on parchment, nor yet on leaves or barks of trees."[4] Similarly, some characters in *Madame Bovary*, like Homais, take Rousseau's ideas as the basis for a science, as a description or recipe for the cultivation of the advantages of civic association. Thinking obviously of Emile, Homais counsels Charles on the benefits of his marital association with Emma and on the proper management of their "natural" resources:

"One should never let any natural faculties lie fallow. Besides, just think my good friend, that by inducing madame to study, you are economizing on the subsequent musical education of your child. For my own part, I think that mothers ought themselves to instruct their children. It's an idea of Rousseau's, still rather new perhaps, but bound to win out sooner or later, like vaccination and breast-feeding." (III, 4; p. 188)

But Rousseau's description of the advantages of society are seen as being balanced against its requirements or conditions, or what is called the "consideration" in light of which the contractual promise is made:

[Man's] faculties are exercised and developed; his ideas are expanded; his feelings are ennobled; his whole soul is exalted to such a degree that, if the abuses of this new condition did not often degrade him below that from which he has emerged, he ought to bless without ceasing the happy moment that released him from it forever, and transfigured him from a stupid and ignorant animal into an intelligent being and a man.[5]

Since the contract limits man's natural liberty in "consideration" of the advantages of civic society, Rousseau wants to know whether the advantages have in fact been gained and whether the trade is worthwhile; this will tell him whether the genuine contract is in force, which is to say, whether the shape of the community is faithful to the sense of its founding contract.

What I find remarkable about Flaubert's treatment of Emma's marriage to Charles is that he avoids the cavils which critics of the social contract so often raise about it, in order to prompt questions of social epistemology, much as Rousseau intended. Critics of the social contract like Hume will always express their dissatisfaction because it is difficult, if not impossible, to point to the moment at which the contract came into being and at which consent was granted. (Judge William comments on a similar difficulty with marriage in *Either/Or:* "The substantial factor in marriage is love. But which comes first? Is the love first, or is marriage, of which love is the equal?" II, p. 35.) But in Emma's case there can be no problem of a contract with hidden origins or of her having granted tacit consent. She knows when she married, and her consent was express. Yet this does not tell her what she needs to know. When she asks, in despair, why she married, she means like Rousseau to question whether or not her present relationship with Charles fulfills the sense of their agreement. She asks whether the "consideration," in light of which a specifically *contractual* promise is made, is being met. She puts into question the "advantage" which is due her as a consequence of the contract, much as Rousseau questioned whether the social contract was in effect by looking to see whether men have gained the reputed advantages of civic association. (Hume would understand Rousseau's project perfectly well: "as no man, without some equivalent, would forego the advantages of his native liberty, and subject himself to the will of another, this promise is always understood to be conditional, and imposes on him no obligation, unless he meet with justice and protection from his sovereign. These advantages the sovereign promises him in return," "Of the Original Contract," p. 150.) Flaubert's narrator says of Emma that "Before marriage she thought herself in love; but since the happiness that should have followed failed to come, she must, she thought, have been mistaken" (I, 5; p. 24). She has read of love and amorous pleasure in books; she knows the words that should describe the condition of someone who has entered into a marriage contract; but she finds, to her dismay, that these descriptions do not apply to her: "Emma tried to find out what one meant exactly in life by the words *bliss, passion, ecstasy,* that had seemed to her so beautiful in books." She questions whether the contract is in effect because she has not gained the benefits which ought to come to her as a result of it.

Emma's question about her reasons for marrying indicates her ignorance of what might serve to validate her marriage. Knowing that she should feel *"bliss, passion, ecstasy"* and finding that she does not, she is at a loss to say what could legitimize the contract into which she has entered. Kierkegaard's ethical individual finds that such ignorance is widespread in society. Some people marry, he says, because "marriage is a school for character" (II, p. 65), others for its educational benefits (Homais would subscribe to this notion). Some marry for the purpose of having children, which means that they take marriage as an expedient for natural processes, something which legitimizes *them* (but then these processes do not legitimize marriage). Some, he says, marry in order to make a home, to find a place for themselves in the world; but marriage can no more *provide* one's domestic relationships than it can legitimize them. There are hosts of similar reasons which one might give for marrying, not one of which will legitimize marriage, and all of which point up a general crisis of social epistemology—"As when one marries for money, or from jealousy, or for prospective advantage, because there are good prospects for her dying soon—or that she may live long and prove to be a blessed branch which bears much fruit, so that by her one may sweep into one's pocket the inheritance of a whole series of uncles and aunts" (*Either/Or*, II, p. 89). Kierkegaard's point, which is consonant with Rousseau and Flaubert, is that if we do not know a valid reason for entering into marriage, then we do not know what it would mean to exist in association with others as one body. This is the crucial problem plaguing Emma's relationship with Charles. Not knowing why she married, Emma is ignorant of the significant social "fact" about herself—the nature of her relationship to him and the meaning of what they hold in common.

I said that Emma's position as an aesthete living in the married state was especially awkward. With the above clarifications made, some of the reasons for that awkwardness may be clear. It is not, I take it, immediately evident that love and marriage do not go together. The awkwardness of her pursuit of immediacy while she is married to Charles is that those pursuits contradict the sense of her contract of association with him. It is difficult to reconcile the aesthete's idea of love with the institution of marriage because marriage depends on the creation of a common body, with one will, which requires the recognition of the will of others who come

[189]

together in it; but the aesthete is disinclined to recognize any will but his own. Rousseau describes the same difficulty in the formation of the "general will" (*volonté générale*) of civil society ("every individual may, as a man, have a particular will contrary to, or divergent from, the general will which he has as a citizen; his private interest may prompt him quite differently from the common interest," p. 21). To enter into marriage, or any civic society, one must learn to conquer self-love (*amour propre*) and private interests, to invest the individual will in the common will, the *volonté générale*.

In the opinion of Kierkegaard's Judge William, the marriage ceremony itself serves a civic function and helps show the individual his relationship to the community: first, by showing him that he is not simply an individual, but a Man, a member of the human race, with a place in the universal scheme of things ("It provides a survey of the genesis of the human race. Thereby it presents the universal, the essentially human, and evokes its consciousness"; "in pointing to the universal it leads the lovers back to the first parents," II, 91, 92); and second by showing him his role as citizen. Marriage is civic because "thereby the lovers belong to the state and the fatherland and the concerns of fellow citizens."[6] The wedded couple stand before the congregation, the larger polity to which they belong through marriage; they recognize that they draw advantages from the community and must contribute to it in return ("The great thing, as I regard it, is to live in the congregation, to bring something finer out of it, if one is able; at all events to subordinate oneself to it and put up with it if one is unable to better it," *Either/ Or*, II; p. 103).

Certainly there is a degree of naiveté in Judge William's idea that the wedding ceremony might in itself be able to awaken a sensibility to the common interest and general will. This is like thinking that the act of signing a contract will automatically "generalize" the sum of individual wills brought together in it. In the case of Emma Bovary, moreover, it is clear that marriage has served no such function. She has entered into a contract, but her pursuits remain private. The contract will not show her the social "facts" she needs to know (viz., with whom she is in community, and why)—just as the contractarian's notion of the prior social contract cannot show such facts. On the contrary, the recognition of one's position in society, as party to certain social relations and obligations, is the *source* of the idea that a prior contract must have been in effect. The problem, which Rousseau takes up, is what happens when a present example of the contract is no longer faithful to the exercise of the general will which it should entail. We fail to exercise the general will, for instance, when we find that we are born free and yet are everywhere in chains. Emma has consented to marriage, which means that a "general will" should be visible. But since she lives at the same time as an aesthete, her life is devoted to the satisfaction of her individual will. In this contract, then, *amour propre* and the particular will are at odds with the common interest, the general will, and Emma's will to the particular or the "private" seriously threatens the validity of her shared, "common" life with Charles.

In arguing the aesthetic validity of marriage, Judge William claims that marriage can incorporate love ethically, and finally religiously, by transforming the aesthete's pursuit of immediacy into a pursuit of a common interest; the words of the Judge in *Stages on Life's Way* echo "A"'s words: they tell of the transformation of aesthetic "love" as a consequence of the union and "generalization" of the wills in marriage: "What am I through her, that she is through me, and we are neither of us anything by ourselves, but only in union" (*Stages on Life's Way*, p. 97). Emma resists the transformation of the aesthetic into the ethical because she exercises her will to the private, to the particular, rather than to the general or the common. Judge William says that marriage also incorporates the aesthetic, again transforming it, in the institution of the family, the creation of which is the ethical end of human sexuality. This is not to say, to repeat an earlier warning, that procreation *legitimizes* marriage (any more than provision for the possession of property, for instance, would legitimize the state), but that *given* our involvement in these activities and relationships, we must be aware of the responsibilities which we have implicitly contracted. Emma finds herself not only married, but with a family; yet she is, until nearly her last moment of life, disinterested in her child. Marriage and a family are superabundant evidence of her consent to the "society" which she is in; yet throughout the novel Flaubert shows her disinclined to recognize those others with whom she stands in community, as if for her society and community are at odds.

In a widely read essay on "Authority and the Family," Max Horkheimer outlined some of the historical tensions between the individual will and the family community that I think are pertinent to *Madame Bovary*. He points to figures like Don Juan, the aesthete, as examples of the "rebellion of eros against authority" and family life: "Such legendary figures manifest the gulf that lies between the individual's claim to happiness and the claim of the family to priority. These artistic creations [he is referring to *Don Juan, Romeo and Juliet, Intrigue and Love*, and *Elective Affinities*] reflect one of the antagonisms that exist between social forms and vital forces."[7] He sees a split between Romantic Love, embodied in the heroes of these works, and its "bourgeois" form, marriage; the family, he says, gained dominance and the "rebels of eros" were unable to prevail over the bourgeois institution:

In general, the authority of the bourgeois male prevails even in love and determines its course. In his concern for his partner's dowry, social position, and capacity for work, in his expectation of advantage and honor from his children, in his respect for his neighbor's opinion, and, above all, in his internal dependence on deeply rooted concepts, custom, and convention—in this male empiricism of modern times, an empiricism which has been learned but which has also become a second nature, there is an imperious urge to respect the form of the family and to affirm it in the individual's existence. (pp. 126–27)

These remarks recall Judge William's warnings to his nephew about those men who are "rebels only in thought," the ones who "sit and sigh over the fact that love has long ago evaporated out of their marriage . . . who . . . sit like madmen each one in his matrimonial cell and shake the iron bars and rave about the sweetness of engagement and the bitterness of marriage" (*Either/Or*, II; p. 33). One thinks, in *Madame Bovary*, not so much of Charles, who is too unaware to be deeply disconsolate behind his "iron bars" of marriage, but of the adulterers, of Emma and especially of Léon. Léon is the image of the "bourgeois male" unable to assert his independence from the social institutions which dominate his life:

Léon finally swore he would not see Emma again; and he reproached himself with not having kept his word, considering all the trouble and reproaches she was likely to bring down on him, not counting the jokes made by his fellow clerks as they sat around the stove in the morning. Besides, he was soon to be head clerk; it was time to settle down. So he gave up his flute, his exalted sentiments, his poetic imagination; for every bourgeois in the flush of his youth, were it but for a day, a moment, has believed himself capable of immense passions, of lofty enterprises. The most mediocre libertine has dreamed of sultanas; every notary bears within him the débris of a poet. (III, 6; p. 211)

Even Emma is unable to circumvent the bourgeois institution of love. As Flaubert remarks of her relationship with Léon, she found in adultery "all the platitudes of marriage." In adultery, she binds herself by the same ties she would break in her relationship with Charles. She is brought to her end in an effort to assert the independence of her will from the authority of marriage and family life; her death by the ingestion of poison is, in an ironic way, an expression of the aesthete's will. But we have seen that it is an act that destroys her as well.

Flaubert's position is not that of the moralizing "ethical individual," like Judge William. The Judge speaks with the voice of authority (even if his voice is eventually undermined by Kierkegaard's larger irony in *Either/Or*); he encourages his nephew to follow the ethical path, to seek out the aesthetic *within* marriage. One senses that Flaubert, by contrast, was himself caught up in, and disillusioned by, the prospects for the aesthete's rebellion. His descriptions of Emma's enticements by adultery are vibrant and lyrical (e.g., "She repeated: 'I have a lover! a lover!' . . . She was entering upon a marvelous world where all would be passion, ecstasy, delirium," II, 9; p. 117). Adultery is, as Victor Brombert said, a "privileged condition, . . . a magic word" for both Emma and Flaubert (*The Novels of Flaubert*, p. 83). Flaubert's dream of an illicit relationship with Elisa Schlésinger was itself fueled by the Romantic ideas of his youth; adultery was a sign of forbidden happiness, an unrealizable dream holding the promise of the Ideal.

Rather than argue that the aesthetic can be incorporated into marriage, and hence argue in favor of marriage, as Judge William does, Flaubert is interested in seeing how far the two can stand apart without divorce. In terms of the contract, this means seeing whether—given prior consent—the individual can withhold his will from the general will to which it has been joined. Judge William chides his nephew: "you dare not enter into an alliance which, when you no longer are *volens* may compel you *nolens* to remain in it" (*Either/Or*, II; p. 148). But Emma has already committed herself to this relationship with Charles. What her adultery teaches her is how difficult it may be to withdraw her consent when she is no longer willing to be party to the contract. Emma is not so radically different from the hypocrites described in *Either/Or*. She remains in part always tied to Charles; her adultery merely puts her on the margin of this relationship; she does not dissolve the original bond but merely puts her faithfulness to it in question. Emma's adultery is her form of dissent, her way of rendering the fact that she does not find in her marriage those things which she expected would fulfill the contract (e.g., "*bliss, passion, ecstasy*").

But Emma cannot dissolve or undo the prior contract to which she gave consent. She can only dissent or dispute what it has come to be. This means that even her attempt to withdraw consent from the contract entails a recognition of the persons and relationships involved in it; that recognition affirms the basis of the contract, and indicates that the community which it founds has not been annulled, but merely protested. Writing of Rousseau, Stanley Cavell said that

Since the granting of consent entails acknowledgment of others, the withdrawal of consent entails the same acknowledgment: I have to say *both* "It is not mine any longer" (I am no longer responsible for it, it no longer speaks for me) *and* "It is no longer ours" (not what we bargained for, we no longer recognize the principle of consent in it, the original "we" is no longer bound together by consent but only by force, so it no longer exists).[8]

To describe the marriage of Emma and Charles in terms of a contract means that they may fail in the duties which they owe one another but that they cannot succeed in divorcing one another, i.e., that it is not in their power to render this contract null. Their consent shows up in ways which they might not have expected, and in contexts which reach far beyond the circumstances in which their consent was originally given. In one of the final scenes of the novel, Emma lies on her deathbed and asks Charles to bring her their child, one of the products of their contract. Emma kisses the child; she recognizes her part in the contract through its fruits. Charles turns to her and asks, with pathetic ignorance, "'Weren't you happy? Is it my fault?'" to which Emma replies, "'Yes, that's true . . . you're good, not like the others.' And slowly she passed her hand over his hair" (III, 8; p. 232). She recognizes Charles as well as the child, but the fact is that these recognitions come too late for the relationship to be repaired. Emma is nearly at her death, and Charles fails to respond to her: "he felt his whole being dissolved in despair at the thought that he must lose her, just when she was confessing more love for him than she ever did. He didn't know what to do, felt paralyzed by fear."

Emma's inability to withdraw her consent from the marriage contract places limits on the extent to which she can exercise her "particular" will, her will to "privacy." She seeks out "idiocy," in the root meaning of the term. The pursuit of self-satisfaction, part of her aesthetic program, would place her outside the community and its rules for order, like the "rebels of eros" that Horkheimer describes, but her aesthetic project fails; the will to the private does not prevail. Perhaps even to his own dismay, Flaubert posits a stubborn presence of the "general will" which brakes the ultimate force of Emma's "idiocy." There is a barrier to the radically "private," and thus proof of our social bonds to others, as revealed for instance by the impossibility of a private language. This follows from Wittgenstein's argument, which I adduced in my discussion of the *Quixote*, that such a language cannot so much as be *imagined* to have any sense, i.e., *be* a language at all. Language is the groundwork of community, the basis for the prior contract, the bar to idiocy, because it cannot but be public, a "form of life," in Wittgenstein's phrase, that is not only ordinary (everyday) but common among us.

Having entered into the contract, Emma must have the capacity to "speak" the common language. The community of which she is a part, or on the margin, and the forms of reciprocity and exchange in which she engages, or which she protests, bar her from the creation of a radically "private" realm. Very near the conclusion of the novel, as Emma lies dying, she hears a blind man recite verses which describe her "private" fantasies:

"Often the heat of a summer's day/ Makes a young girl dream her heart away." . . . And Emma began to laugh, an atrocious, frantic, desparate laugh, thinking she saw the hideous face of the poor wretch loom out of the eternal darkness like a menace. "The wind blew very hard that day / It blew her petticoat away." A final spasm threw her back upon the mattress. They all drew near. She had ceased to exist. (III, 9; p. 238)

The voice of madness, of Emma's fantasy of "privacy," comes from outside her. She fails in giving voice to it herself, which failure points up her inability to "create the realm of the private." Despite her dreams or her wishes, she remains bound to a common, public form of life.

Writers I mentioned earlier—Dominick LaCapra and Tony Tanner in particular—have advanced descriptions of *Madame Bovary* which view Emma's transgression of the marriage pact, and her outsideness to society, in a rather different light. LaCapra, who follows Sartre, explains Emma's adultery in terms of Flaubert's sense of alienation from a language-speaking group which existed prior to him: "he never outgrew the feeling of being its spoken object rather than its active speaker. Language came to him from the outside and put words into his mouth or under his pen" (*Madame Bovary on Trial*, p. 87). Tanner says that the society from which Emma dissents is itself in the midst of a language crisis: "Emma's problem is in part a crucial problem concerning distinctions and differences [i.e., those that language makes; he refers to Lévi-Strauss and Derrida] (hence the fog in her head), and in turn this problem reflects a society losing its ability to maintain differences and distinctions" (*Adultery in the Novel*, p. 362). If Emma's transgression of the marriage contract were more than the expression of dissent, if in adultery she were successful in divorcing herself from the "platitudes of marriage," these suggestions would carry considerable force. But the ultimate failure of her transgression, the fact that her will to separate herself from the established social order brings the destruction of her private world, suggests that there is no such possibility for radical "outsideness" to the public language, nor the radical linguistic dystrophy which Tanner and LaCapra see.

What we find in Madame Bovary, as in much of Flaubert, is instead a crisis of the "common"-ness of language. This shows up in two senses. We see a language in which expression has been reduced to the level of fausse monnaie; and we see a language which is too weak to galvanize the life held in common, the civic and political forms of association which ought to reflect the general will. Stylistically, Flaubert makes expert use of cliché and silence to render this crisis of the common language; Victor Brombert said that "the language of banality is caricatured and at the same time transmuted into poetry" (The Novels of Flaubert, p. 78). Charles, for instance, will describe his dire situation in terms of "fatality"; Léon will lace his speech with such worn topics as the "limitlessness of the ocean"; Emma speaks of a "constant universal pain" ("une courbature incessante et universelle," III, 7); her reveries are animated by a verbal repertoire drawn largely from "the love-songs of the last century" (I, 6; p. 26). (In Bouvard and Pécuchet, as I will discuss, Flaubert's "literary" use of cliché for similar ends is of first-order thematic concern.) Brombert saw in the novel a "drama of incommunicability" (p. 71). The failure of Charles' and Emma's marriage is of a piece with their failure to find meaningful conversation. At home together, they spend hours in silence. Emma "confided many a thing to her greyhound." In this she resembles Kierkegaard's "rebels in thought": "she would have done so to the logs in the fireplace or to the pendulum of the clock" (I, 9; p. 44). The situation is not vastly different with her lovers. She hopes to find new strength and energy, a greater potency of expression in illicit love, but instead she discovers "platitude."

These crises of language do not rend the social order asunder (as Tanner's analysis implies); they are not that powerful. None of the characters is wholly outside the common language (as Sartre and LaCapra would lead us to expect); the common language plagues them. It is there to be found, and possibly to be made significant, even if it is at present largely spent of meaning. The novel is suggestive of a society undergoing a crisis in the civic life, but for rather different reasons. That life (as it is expressed, quintessentially, in politics) depends for its well-being on the ability to join one's own words, along with one's private will, to the common voice and general will. This means not only finding others who can speak for you (i.e., represent you and your will), but speaking for yourself (e.g., voicing an opinion). But in *Madame Bovary* the characters fail to find what words they have in common *and* they fail to find their own language.

At the opening of this section my claim was that "social epistemology" shares with all other kinds of epistemology a concern for the community as the validating basis of human knowledge; as the *Quixote* has shown by example, the search for criteria, which founds human knowledge, is the search for community. In *Madame Bovary*, the durability of the community provides an antiskeptical bias similar to that of *Don Quixote*. The existence of something like a prior contract from which consent cannot be withdrawn (Emma's marriage to Charles) as a bar to privacy puts the will to marriage, and the founding of the common in that way, on a par with the will to knowledge. Marriage, as conversation, does not require certainty of us in our knowledge of others. That is because the condition for marriage is simply an ability to put a relationship into words (i.e., make the contract binding).

In Cervantes, a basis for agreement is mirrored in the successful conversation, the dialogue between Don Quixote and Sancho, in what Bakhtin called the purest form of the dialogic novel. In the essays in *The Dialogic Imagination*, Bakhtin has little to say about *Madame Bovary* as a dialogic novel, and no wonder: In *Madame Bovary*, conversation fails. Knowing that there is a basis for community (knowing, for instance, that she gave her consent in marriage) does not mean that agreement will necessarily be reached (any more than knowing that a prior contract must have been in effect will mean that we are not still "everywhere in chains," or behind bars in marriage), but rather that a failure to reach agreement will not undermine the *basis* for assent; such failures will simply take the form of dissent, not the withdrawal of consent. Emma cannot avoid, for instance, recognizing that she holds in common with

Charles the offspring of their relationship. This is another way of saying, by introduction to *Sentimental Education* and *Bouvard and Pécuchet,* that not every antiskeptical position will lead to a positive epistemology. We have already seen the pattern where both skepticism *and* epistemology are rejected in favor of a form of knowledge that goes beyond the bounds of reason. In Flaubert's work, as I will discuss in the following sections, knowledge takes the shape of a distinctively "negative" epistemology, a process of "unlearning" (in *Sentimental Education*) and of increasing ignorance (in *Bouvard and Pécuchet*).

MORAL EDUCATION

"Adieu, Paris. As we are looking for love, happiness, and innocence, we shall never be too far away from you."

—Rousseau, *Emile*, Book V

THE FOREGOING DISCUSSIONS of *Madame Bovary* in light of Kierkegaard and Rousseau have suggested that Flaubert shares the nonrational bias that we saw in the novels of Cervantes and Dostoevsky. Emma Bovary is an aesthete, and tries to appropriate the world by means of the senses, not the mind; and the principal relationship in which she is cast requires of her the work of *social* epistemology, as opposed to the work of reason. The major difference between *Madame Bovary* and the novels of Cervantes and Dostoevsky is that in Flaubert neither of these nonrational ways of knowing succeeds. In Cervantes, we see that Don Quixote's embodied nature brings him knowledge of the external world that he cannot possibly doubt, but in *Madame Bovary* the project of knowledge by the senses issues in catastrophe. Don Quixote and Sancho engage in dialogue and conversation, understand one another, and change as a result; but in *Madame Bovary* we see the failure of a married couple to engage in successful conversation.

It is essential for the discussions that follow to see that these failures do not necessarily support skepticism. Flaubert can be and in fact is thoroughly pessimistic about the achievements of knowledge; he sees pervasive ignorance in the world, as *Bouvard and Pécuchet* makes plain. Yet this is no basis for philosophical skepticism. For skepticism to take hold, one would have to deny something like the present *and* future prospects for knowledge, to charge not only that we do not but that we *cannot* know. There is a difference between the aesthetic project and social epistemology in *Madame Bovary* which points this up. In the case of Emma's aestheticism, her attempt to know the world by the senses, we can say that it fails her, and that she is greater than it. Thus she assumes heroic dimensions in its light, as at the end of the novel where, in an "ecstasy of heroism," her plight "like an abyss, loomed before her" (III, 8; p. 229). But the basis of social epistemology is something which *cannot* fail her. On the contrary, she fails it in failing to achieve the purpose for which she entered into the contractual relationship with Charles. Frédéric Moreau makes a comment at one point in *Sentimental Education* that broaches the same subject. He says to Rosanette that "'We come across precipices or morasses, in ourselves or in the other person, which bring us to a halt; in any case, we feel that we would not be understood; it is difficult to express anything at all with any degree of exactness, so that complete relations are few and far between.'"[1] Our failure to achieve "complete relations," which roots in a failure to say exactly what we mean, may show up in a grave "crisis of the common" (the common language, the common weal), as in *Madame Bovary*, but this is no reason for acceding to the skeptic's charge that we *cannot* mean what we say and therefore have no basis at all for such relations with others. In *Sentimental Education*, we see a society in chaos, a world in political ruin. But the revolution fails to overturn society, just as Emma's transgression of the marriage contract fails to withdraw her from association with Charles. In these next pages, I want to discuss the bases of moral knowledge in *Sentimental Education* in this light. My claim, as already suggested, will be that Flaubert's pessimism fails to do the work that skepticism would require because, like the revolution, it fails to overturn the foundations of moral knowledge.

In a letter to Mlle. Leroyer de Chantepie in 1864, when he was beginning the second version of *Sentimental Education*, Flaubert said that this novel was to be "the moral history—sentimental would be truer—of the men of my generation."[2] One advantage of introducing *Sentimental Education* after a discussion of aestheticism in connection with Kierkegaard and social epistemology in connection with Rousseau is that it helps bring to light the sense in which these crucial terms, "moral," "sentimental," approach equivalence; indeed, *Sentimental Education* cannot properly be read without recognizing that Frédéric's "sentimental education," his itinerary of disillusionment, is the description of a moral process. By equating "moral" (*moeurs*) with "sentimental" (*sentiments*), Flaubert places himself squarely on one side of the debate over morality of the previous century. Hume, for instance, outlined that debate by saying that

There has been a controversy started of late . . . concerning the general foundation of Morals; whether they be derived from Reason, or from Sentiment; whether we attain the knowledge of them by a chain of argument and induction, or by an immediate feeling and finer internal sense; whether, like all sound judgment of truth and falsehood, they should be the same to every rational intelligent being; or whether, like the perception of beauty and deformity, they be founded entirely on the particular fabric and constitution of the human species.[3]

French Encyclopedists like Jaucourt and Voltaire expended major efforts in the affirmation of *sentiment* and *sensibilité* as high moral guides for man. Jaucourt's 1765 *Encyclopédie* article, for instance, stated a preference for *sensibilité* over *reflexion*: "The authority on morals [Voltaire] says quite correctly that the sensibility of the soul [*âme*] gives man a kind of wisdom about common things, and goes far beyond what the mind [*esprit*] can penetrate alone. . . . Reflection can create a man of probity; but sensibility makes him virtuous." I will discuss some important ways in which *Sentimental Education* is severely critical of the Enlightenment's moral project, but these initial resemblances are enough to provide the grounds for my discussion, and to suggest that, whatever his response, Flaubert was seriously interested in engaging the Enlightenment's beliefs in this novel. Insofar as one finds this direction of inquiry at all valid, Flaubert's equation of "moral" and "sentimental" in his letter may indicate a further relationship of moral knowledge and what we have discussed as social epistemology. If morality lies in "sentiment," in what Hume calls the "immediate feeling and finer sense" that are part of the "particular fabric and constitution of the human species," then moral knowledge would *require* knowledge of what this "fabric and constitution" are, which is to say, knowledge of human nature or of the nature of the human species. But the thorny problem is that no one has ever seen this "*human* nature"—some would say because it does not exist at all, others would say because it does not exist apart from man's *social* nature.

Rousseau outlined this point at some length in the *Emile*, a book which completes many of the basic ideas expressed in the *Social Contract*: "Society must be studied through men, and men through society; those who would treat politics and morals separately will never understand anything of either."[4] This is why Emile must be brought to the city and instructed there ("He knows what is done in the world, and it remains for him to see how men live in it," p. 241). Even though Paris is known for poor taste, bad manners, and corruption, it is still the best setting for the education of men ("If you have a spark of genius, come spend a year in Paris; you will soon be all you are capable of being, or you will never be anything," p. 249). In the city, one can see what it means to be a man, to live in the world among others: "Emile is not made for living always in solitude; as a member of society he ought to fulfill his duties. Made to live with men, he ought to know them" (p. 240).

The moral education of man is training for membership in the polis. For Flaubert, as for Rousseau, and as for most political thinkers before them, political life is imaged in the activity that centers in and around the city. As we begin *Sentimental Education*, Frédéric Moreau is leaving Paris to return to Nogent sur Seine, but he will never be far from the city and he will complete his "sentimental education" there. His expectations of city life recall a comment near the end of the *Emile*: "Adieu, Paris. As we are looking for love, happiness, and innocence, we shall never be far away from you" (p. 258). As Harry Levin said, the city is in the foreground in this novel. The characters who live and move in it are spectators more than actors, and we perceive through them the special ambiance of urban life—"intermittent rain on the streets, the smell of gaslight, the rumbling of the omnibusses." Flaubert felt an affinity for the "great city with all the noises"; each time Frédéric leaves Paris, he experiences a poignant "nostalgia for the boulevards" (*The Gates of Horn*, p. 230).

As the setting for the moral and political education of man, however, the city is also the locus of disillusionment. A sharply contrasting quotation from Rousseau makes the point forcefully: "Adieu to Paris, therefore, city of renown, of noise, of smoke, of dirt, where women no longer live in honor, nor men in virtue" (p. 258). Frédéric's experiences in the city bear out Rousseau's comments. His "sentimental" life is corrupted in the affair with Rosanette, who turns out also to be the mistress of Jacques Arnoux; he is overrun by mercenary concerns in his dealings with Madame Dambreuse and *L'Art Industriel;* his romanticized image of his beloved Madame Arnoux is shattered at the auction of her possessions. One senses that he would have fared better had he limited his sights to Louise Roque, his boyhood fiancée. Thus at the end of the novel, Frédéric and his friend Deslauriers can look back on the past and say that the time they treasure most was when they went, like two naifs, to the local house of ill repute bearing flowers for the girls: "'C'est là ce que nous avons eu de meilleur!'" ("'That was the happiest time we ever had'") (III, 7; p. 419). Harry Levin saw this nostalgia for the past as a sign of a natural "revulsion from guilty knowledge"; it is an indication, he says, of Flaubert's "lifelong desire to be sheltered from the contingencies of adult existence" (*The Gates of Horn,* p. 224). But the course of Frédéric's sentimental education, which begins at his passage into adulthood, is an irreversible process. As he and Deslauriers look back from middle age to their boyhood escapades, the time of innocence is definitively out of reach.

As the novel opens, Frédéric is eighteen years old; he has already reached what one would call the "age of reason." This means that he has the ability to tell good from evil and is ready for membership in the polis. As we saw in connection with *Madame Bovary,* participation in political life requires that one lend one's opinions, will, voice, and mind, to the polis. (The "age of reason" is also called the "age of consent"; in the *Emile,* Rousseau sets it at fifteen years.) Like participation in a society bound by a prior contract, command of one's own mind is not something which one can, at will, attain. It is not an intellectual accomplishment but a moral one, a consequence of the knowledge of good and evil rather than a requirement for it.

The final retreat from the city, after a long, slow process of disillusionment, is not a catastrophe of any sort; there are no signs of the heroic defeat that we see in the case of Emma Bovary as she fails in the effort to withdraw her contractual consent. Flaubert himself saw only dim prospects for the political education of man. We know from his correspondence that he was deeply affected by the revolutionary history of France; by the time he wrote the second *Education*, he had witnessed the upheavals of 1848 and 1851 and could lament that "'89 [1789] had destroyed the nobility, '48 the middle class, and '51 the people." He described himself as "blasé at eighteen!"[5] When he wrote to Mlle. de Chantepie that *Sentimental Education* was to be a history of the *moeurs* or *sentiments* of his generation, it is not surprising that he should have portrayed political life as senseless and effete. Indeed, the novel abounds in testimony of the general idiocy of politics, all pointing to some deep misconception of its very nature, its basis, and its goals. Under different circumstances, Frédéric's ambitions in this direction might well have been a boon to his moral education; but in this environment they yield no significant results.

This is especially to be lamented, because Frédéric needs practice living among men, having reached the age of reason. This is the experience that the city might impart to him, but it is impossible under a reign of political ignorance. When the members of the Club de l'Intelligence send out a call for a man who is "new to politics," (III, 1; p. 306), it is only natural for Frédéric to respond; he is greeted by a "buzz of approval created by his friends," but fails to win confirmation: only Dussardier and Pellerin the painter can vouch for his principles; he is thrown out of the caucus at vicious shouts of "Aristo!" Pathetically, Frédéric himself is wholly unable to sustain his support for the Republic: "He reproached himself with his devotion to the Republic, forgetting that the accusations leveled at him were, after all, perfectly just. What a mad idea it had been to put up for election! But what fools they were, what cretins! He compared himself to these men, and soothed his wounded pride with the thought of their stupidity" (p. 307).

After his defeat, Frédéric decides to visit Rosanette, whom he finds unsympathetic. Nonetheless the dialogue with her suggests some of the deeper reasons for this political failure:

[205]

She was sitting by the fire, plucking the lining of a dress. This occupation surprised him.

"Hello! What are you doing?"

"You can see for yourself," she answered curtly. "I'm patching up my old clothes. *All because of your Republic.*"

"*What do you mean, my Republic?*"

"*I suppose it's mine, then?*"

And she started blaming him for everything that had happened in France during the last months, accusing him of having started the Revolution; it was his fault if everybody was ruined, if the rich were leaving Paris, and if she died later on in the workhouse. (p. 308; italics added)

The underscored portions of this passage in particular show the vacuities of their conception of political life: Rosanette labels the Republic—literally, the "public thing"—Frédéric's, which implies that it is not hers, and therefore is not public but private; Frédéric disclaims it as his, which, together with his cynicism following the election, also confirms his failure to take a role in the public life. Both Frédéric and Rosanette have replaced the public by the private; the communal goals of the Republic degenerate into the irreconcilable interests of particular individuals. Thus Frédéric becomes Rosanette's scapegoat, blaming him for the private misfortune she may have to suffer for the Republic. But by her own words she implies that private interest cannot long be sustained without support from the public sphere: "'You're all right with your private income,'" she says to Frédéric, "'Though the way things are going, you won't have that very much longer.'" At these charges, Frédéric turns pensive: "'The more public spirited you are, the less you are appreciated; and if you hadn't your conscience to support you, the boors you have to deal with would soon make you sick of self-sacrifice.'" Rosanette is not so mild; her reply to Frédéric makes a mockery of the very idea of politics: "'What self-sacrifice? It looks as though the evening hasn't been such a great success. Serve you right! That'll teach you to go playing the generous patriot. Oh, don't deny it! I know you've given them three hundred francs, for she's an expensive mistress, your precious Republic. Well, go and enjoy yourself with her, my lad!'"

Flaubert makes no effort to conceal his own disgust for the pious sentiments which are spoken in the name of the Republic or in favor of the common people. On the one hand that is because he sees them frankly as "imbecilic rabble," as masses of "filthy workers"; he has little tolerance for men like Sénécal or Homais, the quintessential bourgeois of *Madame Bovary*. But, more deeply, it is because the sentiments spoken in favor of the ideals and interests of the common people are just as liable to pervert the nature of the political life as the private interests of the aristocrats are. Indeed, the reason why the prospects for Frédéric's moral education are so bleak is that there are equally grave crises on both sides of the specific political ideologies; both point, although from different directions, to gross misconceptions about what life in the polis can or should be, about the very nature of what is held in common among men. Mademoiselle Vatnaz for instance argues that the work of civilization was "common to both sexes" and that therefore "woman ought to have her place in the State" (p. 309). This can be taken easily enough as a practical recommendation for achieving one of the goals of the previous century's revolution, *égalité*. But the idea becomes horrifyingly dangerous as part of any program to base political equality on an *absolute* equation of human beings. In *Sentimental Education*, we see mass murder and imprisonment—sure enough signs that man is still everywhere in chains—as the result of the Revolution's effort to achieve its goal of "equality." In the prisons, where the National Guards keeps watch,

equality—as if to punish its defenders and ridicule its enemies—asserted itself triumphantly: an equality of brute beasts, a common level of bloody atrocities; for the fanaticism of the rich counterbalanced the frenzy of the poor, the aristocracy shared the fury of the rabble, and the cotton nightcap was just as savage as the red bonnet. The public's reason was deranged as if by some great natural upheaval. Intelligent men lost their sanity for the rest of their lives. (III, 1; p. 334)

This does not describe a "common" life, in the political sense, but something more like anarchy, the veritable harrowing of the common(weal).

The glaring weakness of such political conceptions points to mistaken ideas about what politics is, about how men might be brought together in their "common" interests, their individual wills made part of the "general will," as Rousseau would say. The communal program which Mademoiselle Vatnaz describes as she continues her remarks certainly sounds worthy enough; she wants to "replace selfishness by fraternity, individualism by association, and the small-holdings system by collective farming" (p. 309). But the collective organization of government or enterprise cannot by itself insure the creation of a valid common weal. What we see of the outcome of the revolution in *Sentimental Education* argues forcefully to the contrary; any plan to implement a value like brotherhood (*fraternité*) where there is no *individual* basis for the founding of a life of common interest and concern will issue only in factionalism and hatred:

Some people wanted the Empire, some the Orleans family, some the Comte de Chambord; but all were agreed on the pressing need for decentralization. Several methods were suggested—dividing Paris into countless high streets with villages round them, transferring the seat of government to Versailles, moving the University to Bourges, suppressing the libraries, or putting everything in the hands of the General Staff—and country life was praised to the skies, since illiterates were naturally more sensible than the rest of men. Hatred abounded: hatred of primary school teachers and winemerchants, of philosophy classes and history lectures, of novels, of waistcoats, and long beards, of any kind of independence, any display of individuality; for it was necessary to "restore the principle of authority." (III, 4; pp. 384–85)

The nagging paradox of this revolution is that nothing changes, or seems capable of change, as a result ("It did not matter in whose name [authority] was wielded, or where it came from, provided it was strong and powerful. The Conservatives now talked like Sénécal. Frédéric was nonplussed; and at Rosanette's he heard the same ideas expressed by the same men"). The basis of the polis, which depends on the common life, is impervious to the threats of revolution, even where the common life is largely degraded.

Frédéric's political disillusionment in Part III of the novel is particularly disappointing because he does move from a more marginal
position to substantially greater involvement. At the end of Part II,
he is still disinterested. Returning home from a luxurious meal with
Rosanette, he hears news of a change in government and sees bay-
onettes, but he is blasé, too engrossed in his aesthetic pursuits to
concern himself with the ethical questions that the revolution
might raise:

The crowd was too thick for them to make their way straight back; and
they were turning into the Rue Caumartin when, all of a sudden, there
was a crackling noise behind like the sound of a huge piece of silk being
ripped in two. It was the fusillade on the Boulevard des Capucines. "Ah!
They're killing off a few bourgeois," said Frédéric calmly. (II, 6; p. 283)

The sangfroid of the comment is remarkable because it is taken up
by the narrator at some length in the following passage and is a good
indication of the stylistic parallels to the moral-political crisis:
"there are situations in which the kindliest of men is so detached
from his fellows that he would watch the whole human race perish
without batting an eyelid."

So far, I have not said much about the problem of Flaubert's style,
which has been discussed at such length by Victor Brombert, Jean-
Paul Sartre, Jonathan Culler and others,[6] but examples like this
from Part II are of special interest. There are a number of narrative
statements, similar to the preceding quote, which fall somewhere
between authorial intervention and direct observation by the characters. One might well wonder, with Brombert, how Flaubert could
allow his narrator such dry disinterest in the face of the revolutionary events told in this novel. Brombert says that these statements
create the effect of two visions merging into one; this recalls, and
may have been the source for, Sartre's view that the Flaubertian
style is always "about" two realities, one ("real") which belongs to
the author, and the other ("imaginary") which belongs to the characters.[7] Jonathan Culler in turn revises Sartre to say that Flaubert's
novels are about *neither* of these "realities" because they are about *no*

[209]

reality. I will offer some final reflections on the connection between this style and the "realism" of the novel, but the examples and critical comments just mentioned suggest that Flaubert's style creates the *insulation* of the two realities; the novel, taken as a whole, is stylistically "about" the failure to synthesize them. As René Girard said, I think significantly,

No real operation is possible among the various elements of the novelistic universe. The elements do not go together, neither are they in concrete opposition to each other. . . . We constantly find the same empty oppositions between aristocrats and bourgeois, between the devout and the atheists, reactionaries and republicans, lovers and mistresses, parents and children, rich and poor.[8]

At one point, Pellerin asks the question which is bound to follow: "'What does it mean, reality?'" In his correspondence, Flaubert said that "What is true is only 'relations'; that is the way in which we perceive objects" (*Correspondance*, VIII, 135); "There are only ways of seeing. Is a photograph a resemblance? No more than an oil painting, or just as much" (*Correspondance*, VIII, 382). This is not skepticism so much as grounds for hope that art might be a way of synthesizing those diverse "ways of seeing," fashioning them into a cohesive world. But even the explicitly moralizing comments which the narrator makes fail to construct a coherent universe of value for the characters. Consider the examples of Flaubertian "moralizing" that Brombert cites:

There is nothing so humiliating as to see fools succeed where we have failed. (I, 5)

There always remain in our conscience some of those sophistries which we pour into it. (III, 5)

In the midst of the most intimate confidences, there will always be found restrictions, false shame, delicacy and pity. (III, 1)

Statements like these, which echo with the voice of the *moraliste*, are scattered throughout the dialogue like so many clichés. Flaubert's narrator maintains a dry distance, allowing the characters to convict themselves, if not by their actions, then by their own language and opinions. He refuses to manipulate them or to assume moral control over them; they are free to choose good and evil, and free to fail to choose.

Indeed, Flaubert speculated that the initial failure of the novel may have been attributable to this very fact, which he called a lack of "perspective." "It is too true, and—esthetically speaking—it lacks the distortion of perspective" ("la fausseté de la perspective") (*Correspondance*, VIII, 309). By presenting reality without the "distortion of perspective," but simply as it is—neither morally good nor morally evil—and by withholding any synthetic moral judgments, Flaubert reserves the purposes of art for aesthetics, not politics or morals. If the novelist could reconcile diverse "ways of seeing" with one another, then he might expect art to serve a political goal, to fashion something like a common view for the common weal. An early letter in which Flaubert reflects on the revolutionary history of France in fact reads "Yes, our century is fertile in bloody upheavals. Goodbye, farewell, and let us concern ourselves always with Art, which is greater than peoples, crowns, and kings" (*Correspondance*, I, 22). In *Sentimental Education*, Sénécal says that art "should aim exclusively at raising the moral standards of the masses. The only subjects that should be reproduced [are] those which incited people to virtuous actions" (I, 5; p. 62). Yet whereas this might be vaguely possible for painting, it is inconceivable for literature. Rosanette says to Frédéric: "how can you expect a poet to know anything about politics?" (III, 1; p. 308). The implication is that the poet is too much of an "individual," too independent and idiosyncratic to have the requisite resources for "perspective," for the "common" or political life. This in turn points back to the paradoxical nature of education for membership in the polis: the common political life demands an exercise of human individuality; this is all the evidence there is of having reached the "age of reason." When Frédéric congratulates himself on his independence in handling his financial affairs with Monsieur Dambreuse (III, 2; p. 185), for instance, the compliment is well-earned and sincere, but the problem is that he is unable to sustain his independence in the face of the many claims on his attention.

His "independence" thus turns out to be a delusion, so easily diverted that in exercising it he is in jeopardy of losing the very moral basis of his existence, viz., that same independence.

To take his mind off his disastrous passion, he took up the first subject which occurred to him, and decided to write a history of the Renaissance. He heaped his desk pell-mell with humanists, philosophers, and poets; he went to the Print Room to see engravings of Marcantonio; and he tried to understand Machiavelli. Gradually his work exerted a soothing influence on him. *He forgot his own personality by immersing it in that of others—which is perhaps the only way to avoid suffering from it.* (II, 2; p. 188; italics added)

Frédéric is immersed in high Parisian society, but he is not a part of it; he is in this respect like Emile, whom Rousseau describes as an amiable foreigner to city life. The difference between them is that whereas Emile maintains his distance in order to resist the leveling effects of "culture," Frédéric makes every effort to become a part of Parisian society, seeking for instance to associate himself with *L'Art Industriel* and to gain the inheritance he needs in order to secure his social status. The tragicomedy of these efforts is not so much that they fail but that Flaubert portrays a world in which there *is* no collective life worthy of such efforts; he shows, as Stanley Cavell said of Thoreau, that education for citizenship is education for isolation.[9] For most of the time that Frédéric is in Paris, he is alone; he spends hours in solitary reverie about Marie Arnoux or in consideration of strategies that might improve his social standing and thus approximate himself to her. Frédéric's personal condition in *Sentimental Education* thus mirrors the political crisis: he does not know how to live in community, but neither does he know how to live alone. In the *Emile*, Rousseau recognized that education for responsible citizenship depends absolutely on knowing how to live alone, training in what it means to be of the "age of reason" or the "age of consent," i.e., in command of one's *own* mind and voice, responsible for oneself:

It is asserted that we are trained for society, and yet we are taught as though each one of us was to spend his life thinking alone in his cell, or in discussing idle questions with the indifferent . . . . I have also taught my

Emile how to live, for I have taught him to live by himself, and, in addition, to know how to earn his daily bread. (p. 244)

The consequences of Frédéric Moreau's moral or "sentimental" education are not limited to the political sphere, although they show up particularly well there. Pertinent facts of his relationship with Madame Arnoux and with Deslauriers are also anticipated in the *Emile*. According to Rousseau, friendship, not love, is in fact "The first feeling of which a young man who has been carefully educated is susceptible"; "The first act of his nascent imagination is to teach him that he has fellow-creatures, and the species affects him before the sex" (p. 201). It is only later, at the conclusion of the *Emile*, that Rousseau's pupil sets out on the project that occupies Frédéric for the majority of the novel. The need for love, which brings Rousseau to discuss the education of Sophie, is a part of Frédéric's education from the very start: "'If I had a woman to love me,'" he says to Deslauriers on his first return to Nogent sur Seine, "'I might have achieved something . . . . Love is the food and air of genius'" (I, 1; p. 28). At this point in the novel, his sights are not unrealistic; he explicitly disavows any intention of looking for the "'woman of my dreams'"; "'Besides, even if I find her, she'll only reject me. I belong to the race of the disinherited, and I shall die without ever knowing whether the treasure within me is a diamond or paste.'" Frédéric contradicts these intentions by his actions; he finds himself involved in the most vulgar of affairs with Rosanette; his friendship with Deslauriers is in fact more durable than his love for Madame Arnoux.

In love as in politics, Frédéric's education is a process of growth in reverse, a trajectory of disillusionment which brings no increase in wisdom as recompense. Flaubert mines, and undermines, the ancient literary topos of education through love, taking it to mean that love educates the individual, bringing out the best in him, and that the individual is educated in the ways of love, especially in the passions. When Rosanette first says that she loves Frédéric, the idea appears as a mystery to him; he seems unable to fathom the school in which *she* might have been "educated":

"How you suffered my poor love!"

"Yes," she said, "more than you think!" "So much that I wanted to put an end to it all. They fished me out of the river."

"What!"

"Oh let's forget about it! . . . I love you, and I'm happy. Kiss me."

. . .

Frédéric was thinking above all of what she had left unsaid. By what steps had she succeeded in emerging from poverty? What lover had given her her education? What sort of life had she led up to the day when he had first been to her house? Her last admission forbade any further questions. He asked her how she had come to know Arnoux. (III, 1; p. 327)

Here, thinking about Rosanette is only a vicarious way of thinking about Madame Arnoux, his "dream"; the moment does not acquire its full meaning until the very end of the novel, and the termination of Frédéric's "education" as he and Deslauriers look back on their naive adventures in the brothel.

What Frédéric gains in his "moral" reverse-education is, if not the courage of his sensibilities, at least his awakening to them. This may explain why the novel ends with a mixture of pathos and irony, rather than on a moralizing note. Flaubert sees that society, as it exists, places obstacles in the way of education, or is itself that obstacle. Hence there is something paradoxical in the very *idea* of education, at least if one thinks about it as learning how to live among men. Madame Dambreuse can praise Frédéric's "manners, his looks, and, above all else, his morals" (III, 2; p. 336) long after they have been corrupted; his interest in her is motivated by mercenary concerns and by the hope that she might establish his "position in society?" (III, 3; p. 360). In this novel, the demands of society and the polis are set against "proper" moral principles; the appeal to the senses as the basis of morality in turn deadens the moral sensibility. As the narrator remarks at one point, "The political verbiage and good food began to dull his sense of morality" (p. 359). Frédéric sounds like the perfect aesthete when he tells Madame Dambreuse that " 'Our grandfathers knew how to love better than we do. Why shouldn't we yield to the impulse of the moment?' " (p. 362). The narrator implicitly agrees by use of *le style indirect libre*: "After all, love in itself was not so very important." To be sure,

Madame Dambreuse is not so naive that she can hear all this with impunity; she raises the very objection that the reader is likely to voice: "'But what you're saying is positively immoral!'"

What Frédéric says *is* immoral, positively so; in the society that Flaubert imagines, love naturally clashes with "morality." The *coup de grace* of this exchange with Madame Dambreuse comes in Frédéric's response to this charge of immorality—or rather, in recognition of it:

"Can't you see that I'm lying? Because to please a woman one has to display a carefree levity or a tragic frenzy. They laugh at us when we tell them we love them, and nothing more. To my mind the highflown humbug they enjoy is a profanation of true love; so that one doesn't know how to declare that love, especially to a woman who is . . . very intelligent."

Frédéric's words are a collective insult—to Madame Dambreuse and to her sex, but also to himself and to society at large. He says that one cannot find the proper ways to express love; and not finding the proper expressions of it, how can one know that it is real? The final irony is that this ignorance of the declarations of love, and hence of love itself, shows up among those who are most "intelligent," those who are at or near the pinnacle of the social order, the aristocrats like Madame Dambreuse.

Frédéric Moreau's moral miseducation, his disillusionment in and through love, is made possible largely through the cultivation of the life of the senses in Paris. He is introduced to a world of luxury, wealth, and power, but still he is not satisfied; on the contrary, he is disillusioned. Rousseau analyzed the problem in *Emile* and said that such images of happiness are of themselves deceptive. They do not provide us with what we need in order to be satisfied, because they do not correspond to what we ourselves want; they are generated by the will of others:

Do not cause pride, vanity, and envy to germinate in him; through the deceptive images of the happiness of men, do not at first expose to his eyes the pomp of courts, the pageantry of palaces, and the attractions of the theatre; do not take him about in social circles and brilliant assemblies; do not show him the exterior of grand society until after having put him in a

[215]

condition to form an estimate of it himself. To show him the world before he knows men is not to form him but to corrupt him; it is not to instruct him but to deceive him. (*Emile*, p. 201)

Frédéric is, to be sure, "corrupted" as he comes under the sway of pleasure-seeking Parisian society; his affections stray from Marie Arnoux toward Rosanette and Madame Dambreuse. But *Sentimental Education* is hardly written in condemnation of the pursuits of pleasure; as we have already seen in *Madame Bovary*, Flaubert finds satisfaction in his own rather sensuous style. The problem lies deeper: Frédéric finds no satisfaction in Rosanette or in Madame Dambreuse, but the crucial fact is that he finds no greater fulfillment in Marie Arnoux. He pursues Rosanette and Madame Dambreuse because he has not yet learned, as Rousseau said a man must, how to judge for himself; this is a glaring deficiency in someone who has reached the chronological age of reason, a sign that he has not attained its moral equivalent. Like Emma Bovary, Frédéric fills his life with illusions, primary among them Marie Arnoux. And, as we discover with him, any pursuit of happiness in matters of love must leave that illusion intact. This latter consequence is far more serious for the moral education of the individual than any of the dangers posed by the aesthetic life.

Rousseau issued certain warnings in the *Emile* which may clarify the point. Emile, he said, "everywhere finds comparisons which make him prefer his dream to the real objects which excite his attention." Frédéric Moreau is chronically beset by this problem. From the start, in the famous first description of Marie Arnoux, she seems to him like a vision, "comme une apparition"; to someone who has been reading *Werther*, "She looked like the women in romantic novels. . . . She was the point of light on which all things converged; and lulled by the movement of the carriage, his eyelids half closed, his gaze directed at the clouds, he gave himself up to an infinite, dream joy" (I, 1; pp. 18,22). As Rousseau goes on to say, and as I think holds strikingly true for Flaubert, love is by nature a product of our dreams; if we try to make it "real," it is bound to end in disillusionment:

[216]

What is real love itself, if not a dream, a fiction, an illusion? We love the picture which we form more than the object to which we apply it. If we saw what we love exactly as it is, there would no longer be any love in the world. When we cease to love, the person whom we loved remains the same as before, but we no longer see her the same. The veil of delusion falls, and love vanishes. (*Emile*, III; pp. 242–43)

Reading Rousseau's warning, one thinks of Don Quixote's devoted pursuit of Dulcinea and especially of the episode in the *Quixote* (II, 10) where the peasant girl falls from a donkey; rather than admit that he is mistaken about Dulcinea, Don Quixote claims that the girl he sees is simply his beloved Dulcinea under an enchanter's spell. Rousseau's comment suggests initially that the pursuits of love and happiness are mutually exclusive, that we cannot find satisfaction if we come to know the true object of our devotion. There is, however, an alternate path toward happiness which Rousseau considers, in consonance with the quixotic vision: that we may measure happiness not only by the successful completion of some "schedule of activities and aims,"[10] but more treacherously perhaps, by attaining a certain state of mind. What this means is that if it is not in our power to execute our aims, we might look instead to adjust the image of our happiness. This is, however, where Flaubert's characters are foiled. Identifying with Werther or the heroines of Walter Scott's romances, they seek out those forms of happiness which are achieved with most difficulty. Their life-plans include goals which are marked as uncommon, difficult, or impossible to attain: infinite wealth, social status and power, ideal love, even encyclopedic knowledge in the case of Bouvard and Pécuchet. Rousseau tries to teach Emile the one truth which might save Flaubert's characters from disillusionment, viz., that happiness is within the reach of all men, and especially of common men, if only we can learn to adjust our image of it accordingly:

The objection will doubtless be made that such [common] amusements are within the reach of all men, and that one does not need to be rich to enjoy them. This is precisely the point I wish to make. We have pleasure when we are willing to have it. It is opinion alone which makes everything difficult, which drives happiness from us; and it is a hundred times more easy to be happy than to appear so. (*Emile*, IV; pp. 257–58)

To this end, Emile's educator sets out to control his pupil's vision of what will satisfy him: "by furnishing the imaginary control, I am the master of comparisons and easily prevent the illusion of real objects" (*Emile*, III, pp. 242–43). In *Sentimental Education*, Sénécal thinks that art can serve this purpose for the masses and hence raise their "moral standards"; Mademoiselle Vatnaz apparently has similar hopes for poetry. She wants to publish an educational book, "a literary and moral anthology entitled *The Young Person's Garland*" (III, 1; p. 128). But, as we have already seen, Flaubert saw these as dim possibilities. Frédéric Moreau's education takes place without any of the benign control imagined by Rousseau, and thus issues in profound disillusionment. As long as Frédéric approaches the "real" objects of his desire, the more certain he is to be unsatisfied. Finally, he sees Madame Arnoux fall from wealth and social power and witnesses the painful process of the auctioning of her possessions.

Love and happiness exclude one another because Frédéric has no benign master to protect him from reality. Frédéric himself tries to be that master and to supply his own illusions; when Rosanette tells him that she is pregnant, for instance, he turns his thoughts to the prospect of fathering a child with Marie Arnoux:

The idea of being a father struck him as grotesque, unthinkable. But why should it? If, instead of the Marshal . . . ? And he became so absorbed in his reverie that he had a sort of hallucination. There on the carpet, in front of the fireplace, he saw a little girl. She took after Madame Arnoux and a little after him. . . . Oh, how he would have loved her! And he seemed to hear her voice calling "Papa! Papa!" (III, 3; pp. 355–56)

But when Madame Arnoux asks him about his engagement to Louise Roque, he can only admit that "'A man falls back on the second-rate when he has given up hope of the ideal he has dreamt of'" (II, 6; p. 257). The fact that Frédéric is unable to sustain his self-delusions will explain the irony of the novel's final pages— his admission that his maximum happiness was coincident with his greatest ignorance.

So understood, the close of the novel is a good indication of Flaubert's aversion to skepticism. Whereas a skeptic would argue that happiness consists in *nothing but* our different (and presumably incommensurate) ideas of what will satisfy us, and will go on to say that happiness *itself* is nothing but an illusion, the progression of *Sentimental Education* toward Frédéric's yearning for lost innocence stands such skepticism on its head. At the end of the novel, Frédéric is not craving any more knowledge but, along with his lost innocence, the recuperation of his youthful *ignorance*. Flaubert and Rousseau have both made comments which, out of context, hint of skepticism (e.g., Rousseau: "What is real love itself, if not a dream, a fiction, an illusion?"; Flaubert: "What is true is only 'relations'"), but they refuse to enter into epistemological debate with the skeptic. The work of reason, as *Bouvard and Pécuchet* will make plain, creates its own special Hell. Better, as Frédéric seems to know at the end of the novel, to be classed with the majority of the people of the world, as Pellerin describes them: "'Some see black, some see blue, *most see stupidly.*'"

It should be fairly clear from the examples already cited that Frédéric Moreau, like Emma Bovary, bases his pursuit of happiness on "aesthetic" goals, not on reason (in Part II, Flaubert says that "Another thirst had come upon [Frédéric]: the thirst for women, for luxury, for everything that life in Paris implies," II, 1; p. 133). Insofar as the "pursuit of happiness" can be identified as a *moral* goal, this places Flaubert unmistakably on the side of "sentiment" in the debate over morals that Hume described. This is not to say that Flaubert holds much hope for the success of a morality based on sentiment. On the contrary: Frédéric Moreau is destroyed by his "sentimental" life, by his fall from youthful innocence, much as Emma Bovary is undone by her aestheticism. But the failure to live a morally good life on the basis of sentiment is not, in Flaubert's eyes, grounds for rejecting sentiment in favor of reason, just as congenital ignorance—Frédéric says at the end of the novel that "stupidity is catching" (p. 417)—is not grounds for philosophical skepticism, as we shall see in *Bouvard and Pécuchet*. To show this

[219]

fully will require some additional evidence that the "pursuit of happiness" might on some account provide a moral basis for living, evidence that it is not *necessarily* the same as the pursuit of our incommensurate private pleasures, as the skeptic would want to claim.

Aristotle said that beings seek what satisfies them because they will thereby flourish and be the best that they can. But his idea of happiness, as *eudaimonia*, is free from the troublesome concept of pleasure, with all its overtones of relativism and hedonism which had become attached to the idea of happiness by Flaubert's time. Indeed, one of the major efforts of thinkers in the century preceding Flaubert was to extricate the idea of the pursuit of happiness from its entanglement with the pleasurable—yet not necessarily moral—sentiments and so to reestablish it as a valid moral and political principle. To do so required a definition of happiness such as Locke gave in *An Essay Concerning Human Understanding* (II, 21, "Of Power"):

Happiness, what. Now, because pleasure and pain are produced in us by the operation of certain objects, either on our minds or our bodies, and in different degrees' therefore, what has an aptness to produce pleasure in us we call *good,* and what is apt to produce pain in us we call evil, for no other reason but for its aptness to produce pleasure and pain in us, wherein consists our happiness and misery.[11]

Even though reason can instruct us in the advantages, disadvantages, and relative utility of various human activities, still it is up to sentiment to direct us toward those activities which will yield our happiness. Reason and sentiment must work together, find their proper balance. Hume wrote that "It is requisite a sentiment should here display itself, in order to give a preference to the useful above the pernicious tendencies. This sentiment can be no other than a feeling for the happiness of mankind, and a resentment of their misery" (*An Enquiry Concerning the Principles of Morals,* Appendix 1, §235, p. 286). By the time that Thomas Jefferson and the framers of the Declaration of Independence had enshrined the notion of the "pursuit of happiness" in its most famous modern context ("life, liberty, and the pursuit of happiness"), it had already been rescued as a valid goal for moral and political philosophy. Voltaire declared that there is no truly *human* happiness that is not also beneficial to society: "We live in society; therefore there is no true good for us except that which promotes the good of society" (*Dictionnaire philosophique*, s.v. "vertu"). The influential Scottish Enlightenment figure Thomas Hutcheson described human happiness as the pursuit of "the greatest happiness of the greatest number."[12] Both Hutcheson and Hume explain obligation (duty) in terms of the gratification of the moral sense, the satisfaction of the moral appetite; as the following passage explains, that appetite is the source of the maximum *public* good:

If by *obligation* we understand *a motive from self-interest* sufficient to determine all those who duly consider it and pursue their own advantage wisely, to a certain course of actions, we may have a sense of such obligation by reflecting on this determination of our nature to approve virtue, *to be pleased and happy when we reflect upon our having done virtuous actions* and to be uneasy when we are conscious of having acted otherwise—and also by considering how much superior we esteem the happiness of virtue to any other enjoyment. We may likewise have a sense of this sort of obligation by considering those reasons which prove a constant course of benevolent and social actions to be *the most probable means of promoting the natural good of every individual.*[13]

By the kind of careful husbanding that Rousseau outlined, we should be able to direct the passions and the interests—products of sensibility—toward morally valuable ends, ends which will, as Hume said, be consonant with "the happiness of mankind." This will require, as we have already seen Rousseau to say, avoiding "pride, vanity, and envy," keeping the passions from generating delusions of happiness, such as that of the "pomp of courts, the pageantry of palaces, and the attractions of the theatre" (*Emile*, IV; p. 201); and it will mean, contrastingly, directing the passions to feel "the true relations of man both in the species and in the individual." With this requirement, it seems we are back to the need for knowing the human species as such that follows from Hume's earlier comment on "sentiment," but with the difference that the *collective* dimension of the moral sentiment should now be apparent: if that "sentiment" derives from an affective sympathy for others of the species, then its gratification through something like the "pursuit of happiness" need not impede the common interest and good at all; on the contrary, it ought to favor that good and foment the concrete possibilities of our sympathy with others.

In the revolution that fails to overturn society, in the social contract which cannot be anulled, Flaubert finds an inalienable basis for public and private morality; for this reason he is no skeptic. But he finds that in practice the pursuit of happiness readily decays into the pursuit of the pleasures of the senses, the cultivation of private interest to the exclusion of the public good; for this reason he is a pessimist and a cynic. The examples we know of Emma's aestheticism and of Frédéric Moreau's initiation into Parisian society will suffice as evidence of Flaubert's outlook in this regard. As the chapters on politics in *Sentimental Education* show especially well, Flaubert viewed the Enlightenment project with much despair and little respect; Hume's effort to balance sentiment over reason is rejected as folly. Recall the close of the novel where Frédéric and Deslauriers admit their failures—"They had both failed, one to realize his dreams of love, the other to fulfill his dreams of power" (III, 7; p. 417); the accounting Deslauriers gives is remarkable: "I was too logical, while you were too sentimental" ("'J'avais trop de logique, et toi de sentiment,'" p. 418); if this book is a study in Frédéric's "sentimental" excess, *Bouvard and Pécuchet* will be a study of the imbalance of logic. The implication is that *neither* "reason" (*logique*) *nor* "sentiment" will allow the individual successfully to satisfy his pursuit of happiness, to "realize his dreams" of power or love; this explains Frédéric's attitude at the end of the book, his yearning for lost ignorance and innocence, for a time before the moral sentiments had been awakened in him, for any age prior to the dreaded "age of reason."

As the novel draws to a close, Frédéric grows increasingly conscious of the impending disillusionment of the senses; this is particularly true of his relationship with Madame Dambreuse:

When he was with her he did not feel that overwhelming ecstasy which impelled him towards Marie Arnoux, nor the happy excitement which

Rosanette had caused him at first. But he desired her as an exotic, refractory object, because she was noble, because she was rich, and because she was devout, imagining that she had delicate feelings as exquisite as her lace, with holy medals next to her skin and modest blushes in the midst of debauchery.

He made use of his old love. He told her about all the emotions which Marie Arnoux had once aroused in him—his yearnings, his fears, his dreams—as if she had inspired them. (III, 3; pp. 360–61)

Ironically, then, one of the best uses of the sentiments in the pursuit of happiness is to excite the more "dangerous" passions and so to forestall disillusionment, as when Frédéric revives his waning love by imaginative simulation: "He admitted at that moment what he had refused to acknowledge until then—the disillusionment of his senses. This did not prevent him from simulating ardent passions; but in order to feel it, he had to summon up the image of Rosanette or Madame Arnoux" (III, 4; p. 369). With this comment, we have come full circle from Rousseau's precept on the education of Emile, i.e., that he should be shielded from the pleasures of the senses until he can judge for himself. We find instead the glaring absence of any benign master to control Frédéric's image of happiness and prevent the "veil of delusion" from falling.

In the novel, the ultimate responsibility for such governance rests with the characters, not the narrator as one might expect were the parallel with Rousseau completely borne out. The Flaubertian narrator, famous for his ironic capabilities, resists the direct control or manipulation of his characters. He will offer his moralizing observations and dicta, half-joining his voice to that of the characters, but he maintains his aloofness and distance. Thus there is relatively more freedom in the moral world of Sentimental Education than in the Emile; in that sense the world of the novel is more "real," less beset by illusions whose source may be undetectable to its inhabitants. Flaubert's narrator may have us conclude that ignorance is bliss, and he may have us recognize, with Frédéric Moreau, the precious value of illusions, but he will not bear the burden of choosing or controlling them for us. What this shows, beyond Rousseau, is that anyone of moral age, the age of reason, must be responsible not only for the truths that he can call his own, but for his illusions as well. Frédéric Moreau, to take the case at hand, must recognize for himself that his days of happiness lie in the irretrievable past. In marking his distance from his illusions he claims them as his own; it is only from this stance that one can measure any advance in his "sentimental" education.

THE ABUSES OF CERTAINTY

"The more ideas they had the more they suffered."
—*Bouvard and Pécuchet*

OF THE THREE NOVELISTS considered here, Flaubert maintains the most equivocal stance with regard to human knowledge; for while he clearly rejects reason as a valid guide, it is not clear whether he sees any other mode of knowledge as capable of taking its place. Knowledge by the physical senses (as in *Madame Bovary*) or the moral sentiments (as in *Sentimental Education*), neither of which is rational, are dismal failures. Might some other way of knowing satisfy the *libido sciendi*, or are the enticements of knowledge mere folly, delusions of the human mind? Flaubert's characters are to be sure attracted by the promise of knowledge; they sense its magnetism and its lure; to the extent that Flaubert himself shares this attraction (and there is strong biographical evidence for this in the circumstances surrounding the composition of *Bouvard and Pécuchet*) he is rather unlike the skeptic, who warns against the dangers of knowledge, who thwarts its efforts and rejects its claims. The paradox of Flaubert's novels, though, is that his attraction to knowledge brings intense dissatisfaction with its results. The prospect of knowledge is a lure and a temptation; it ends in betrayal and repulsion—hence the temptations of Saint Anthony, hence Frédéric Moreau who looks back wistfully to a time before his exposure to such threats. In the following pages, I want to examine this contradiction in connection with *Bouvard and Pécuchet*, Flaubert's tragicomedy of knowledge. I do not expect to resolve the paradox, which proves to be an important index of Flaubert's nonpartisan rejection of both skepticism *and* reason. *Bouvard and Pécuchet* thus places Flaubert squarely in the line of Cervantes and Dostoevsky, who likewise reject rational answers to skepticism's threats.

[225]

In our analyses thus far, we have seen numerous instances where the demands of knowledge cannot be met by additional facts, rules, or information. This is especially true where what is required is wisdom—as in the case of Dostoevsky's suicides, who need self-knowledge—which reason cannot supply, or where the knowledge we require can be told only by the body, as in Don Quixote's clashes with the external world. In *Bouvard and Pécuchet*, there are more facts, rules, and information, but also less satisfaction and learning than in any novel we have seen. The failure of Bouvard and Pécuchet to know the world by rational method and empirical observation is in proportion to the gargantuan magnitude of the effort they make.

Flaubert's two heroes—"simple, lucid, mediocre," as Maupassant said—range over the gamut of the sciences and disciplines, amassing an encyclopedia of useless knowledge. In part, this is a satire of the efforts of the Encyclopédistes of the previous century. As Lionel Trilling said, "*Bouvard and Pécuchet* in its despair that anything at all can be done is the negation of the morning confidence and hope of the *Encyclopédie*."[1] As another critic said, Flaubert's heroes are stricken by the "virus of Encyclopedism";[2] their intellectual tourism brings them through the different fields of human learning. They are fascinated by rules, by formulae, and by the certainties of science; they relentlessly pursue the "causes of things." Their quest for knowledge runs to epidemic proportions; it is as wasteful of human effort as the skeptic's denials.

Bouvard and Pécuchet is more than the story of another failed "pursuit of happiness," comparable to *Madame Bovary* or *Sentimental Education*. The despair in the face of the self-confidence of the *Encyclopédie*, of which Trilling speaks, is not simply a matter of disillusionment after dogged effort. It is the indictment of a culture which had made reason its god, its idol. If we take Kant's 1784 essay "What is Enlightenment?" as a guide, that culture saw its purpose as freeing the human mind from "prejudice" by providing reliable (i.e., rational) foundations of human knowledge. The Enlightenment could claim the expansion of human knowledge to encyclopedic proportions, and it could claim having responded to skepticism, in fact, only *because* it founded knowledge on reason. But in Flaubert's eyes, the price of such putative accomplishments was inordinately high. As Bouvard and Pécuchet move from one field of learning to another, passing through the physical and natural sciences, through philosophy, education, and religion, entire disciplines are successively trivialized, rendered useless or effete; like Faust in this sense, they find all the fields of learning inadequate. Founding human knowledge on human reason, and uniting the disciplines on this ground, all the fields of learning are equated, and all are rendered equally banal. We note the glaring loss of a master discipline, a single field to give direction and value to the rest. Bouvard and Pécuchet ceaselessly seek *final* answers to the world, a single paradigm in which to explain its diverse phenomena; they find instead that the chaos of reason reigns, and so their totalizing efforts produce what Sartre liked to call a "detotalized totality."

This is not to say that Flaubert expresses nothing more than contempt or disgust for the Enlightenment project; as Lionel Trilling said so well, "[Bouvard and Pécuchet] are the butts of his humor, which is strongly qualified by affection" (*The Opposing Self*, p. 166). Indeed, Flaubert himself felt the attraction of knowledge, the temptation and lure to which his characters succumb; hence his compassion toward them. Some details surrounding the composition of the novel are particularly illuminating of this fact. Flaubert boasted that he had read some 1,500 works and filled countless notebooks in preparation for this encyclopedic farce—which suggests that he valued it not only as comedy but also as a chance for self-indulgence. In response to Turgenev and Taine, who urged him to be brief, Flaubert insisted that a travesty of encyclopedism must itself be of encyclopedic proportions; he wanted, he said, a work that would take in the whole intellectual life of France. Trilling compares him to Diderot, canvasing France for the right information on this new chemical process or that new invention to fill his *Encyclopédie*. The major trouble, as Flaubert lets us see, is that such a project, taken as a whole, makes no more sense than its isolated parts. An encyclopedic collection of knowledge fails to give meaning to the facts and information that are amassed. The virtuoso efforts of Bouvard and Pécuchet, as of Flaubert himself, conceal an emptiness at the core.

Stylistically, this central vacuity shows up in Flaubert's sentence structure and in the rhythm of his phrasing. He proceeds by the juxtaposition and slow accretion of details; each promises to give significance to the last, but none gives any final meaning to the constructed whole. Flaubert once wrote that this book could be subtitled "Encyclopedia of Human Stupidity."[3] In René Girard's analysis, Flaubert's style is his solution to the problem posed by that theme: "To resolve the problem Flaubert invents the style of false enumerations and false antitheses . . . . this impassive juxtaposition reveals the absurdity. The inventory grows longer but the total always remains zero" (*Deceit, Desire, and the Novel*, p. 151). The same could be said of the larger plan of the book: the plot is almost nonexistent and, as more than one critic has remarked, the principal characters are scantily drawn. In these respects, Flaubert anticipates the modern "novel of ideas," and the demise of character as a viable literary vehicle of values. Those literary developments may well be linked to a decrease of confidence in the rational mind, but in the case of *Bouvard and Pécuchet*, which overtly parodies the cult of reason, the claim can be made with no conjecture or speculation.

Indeed, one of the clear advantages in any reading of this book is that it is so culturally well-aimed and specific in intent. Virtually the whole of its attack is pointed at the pillars of Enlightenment thought: faith in human reason and its totalizing capacity, confidence in man's ability to learn, hope in mastery of the world by the methods of science (experiment, observation, analysis), the formulation of principles and rules directed toward practical ends, and "progress" through technology. As a satire, though, it mounts this attack by subversion, employing the manners and techniques of the very culture it opposes. Bouvard and Pécuchet set out to manage a farm, armed with little more than blind faith in the power of reason. They attempt arboriculture and agronomy, the confection of cremes and preserves, the bottling of wines and champagne. They learn these arts by experiment and analysis, the study of books and of manuals. They presume that the world is governed by knowable rules, the mastery of which will allow them to improve upon nature. But they become slaves to their "scientific" projects, which turn out to be dismal failures. The results, moreover, are out of all proportion to the amount of effort invested. When their soups and syrups spoil, when their vegetables rot and their cooking utensils shatter, they are driven to study chemistry. They are set on the path of a constant regression to know the first causes of things, to discover the principles and formulae at work in the world.

This dauntless search for the foundations of knowledge is the driving force behind their encyclopedic tour through the disciplines of human learning. The idea that there are such first causes, and one language to relate them, is a satiric attack on Leibniz and Spinoza, on the hope for a *mathesis universalis,* and on the notion of God as self-caused (*causa sui*). Bouvard and Pécuchet are of course incapable of understanding Leibniz or Spinoza, but this incompetence is masked by their boundless naiveté, by their unstinting faith in the existence of the "final cause" that they seek:

The stomach is made for digesting, the legs for walking, the eyes for seeing, although dyspepsia, fractures and cataract can occur! No arrangement without a purpose! Effects happen now or later. *Everything depends on laws. Therefore final causes exist!*

Bouvard thought that Spinoza might provide him with arguments, and he wrote to Dumouchel to get Saisset's translation.

The ethics frightened him with their axioms, their corollaries. They read only the passages marked in pencil, and understood as follows:

Substance is what is of itself, by itself, without cause and without origin. That substance is God.[4]

Bouvard and Pécuchet become hyperbolic parodies of the antiskeptic, so obsessed with finding certainties in nature that ironically they undermine their own efforts; eventually they see only relativity, evanescence, constant flux; they are fascinated by the changing shape of wind-driven clouds, by contradictions, polar opposites, and the variances of perspective. When they become disgusted with geology, for instance, Pécuchet exclaims that "'Creation is put together in such an elusive and transitory fashion'" (III, p. 99). Because of their own strenuous efforts, they are dissatisfied with nearly every attempt to find a master discipline or single science of nature; studying medicine, for instance, they note that "The springs of life are hidden from us, ailments are too numerous, remedies questionable, and none of the authors offers any reasonable definition of health, sickness, diathesis or even pus!'" (p. 81). At one point in the text their large investment of hope in science brings near total disillusionment, for their own achievements have been so meagre. "Science is built up of data provided by one corner of the whole expanse. Perhaps it does not apply to all the rest that we do not know, which is much bigger, and can't be discovered!'" (p. 85).

This does not mean that Bouvard and Pécuchet will abandon their project; rather, they will direct themselves toward more congenial fields, toward the "human sciences" rather than the sciences of nature—toward philosophy, religion, and education. They never lose conviction that there must be final answers to the mysteries of the world, and that it is within their capability to apply their knowledge to the improvement of their lot. Their boundless optimism—which seems to thrive on disappointment—makes tacit reference to Voltaire's *Candide*, which Flaubert once called the "greatest moral lesson that exists" (*Correspondance*, VIII, 203). Voltaire's Pangloss, who revels in his discovery of the commonplace, looks ahead to Flaubert's bourgeois intellectuals, who in their own quixotic way take the most ordinary things of the world—things as common as sex—as marvels and discoveries:

Pangloss taught metaphysico-theologo-cosmolo-niology. He proved admirably that there is no effect without a cause and that, in this best of all possible worlds, My Lord the baron's castle was the finest of castles, and My Lady the best of all possible Baronesses.

"It is demonstrated," he said, "that things cannot be otherwise, for everything being made for an end, everything is necessarily for the best end. Note that noses were made to wear spectacles, and so we have spectacles. Legs were visibly instituted to be breeched, and we have breeches. Stones were formed to be cut and to make into castles; so My Lord has a very handsome castle; the greatest baron in the province should be the best housed; and, pigs being made to be eaten, we eat pork all year round: consequently, those who have asserted that all is well have said a foolish thing; they should have said that all is for the best."[5]

This parody of intellectual optimism, so kindred to what we find in Flaubert, is quixotism with a new twist: these optimists do not look to change the world, as Don Quixote did; they do not want to revive the glories of an age gone by. On the contrary, they proclaim to the masses that *this* is the best of all possible worlds—despite its manifest failings and faults. Yet as in *Don Quixote,* the world of the commonplace is filled with excitement, mystery, and suspense; it is the source of authentic wonderment:

Pangloss sometimes said to Candide: "All events are linked together in the best of all possible worlds; for after all, if you had not been expelled from a fine castle with great kicks in the backside for love of Mademoiselle Cunégonde, if you had not been subjected to the Inquisition, if you had not traveled about America on foot, if you had not given the Baron a great blow with your sword, if you had not lost all your sheep from the good country of Eldorado, you would not be here eating candied citrons and pistachios." "That is well said," replied Candide, "but we must cultivate our garden." (p. 101)

The return home to the garden, to the labors of the hands and not of the mind, is echoed at the end of *Bouvard and Pécuchet* as Flaubert's two heroes take up their life together at their two-sided copying desk, having forsaken their hopes for an intellectual career. Given the travails to which the life of the mind and pursuit of the rule of reason have subjected them, this final consignment to the meager task of copying is in fact a relief; one thinks of the words of Voltaire's Martin: "'Let us work without reasoning . . . it is the only way to make life endurable'" (p. 101).

But until their moment of retreat, Bouvard and Pécuchet are sustained in their projects by an infinite hope in the human capacity to know and to learn, using reason to master the surrounding world. They are confident for instance that the "moral sensibility," which we discussed in connection with *Sentimental Education,* can be clearly distinguished from the physical senses, and that it must be described in terms of its own peculiar structures and laws:

Within the faculty of feeling let us distinguish physical sensibility from moral sensibility.
Physical sensations fall naturally into five classes, being conveyed by the sense organs.

[231]

The facts of moral sensibility, on the other hand, owe nothing to the body: "What is there in common between Archimedes' pleasure at discovering the laws of gravity and Apicius' filthy delight at devouring a boar's head!"

This moral sensibility has four types, and the second type, 'moral desires,' can be divided into five kinds, while the phenomena of the fourth type, 'affections,' are subdivided into two other kinds, among which is self-love, 'a legitimate tendency, no doubt, but which, when exaggerated, is called egoism.' (VIII, p. 207)

They cite Locke on the nature of ideas, Condillac on sensations, Voltaire on matter and movement; their conception of ethics shows the influence of Diderot. Yet because they are incapable of learning these things for themselves, but only collect the favored phrasings and catchwords from books they have read, few of these ideas leave traces of any depth. As Harry Levin said, *Bouvard and Pécuchet* is "an anti-educational novel, a *Bildungsroman* in reverse" (*The Gates of Horn*, p. 298). In one desperate letter, Flaubert said to Maupassant that "I want to show that education, no matter of what kind, doesn't mean much, and that nature does all or almost all" (*Correspondance*, VIII, 353).

As in *Sentimental Education*, the presence of Rousseau is deeply visible in *Bouvard and Pécuchet*, although here Flaubert's response is notably more pointed and dyspeptic. An entire chapter (10) is devoted to Bouvard's and Pécuchet's attempt to educate Victor and Victorine, the children of a criminal; the effort is an abysmal failure, and leaves us with the sense that there is nothing man can do to improve upon his own base nature. Attempts to embellish or otherwise to alter it are likely to produce grotesque results, as in the absurdly crafted garden which the two heroes design near the beginning of the book—with its Venetian bridge spanning the patch of kidney beans, yews shaped like armchairs, and tomatoes hanging like stalactites: "here and there a sunflower displayed its yellow disk. The Chinese pagoda, painted red, seemed a lighthouse on the mound. The peacock's beak, struck by the sun, reflected its beams; and behind the lattice, unframed by its slats, the flat fields bounded the horizon" (II, p. 61). This description, memorable in its own right, could well stand for the useless pursuits to which the search for the foundations of knowledge leads.

In Lionel Trilling's analysis, *Bouvard and Pécuchet* is Flaubert's rejection of the idea of culture as such.[6] The remarkably unoriginal assemblage of book learning and technique is in his view the sign of a culture grown dissatisfied with its past:

The human mind experiences the massed accumulation of its own works, those that are traditionally held to be its greatest glories as well as those that are obviously of a contemptible sort, and arrives at the understanding that none will serve its purpose, that all are weariness and vanity, that the whole vast structure of human thought and creation are alien from the human purpose. (*The Opposing Self*, p. 171)

In the analysis he gives, Flaubert's rejection of culture roots in a hatred of the leveling effects of bourgeois democracy; that in turn rests on the egalitarian principles of the Enlightenment, whose revolutionary values, we saw in *Sentimental Education*, were particularly suspect. Indeed, Flaubert's correspondence corroborates the idea that he sensed human culture to be in a period of decay, of unalterable decline; he writes: "Can one believe in progress and civilization with all that goes on? What is the use of science, since this nation of scientists commits abominations worthy of the Huns?"[7] In light of the content of *Bouvard and Pécuchet*, it is clear that Flaubert's objections to reason and science have to do with the use to which the Enlightenment put them, to their elevation to the status of a culture's sole values, i.e., that culture *itself* should be considered as synonymous with science and reason. Where culture has so limited itself, the results have been absurd; consider the garden described above, which suffers under the excess of rationally planned cultivation.

Uncritical faith in reason and science, unrestrained hope in progress, boundless optimism such as Bouvard and Pécuchet display, are founded on the expectation that the worlds of man and of nature can be understood and explained in the language of reason, that the causes and effects, principles, rules, and natural laws which we discover are basic and original Truths; this is a principal Enlightenment myth which Flaubert rejects. He shows that the language of reason simply makes possible the various descriptions, classifications, and systemic representations which we perceive in the world; *Bouvard and Pécuchet* is written forcefully against the prevailing supposition that the rational explanations we make are something more than convenient descriptions of it, that they are *absolute* truths.[8] At the end of the novel, as Bouvard and Pécuchet take their positions at the two-sided copying desk, it becomes clear that such verities are and always were beyond their reach; the copying which they undertake—notably unoriginal, derivative, archival in quality—brings them no closer to the truth than their former search for the basic explanations and first causes of things; in fact, it points up how *unoriginal* and derivative all their other work had been: much of what they tried to learn and discover was itself derived from books; it has brought them no closer to the absolute Truth than their copying does.

Two statements from Flaubert's correspondence, cited earlier, confirm the general sense of *Bouvard and Pécuchet* in this regard; one is that "What is true is only 'relations'"; the other is that "The True does not exist [*Il n'y a pas de Vrai*]. There are only ways of seeing" (*Correspondance*, VIII, 135, 170). In light of Flaubert's manifest dissatisfaction with the tenets of a culture based on Reason, it is evident that his position is not skepticism—which would reject the very possibility of human knowledge, in any form—but primarily a stance against the rational idea of a Truth beyond our provisional representations. Something like knowledge is possible, given Flaubert's position, but only if we recognize that it is a way of organizing the "relations" we perceive among objects, a form of mediation between ourselves and the world, something that might be thought of as a pragmatic "discourse."

In *Deceit, Desire, and the Novel*, René Girard saw the mediation of experience by books as characteristic of certain major novels, among them *Don Quixote* and *Bouvard and Pécuchet*. In the novel as a genre, if we follow Girard's analysis, a stable truth is invariably arrived at in the conclusion. "The conclusion," he says, "is the temple of truth. The conclusion is the site of the presence of truth, and therefore a place avoided by error" (p. 370). Yet Flaubert resists

[234]

the idea of a conclusion and what it represents for our conception of knowledge; indeed, one of the best-known remarks from his correspondence says that "L'ineptie consiste à vouloir conclure" ("Ineptitude is wanting to conclude"). Bouvard and Pécuchet are on an interminable course "in search of an ending," but Flaubert shows that this search is an eternal regression. The only conclusion they reach at the end of the book thus insures the disruption of closure, for to copy other books is a process with no end. Relative to their former search for final answers to the phenomena of the human and natural worlds, though, this does mark an advancement of their learning.

Seen in light of this inconclusive conclusion, the rational pursuit which occupies Bouvard and Pécuchet for the major portion of the book appears to be a form of gross self-delusion, enslavement to a false image of what knowledge can and should be. Socrates said that knowledge must begin in an awareness of ignorance, not in boastful claims of learning. This image of inauthentic knowledge, which masquerades as reason, is one of the most ancient enemies of the pursuit of wisdom, to which the philosopher is devoted. We see it in Plato's dialogues under the guise of sophism, philosophy's counterimage. In direct contrast to the skeptic, who undermines knowledge by limiting it through doubt, the sophist is too liberal in what he admits as knowledge, and undermines it in that way. We see him in all practitioners of the sham arts of knowledge—in Homais of *Madame Bovary,* who is a pharmacist, not a physician, and in Bouvard and Pécuchet, who attempt by technology to amend the natural world, failing as long as they do to discover the truth in themselves. Throughout his works, Flaubert demonstrates a special sensitivity to sophism and its voice, to the empty sound of learning where there is no wisdom to be found. Again it shows up in Homais, the bourgeois intellectual, who is ready to presume the ignorance of others in light of this own "enlightened" nature; and we see it in Bouvard and Pécuchet, who are convinced that they can gain access to the truths of nature which others have not found: at one point in the novel, the narrator notes that "a *lamentable faculty* developed in their minds, that of noticing stupidity and finding it intolerable" (VIII, p. 217; italics added). Like Plato, Flaubert is intolerant of such presumptions to "wisdom," which turn out only to be pseudoknowledge, and he reacts dyspeptically to the bloated sound of its voice.

It would seem possible to turn from a repudiation of the idea of any absolute Truth, and of the notion of a single language or discipline capable of expressing it, to an espousal of skepticism. But *Bouvard and Pécuchet* shows that such a definition of truth is itself an illusion—the illusion on which the culture of Newton and Leibniz was based. It is the equation of truth with (scientific) certainty—which we know from our discussions of Cervantes and Dostoevsky are not the same—that stands at the root of this illusion. Any kind of truth or knowledge worth anything is a form of wisdom with dimensions that cannot be reduced to certainty or reason. We have seen that to be the case for instance in the responsibility which association with others entails, as Emma Bovary acknowledges in the moments before her death. In *Bouvard and Pécuchet* this human dimension of knowledge, which supplements reason and wholly outstrips it in terms of value and worth, takes the form of the loyalty of the two men; their friendship binds them together, supports the life they have in common, and enables them to know each other. It is the fact of their companionship, and the benevolence that it implies, that relieves this tragicomedy of knowledge of its otherwise oppressive effects.

When Plato rejected sophism because of its interest in the sham arts of knowledge, he reformulated the bases of knowledge on the grounds of dialogue, in which interlocutors respond to words spoken by persons, not only to the "referents" of their statements. This dialogue of open learning, which implies sharing one's life with another, is continued in the *Quixote*, where the Knight and the Squire love and learn under each other's influence, and where they change as a result. And it is continued in the lives of Bouvard and Pécuchet, these two middle-aged bachelors, one fat the other thin, who are bound together in a common pursuit; as Lionel Trilling said, "Flaubert, like Plato, conceived of friendship as one of the conditions of thought. Love and logic go together" (*The Opposing Self*, p. 163). Their encyclopedic adventure through the fields of human learning has value and meaning not because of what they know but because of their devotion to one another. What they "discover" as they grow in disillusionment is the permanence of their own relationship; this tells them the true nature of their love.

Like Cervantes' *Don Quixote, Bouvard and Pécuchet* is an overtly satiric novel. They mock in different ways the distortions of human reason. Yet in both cases the comedy is qualified by warmth and affection. Flaubert, like Cervantes, is sympathetic toward his characters; he laughs at their foibles and follies, and refuses to condemn them at the end. He looks kindly toward them because, beyond the learning and useless knowledge which they amass, they demonstrate a faithfulness to one another, which confers value and worth. Such faithfulness is not in their case given in terms of devotion to an ideal of Beauty or Love; they worship the gods of Truth and Reason, and find them to be bankrupt; it is given in the constancy of their response to, and responsibility for, one another. This is more like Don Quixote's friendship for Sancho, and Sancho's devotion to him, than the Knight of La Mancha's love for Dulcinea. Their relationship has been described on various occasions in terms of marriage. That is an appropriate image to keep in mind in light of the discussion that follows, for the skeptical predicament as it bears on our relations to others points up the *limitations* of marriage which, like human knowledge under the pressures of radical doubt, can be shattered and destroyed. However, the vulnerability of knowledge, or marriage, is only apparent in light of the alliance of knowledge and power which I will discuss next.

IV.
KNOWLEDGE AND POWER

"One that loved not wisely but too well"
—Othello (V.ii.346)

AT SEVERAL POINTS in the preceding discussions, I left open the problem of skepticism and our knowledge of others, promising to take up the question at the end of this study: there is the case of Raskolnikov at the close of *Crime and Punishment*, for instance, who seems so solitary, so dark to his fellow men, despite the love of Sonia; there is Emma Bovary, who acknowledges her relationship with Charles, and the fruits of their marriage, only moments before she dies; there are Marcela and Grisóstomo in *Don Quixote*, who remain virtually unknown to one another; there are Prince Myshkin, Aglaya, Rogozhin, and Nastasya Filippovna, who live in a society which seems to be made up exclusively of "outsiders," unable, or unwilling, to know one another. And yet there are Don Quixote and Sancho, Bouvard and Pécuchet, the "eternal couples," in whose friendship and love we find buoyant hopes for the prospect of our knowledge of others.

How are we to take this variety of cases, this mixture of failure and success? At one point, in the discussion of Dostoevsky, I proposed the term "alienation" to describe our knowledge of others, a term I said was more appropriate than what Hegel meant by "mediation" because it responds to the intactness of the self and the other, to our mutual privacy, if you will. In reviewing the list of cases in which the problem of our knowledge of others might conceivably arise, this description seems all the more apt insofar as it also tells something about what it might mean to seek to know another, independent of the success or failure of the enterprise itself. In the cases at hand, it might show us something about our *position* with respect to others, which in my discussion of Dostoevsky I described in terms of our "outsideness" to them. But one might also think of Don Quixote and Sancho in this regard, and of their respective lives: they come to know one another, and to change as a result; this change is evidence of their mutual understanding, but it leaves them once again apart. The deepest evidence they have of each other points to the fact that they are and always will be outsiders to one another's lives.

The discovery of our mutual outsideness, or "otherness" as it is sometimes called, is on the one hand a function of skeptical doubts (e.g., the skeptic's worries about his outsideness to the world, or his displacement from it); but it is also a discovery which may be made as part of any effort to overcome skepticism which starts from an acknowledgment of the skeptic's threats. In this final chapter, I will take as a guide to this problem the contrasting epistemologies of our knowledge of the external world and our knowledge of others, a contrast which lies more in their methods and procedures than in their results. The fact that our knowledge of others is not open to confirmation by evidence has been implicit in discussions of skepticism since at least Descartes. In the *Meditations,* Descartes looks to God in order to confirm the fact that he is not alone in the world, that there exist others like him. In the texts I shall discuss, the role assumed by Descartes's God is taken on by us, regardless of whether any human may be able to meet such a task, and regardless of the consequences which it may entail. In trying to know others as spies of God, we implicitly claim a power over them and estrange them from ourselves; thus despite the operations or even the availability of such a power, others remain outsiders to us, and we to them, as the discussion of Dostoevsky's *The Idiot* has already shown.

On one interpretation of the question of skepticism, the fact that our knowledge of others is not a matter of empirically verifiable fact leads to the conclusion that our efforts at knowing others leads to a *denial* of them.[1] This is the driving force behind Stanley Cavell's interpretation of *Othello* and specifically of Othello's image of Desdemona as a statue, or as stone ("whiter skin of hers than snow, / And smooth as monumental alabaster"[2]); in addition it gives the significance of the murder in that play. However, this interpretation overlooks the fact that in Act V Desdemona appears briefly to revive, as if in expression of the hope, now imputed to us, that some force (perhaps the power of our merely wishing it) would somehow

[240]

bring her back. This wish implies some godlike power, and is a function of the desire to know (to know "transcendentally," as it were); hence it is not just that skepticism leads to a discovery of our outsideness to others, but that the requirement of knowledge, which is power, leads to that discovery as well. In *King Lear*, to take a complementary case, these requirements involve the projection of godlike powers (in *Lear* this is clearly a function of madness), as in the scene in Act V where Lear entertains the fantastical hope of finding life in the body he well knows is dead:

LEAR. . . . She's gone for ever.
    I know when one is dead, and when one lives.
    She's dead as earth. Lend me a looking glass.
    If that her breath will mist or stain the stone,
    Why then she lives. (V.iii.260–64)

In *King Lear*, as in *Othello*, images of our community with others are given together with images of our separation from them: when Lear returns with Cordelia, he is carrying her as he would a baby; when Othello murders Desdemona, he also joins her at their bridal bed. These might be taken as further images of what earlier I called our "separateness in society," a fact which is confirmed in the novels of Cervantes, Dostoevsky, and Flaubert. But as a reminder that the fact of our separateness from others is not only discovered in their death, or in our outright denial of them, but is also a function of our knowledge of others, and of the power which that knowledge requires, I would set the Pygmalion myth beside the final scene of *Othello*, for that myth can be said to *begin* from a vision of the other as a statue or as stone, and go beyond the place at which *Othello* stops. The bringing of a statue to life in *Pygmalion* is predicated on the existence of some godlike power, but as Paul de Man has said in his reading of Rousseau's dramatization of that myth, *Pygmalion* offers no significant hope for communion with others. Even here, where the other is as if by magic returned to humanity, self and other remain apart. At the close of Rousseau's brief *scène lyrique*, Pygmalion and Galathea address one another, each with an astonished "Moi!" Pygmalion touches the flesh-from-stone which he has made, and wanting to see himself in it he also sees it as his

[241]

alienated self. Galathea's response, "Ah! encore moi," which de Man takes as meaning "de nouveau moi" ("me again," which is a disappointment), is then a sign of the separation of these two selves. The fact of their isolation from one another thus remains, despite the fact that *Pygmalion* could be said to reverse the tragic pattern evident in more skeptical plays. On Cavell's reading of *Othello* we can be seen as wanting to deny the humanity of the other, a fact which is said to be motivated by a desire to mask the fact of our own finitude and embodiment; but in *Pygmalion* we see the fulfillment of the wish which remains repressed in *Othello* and *King Lear*—the wish to bring the other back. In the case of *Pygmalion*, however, the failure of our knowledge of others may be seen as a function of our unwillingness to be *loved by* another. This would in turn provide one explanation of the need to gain power over the other as if by some superhuman force, viz., as a way to ward the other off.

Thus before turning to some final readings of Cervantes, Dostoevsky, and Flaubert, I would point out that if the wish for the revival of the other is repressed in *Othello*, the wish for power which motivates it is not. Of course the falseness of that hope is registered by the fact that this power is seen as a form of magic, and that both are from the start tied up with Othello's denial of Desdemona and with her eventual death. In the first Act, for instance, Brabantio says that his daughter—"abused, stolen from me and corrupted / By spells and medicine bought of mountebanks" (I.iii.60–61)—is already "dead" to him because she has married the noble Moor. Othello, for his part, takes Brabantio's accusation and turns it into a boast; he claims to have won Desdemona by magic charms:

I will a round unvarnished tale deliver
Of my whole course of love: what drugs, what charms,
What conjurations, and what mighty magic—
For such proceedings I am charged withal—
I won his daughter.

(I.iii.90–94)

Othello claims power over Desdemona, a control over her life which a god might claim over his creature; he thinks that winning her love can be accomplished by witchcraft. His idea of his knowledge of her, as he imagines it in this fantasy of power, expresses the wish for him, as knower, to be free from the conditions and limitations of human knowledge. His search for "ocular proof," for evidence and convincing argument, could then be said to conceal his reluctance to recognize the limitations of his powers and the human conditions of knowledge. This may be taken as the theme at work in the texts I will turn to next. In them we see that the wish to know another from a transcendental point of view, and the assumption of power that this would entail, is the attempt to stand outside of human nature, to escape the human condition by the unlimited power of reason. As the following readings of Cervantes, Dostoevsky, and Flaubert will show, the consequence for others of that wish is not a liberation from the conditions of humanity but, on the contrary, a denial of the other's human nature.

CERVANTES

OSTENSIBLY, the "Story of the One Who Was Too Curious for His Own Good" which is read at the inn in chapters 33 and 34 of *Don Quixote*, Part I, is about conjugal love and mistrust, about the doubts and the fears of an honor-conscious husband concerned beyond reason for the faithfulness of his wife. His suspicions are generated by an excessive and "impertinent" curiosity (the story is called the "Curioso impertinente") which is, apparently, the eventual cause of his undoing. Anselmo demands proof, tangible evidence and convincing argument, *more geometrico*, of his wife Camila's faithfulness to him ("'palpable examples, readily understood and demonstrable, and such as admit of undeniable and indubitable mathematical proof,'" I, 33,— as his friend puts it). To this end he secures the aid of Lothario, who is asked to lay a trap for Camila. Much like Shakespeare's Othello, who takes Desdemona's faithfulness as a matter of mortal importance, Anselmo is convinced that Camila's faithfulness is something worth his life, even though Lothario warns him against such foolishness:

"which of these—your life or your honor—is now imperiled that I at risk to myself should oblige you by doing a thing so detestable as that which you ask me? Neither of them, certainly. What you are demanding of me is, rather, as I understand it, that I seek and endeavor to deprive you, and myself at the same time, of both honor and life. For if I take away your honor, it goes without saying that I am also robbing you of life, since the man without honor is in worse plight than a dead man."

Lothario tries to dissuade Anselmo from his foolish curiosity, arguing that his certainty of his wife's faithfulness needs no proof or empirical testing ("'Did you not tell me that I am to pay court to a

[244]

woman of reserve, bring my persuasive wiles to bear upon a respect-able matron, make advances to one who is not looking for anything of that sort, and offer my attentions to a lady who is noted for her prudence? Yes, that is precisely what you told me. *Well, then, if you know that you have such a wife, reserved, respected, prudent, and retir-ing, what is it that you seek?'"* italics added).

For the first part of the story, Anselmo's certainty of Camila's faithfulness is secure; she is in fact faithful, and his search for evidence and demonstrable proof purchases him nothing. But even-tually Camila falls to Lothario's advances, while Anselmo remains ignorant of the fact; he sees clear enough signs of her sexual "wound-ing" and "death," but this evidence of her unfaithfulness likewise proves useless to him. Thus Anselmo seeks certainty when he does not need it—in order to prove Camila's faithfulness, which he knows to be true—and, when he finds it, does not know what to do with it. Lothario explains this to Anselmo early on, but precisely because Lothario is right in his advice Anselmo cannot understand him: "'Is it that you do not believe her to be what you say she is, or that you do not realize what you are asking? If you doubt her virtue, why trouble to test it? Why not treat her as guilty and take what action you may see fit?'" Lothario's warning proves all too true; a trap is laid for Camila because Anselmo sought certainty where it could be of no use; more important, the story reveals that An-selmo's own undoing was brought about in this same way.

Seen in this light, the story of Anselmo and Lothario reverses the pattern evident in *Othello.* Both Anselmo and Othello are mistaken about their wives; but Anselmo is unable to see that Camila was unfaithful, whereas Othello is unable to see that Desdemona was not. In contrasting ways, both husbands not only fail to know their wives; they in fact deny them in their claims of power over them. In *Othello,* the image of Desdemona's body as "monumental alabaster" might be taken as one projection of the magical powers which Othello claims. There is a sequence of related imagery in the story of Anselmo and Lothario where Anselmo compares his wife to gold and diamonds, as if to suggest that his efforts at knowledge have an alchemical effect.[3] Anselmo attempts to know his wife, to deter-mine her worth, and to measure her value for him, as one would test a precious metal or stone. Anselmo's friend Lothario compares Camila to ermine; he says she is like a mirror. The sense of these metaphors is that she is not to be approached, either because she is clean and may be dirtied, or because she is fragile, and may be broken. She is like a relic, to be beheld from a distance, "adored, not touched." In comparing Camila to gold, diamonds, ermine, and glass, Anselmo and Lothario deny what is most human about her: her vulnerability to the power of another, and her suscep- tibility to sexual contamination. To expect her to respond like a precious metal or stone is, as Anselmo recognizes at his death, to expect the inhuman of her: "'If the news of my death should reach Camila's ears, let her know that I forgive her; for *she was under no obligation to perform miracles* and I had no right to ask them of her'" (I, 35, italics added).

If it can be said that skepticism is often a cover for our failure to face human finitude and limitation, and if the requirement of knowledge is the assumption of power over others, then as Anselmo relinquishes his control over Camila he also comes to recognize the limitations of his own powers. But this occurs only at the close of Cervantes' story, which is to say only once it is too late. For the greater part of the tale, Anselmo's relationship to Camila is marked by a series of ironies which follow from his assumption of power and the denial of finitude which it entails. Although Cervantes is never explicit about the fact, there is one passage in the text which prompts us to suspect that Anselmo and Camila never consum- mated their marriage, hence that Anselmo failed to know Camila in a conjugal way. After Anselmo's second absence from Camila, he returns but fails "to perceive what was missing there: namely, the thing he had treated so lightly yet had treasured most" (I, 34). We know from this hint and from explicit statements elsewhere in the text that Lothario has slept with Camila ("Camila surrendered, yes, Camila fell. Was it to be wondered at if friendship in Lothario's case could not keep its footing?"). But why should Anselmo have ex- pected that "what he most treasured" of Camila (i.e., her honor) would be intact, and why did he not notice its absence? The in- ference is that Anselmo, who is so concerned for the fragility, the vulnerability, and the cleanliness of his wife, has not himself slept with her. Avoiding the fact of Camila's human finitude, he treats her like polished glass or white ermine; in so doing, he avoids her sexuality, and thus could not help ignoring the absence of his "greatest treasure." It is this aversion to human sexuality, the avoidance of the fact of human finitude, covered by the seemingly "impertinent" desire for certainty, which skepticism serves in the story of the two friends.

What is the source of this aversion? We know from Lothario's earlier remarks that Anselmo tried to test Camila's faithfulness because he saw the matter of her honor as implicating his own. The idea that one's honor should depend on the virtue of another is conventional enough and would not warrant further remarks if Lothario did not give an explanation pointing to the much more literal sense of Anselmo's dependence on Camila. Lothario tells Anselmo that his honor depends on Camila because, as husband and wife, they are of one flesh and, being of one flesh, any injury to her is an injury to him: "'the woman's flesh being one with that of her husband, the stains and blemishes that she incurs are reflected upon his flesh, even though, as has been said, he has given no occasion for her sinning.'" That Anselmo should depend on Camila, who is of flesh and hence may be flawed, blemished, or stained, would force him to recognize the fact of his own finitude. He avoids recognizing this, and sustains his fantasy of power over Camila, through his designs for perfect knowledge of her, staking his life on the possibility of *proving* her faithfulness to him just as Othello stakes his life on the faithfulness of Desdemona ("My life upon her faith," I.iii.294). Yet in so doing, Anselmo implicates himself in what amounts to an obscenity committed against Camila, as if to suggest that his claim of power over her were itself a violation of her. This claim of power, and the violation or loss of honor which attaches to it, may be compared to what Kenneth Burke saw as Othello's fantasy of ownership or possession of Desdemona and of the violation of privacy which is evidenced by the handkerchief in that play:

[The handkerchief] will be public evidence of the conspiracy which Othello now wholly believes to exist. . . . And, by the same token, it will

[247]

be the privacy of Desdemona made public. . . . Since it stands for Desdemona's privacy, and since this privacy in turn had stood magically for his
entire sense of worldly and cosmological order, we can see readily why, for
Othello, its loss becomes the ultimate obscenity.[4]

In the final scene of Cervantes' story, Camila contemplates suicide and is wounded by the dagger which Lothario seizes. The scene
is suggestive of her violation or wounding, which in turn hints at
the fact of her vulnerability to the effects of power and to her
sexuality. The details of the incident are given with meticulous
care: Cervantes insists that the wound is shallow, and he notes that
blood is spilled. This is a miniature "drama of conjugal fidelity," a
"*comedia* about the death of Anselmo's honor," made to look strikingly real. It is an expression, via metaphors of human sexuality, of
what Camila's "fall" to Lothario means: that she is finite and vul-
nerable, an embodied creature, not someone of whom we can expect miracles, as Anselmo later says.

Camila's searing experience in this scene, which borders on madness, seems to outstrip the surrounding reality, but Anselmo remains a passive spectator to the wounding, as if the power of which
he is in one sense the agent were independent of him: "[Camila]
paced up and down the room with the dagger unsheathed, swaying
and staggering and making such wild gestures that she appeared to
be out of her mind, and one would have taken her for some desperate ruffian rather than a woman who had been gently bred and
reared. Anselmo watched her from behind the tapestries where he
had hidden and was vastly astonished by it all." When the story of
Anselmo and Lothario concludes in chapter 35, Anselmo is awake
to the meaning of what he has seen; here *he* is described "as if he
were losing his mind," which we know represents a real danger for
him. His madness and eventual death are not only his just desserts,
but consequences of the power which he takes on for himself. Yet
Anselmo does not bear sole responsibility for these disastrous
events. At the very least Camila is to blame for having been unfaithful to him, and Lothario is guilty for his part in the scheme of
virgin-baiting. Indeed, Lothario is implicated from the very beginning of the story: Anselmo is not alone in taking Camila as an

object, as having a value that could be determined by ocular proof. When Lothario tells Anselmo that Camila is like ermine, or polished glass, he shares his friend's misconceptions. Although Lothario objects to Anselmo's initial plans, he understands as little about Camila, and about what knowing her would mean, as Anselmo does.

As a friend, Lothario feels a certain allegiance to Anselmo; this is apparently why he resists participating in Anselmo's scheme at first. But his unwillingness to test Camila also suggests that he shares Anselmo's ideas about her. His initial reluctance appears to stem from his friendship for Anselmo, but it turns out that their relationship is premised on very grave misunderstandings about the nature of friendship itself; neither fully knows what it would mean to know another individual, to be willing to stake something of infinite value, such as one's life, on a relationship to them. As Lothario sees it, a friend is only an ombudsman for a husband ("every married man should have some friend of his own sex who would call his attention to any negligence on his part"). Before Anselmo married, Lothario would visit him regularly; but after the marriage he suspended his visits. This is not simply an act of discretion; as the passage below reveals, Lothario regards marriage and friendship as incompatible, as if they were forms of life that should not be mixed:

When the wedding days were over and congratulatory visits became less frequent, [Lothario] was careful not to go so often; for it seemed to him, as it must to all men of good sense, that *one should not continue visiting the homes of married friends* with the same frequency as in their bachelor days. *Good and true friendship neither can nor should be at all suspect; but, nevertheless, the honor of a married man is so delicate a matter that even blood brothers may give offense,* to say nothing of those who are no more than friends. (I, 33; italics added)

The story of Anselmo and Lothario is ostensibly about marriage, conjugal love, mistrust, and idle curiosity. But it is also about the failure of friendship. By a coincidence essential to the Cervantean shape of things, Anselmo and Lothario are known at the start of the story, as "los dos amigos," "the two friends." The epithet under-scores the bond which unites them prior to Anselmo's marriage; the gradual dissolution of that bond over the course of the story is, by virtue of contrast, all the more remarkable. In an almost Platonic way, Cervantes sees in friendship (as in marriage) the possibility for a knowledge of others which recognizes the demands of reason and the power which knowledge implies, but which relieves that power of its most devastating effects by relying instead on trust. This implies no guarantee that friendship will be achieved. Cervantes also sees the possibility of callous ignorance, estrangement, and denial. In the story of Anselmo and Lothario, for instance, friend-ship fails under the pressures of knowledge and power because the two friends do not recognize that friendship also requires trust.

The images of the dissolution of friendship and of the transgres-sion of trust present a stark contrast to the general grain of Cer-vantes' novel. From other episodes in it we know that dialogue provides sufficient grounds for agreement where individual perspec-tives clash, and that a human community of knowers generates the criteria essential to their work together. Perhaps most important, we see throughout the novel the friendship of Don Quixote and Sancho; their friendship is an adventure and so, by definition, requires risks. The *Quixote* thus shows that there are grounds for knowing others which recognize but overcome the effects of power, and it shows that those grounds are friendship and trust. We simply must recognize that the desire of perfect knowledge of another, which generates fantasies of perfect power over them, cannot be met. When, near the end of Part II, Don Quixote decides to forsake knight-errantry, Sancho wants desperately to continue in their pur-suits. He has understood Don Quixote so well that he has taken on his desires (this might provide an answer to Raskolnikov's rhetorical question of Sonia at the end of *Crime and Punishment*: "'Is it possi-ble that her convictions can be mine, too, now? Her feelings, her yearnings, at least . . .'"). However, the moment is bittersweet. Sancho's understanding of Don Quixote has come too late, because Don Quixote has now changed. Where our knowledge of others is in fact so deep that we are changed by it, there is always the risk of missed understandings like this.

[250]

On balance, there is no failure of friendship in the *Quixote*; misunderstandings are in general the result of the characters' growth and provide evidence of their willingness for risk and of their mutual trust. But in the story of Anselmo and Lothario, as in some of the other intercalated tales, the situation is vastly different. This story charts the breakdown of friendship and of the community of relationships which support understanding; it gives the outlines of a world in which authentic dialogue is lacking, and where trust is subverted by the demands of knowledge and power. Thus we have reason to doubt whether these two "friends" share any basis for knowing one another at all, as is shown by what Lothario says here:

"Either I do not know you, or you do not know me. But that cannot be; for I am well aware that you are Anselmo, and you are conscious of the fact that I am Lothario. Unfortunately, however, I cannot regard you as the Anselmo that used to be, and you likewise must have thought that I am no longer the Lothario of old. For the things that you have said to me are not those that my friend Anselmo would say, nor are the things you ask of me such as you would ask of the Lothario that you know. True friends, as the poet has said, will prove and make use of each other *usque ad aras*, which is to say, they will not put their friendship to the test in a manner that is contrary to God's will."

Their friendship is indeed tested in a way that might be considered contrary to God's will, just as marriage is so tested. Under the conditions of such proofs, both are found to fail. If we take the remainder of the *Quixote* as a guide, the appropriate conclusion to be drawn is not that Cervantes views the possibility of our knowledge of others with despair, but rather that knowledge in alliance with power will subvert the trust on which the very possibility of our knowledge of others relies.

DOSTOEVSKY

"He might marry her tomorrow and, perhaps, murder her a week later"
—*The Idiot*

ANY READER is likely to be struck by the resemblance of *Othello*, and in particular the images of magic and power in that play, to the final chapters of *The Idiot*. In his notes for the novel, Dostoevsky outlined a scene between Nastasya Filippovna and Prince Myshkin on the morning of their wedding, and another between Aglaya and the Prince, where the name of Othello appears twice. My discussion of *The Idiot* in connection with Cervantes' tale and the problem of knowing the existence of others is prompted by one of those two references: "The Prince simply and clearly (Othello) tells [Nastasya] why he loves her and that it is not merely from compassion (as Rogozhin intimated to her and with which Ippolit plagued her) but from love."[5] Apparently, the reference is to the moment in Shakespeare's play where Othello says that Desdemona loved him for his acts of bravery and that he loved her for compassion or pity for him ("She loved me for the dangers I had passed,/ And I loved her that she did pity them," I.iii.167–68). Like *Othello*, and like Cervantes' story of Anselmo and Lothario, *The Idiot* explores what it would mean to know the existence of another in terms of what it would mean to trust another or to deny that person our trust. Earlier in this discussion I said that the requirements of our knowledge of others may entail projecting certain powers over them. Those powers may be masked as trust, or as love, and indeed the relationship between knowledge and power in *The Idiot* begins from a consideration of how we might recognize authentic love; how might we tell it from pity, for instance, which unlike love is a projection of the will to power? The success or failure of our knowledge of others turns on our ability to make such distinctions as these, and Prince

[252]

Myshkin learns them too late. It is only after his relationship with Nastasya is beyond repair that he recognizes what it would mean to love her out of love, and not out of pity. This confusion of love with pity, as an expression of the will to knowledge as power, will form the basis of my discussion of *The Idiot* in what follows.

The Idiot exemplifies certain truths about skepticism, reality, and the nature of conviction, which at the end of the novel converge around the problem of knowing the existence of others. We can see for example that the murder is carried out in such a way that it resembles a denial of reality parallel to the skeptic's denial of the existence of the world. We know that denials of the world, like the ones that Don Quixote attempts, are likely to rebound with our "conviction" at its hands, and we can say that the same is true of the murder of Nastasya Filippovna. As in *Crime and Punishment*, the body leaves traces and tracks (its natural odors, for instance) which finally "convict" the Prince of his denial of her, even though he was not the instrumental cause of her death. Yet we have seen that skepticism with respect to others is fundamentally different from skepticism with respect to the external world. One measure of that difference is the following: once we deny the existence of others through the power of knowledge—once we kill them, turn them to stone, or make them in some other way dead to us—there is then no power strong enough to bring them back. When the Prince comes upon Nastasya in the final scenes of the novel, that is, when he comes upon her body, her corpse, there is nothing which he can do to make her human. His only wish would be the impossible inversion of his denial of her: to see her body, now an object of the external world, as human.

As Rogozhin and the Prince stand over the corpse of Nastasya Filippovna, Rogozhin suggests, in a moment of madness, that the two spend the night beside the body:

"We'll stay the night here—together. There's no bed except that one there—so I thought we might take the pillows from the two sofas and I'll make up a bed here, near the curtains, for you and me—see?—so that we can be together. For if they come in and start looking around or searching, they'll see her at once and take her away. They'll start questioning me, and I'll say it was me what [sic] done it, and they'll take me away at once. So let her lie there now beside us, beside you and me." (IV, 11; p. 653)

Rogozhin knows that he is guilty of the murder, and that he is liable to be arrested if found beside the corpse; he is naturally afraid, but he also finds peace and satisfaction in the prospect of lying next to Nastasya Filippovna. His words bespeak a desire to be near her, to bind himself to this object of his love. But if his love could be satisfied in this way, then Nastasya can only be for him as Desdemona for Othello, "monumental alabaster." His knowledge of her involves the assumption of a certain power, which is both the power to deny her (to turn her to stone) and to deny her his love. But regardless of what powers we might assume—even if we imagine ourselves capable of something like metempsychosis—we can only succeed in knowing our outsideness to others, which is also to say their independence from us. We are sealed off from others by the body, and our greatest powers over others can only confirm this fact.

Rogozhin's remarks indicate his separation from Nastasya, his outsideness to her, even though he fails to recognize the force of his own words. The resonances of what he says, and of this final scene, though, reach well beyond his own interests. As I have said, neither Rogozhin nor the Prince has adequately loved Nastasya Filippovna—Rogozhin most obviously because he has killed her, and the Prince because he has failed to grant her his love. By placing Rogozhin and the Prince together beside the corpse, Dostoevsky suggests that Rogozhin's deed, his murder of Nastasya Filippovna, images Prince Myshkin's silent denial of her. At the very least it prompts him to realize that he has denied her his love. It brings him to the sudden recognition "that at that moment, and for some time past, he had been saying not what he had been meaning to say and had been doing what he should not have been doing" (p. 656).

In order for us to understand what the Prince finally understands here, we must understand something about his relationship with Nastasya Filippovna and with her rival, Aglaya. Throughout the novel, his love for the one is refracted through his relationship with the other, in part because they are such vastly different personalities which function as competing objects of his affection. It is only because of his relationship with Aglaya, for instance—the demands she makes on him and the questions she prompts—that he is able to recognize what it would mean to know and to love Nastasya Filippovna.

At one moment in Part III, just after Ippolit's attempted suicide, the Prince and Aglaya themselves broach the subject of knowing other persons. Aglaya accuses the Prince of having sent her a letter of suspicious intent; he claims that the letter was written in candor and honesty—"'straight from my heart at a most painful moment of my life'" (III, 8; p. 470). He says that he regards her as someone "very dear," but she accuses him of laying a trap, of contriving to be discovered with her so that they would be forced to marry. The accusation is of course untrue, and the Prince responds defensively: "'How could such a sordid idea enter your pure, innocent heart?'" he asks her, "'I bet you don't believe a word of it yourself—you don't know yourself what you're saying.'" The Prince, as an outsider, claims sufficient insight into Aglaya to see that she has not yet come to self-understanding, but it is her question to him, which had prompted this response, which goes to the root of the problem of our knowledge of others: "'How do you know that my heart is innocent?'" she asks. She admits trying to test the Prince, and despite her suggestion that he cannot know her heart, she claims to be able to know *everything* about him, especially the nature of his relationship with Nastasya Filippovna:

"Oh, if you could know everything!"
"I do know everything!" she cried with renewed agitation. "You'd been living at that time for a whole month in the same flat with that abominable woman with whom you ran away."

To be sure, Aglaya feels betrayed, and those feelings are evident here. But beyond that, her assumption of what it would mean to know the Prince, to know "everything" about him, leads her to avoid knowing him as a person, i.e., responding to him with demonstrations of her love. Recall the lie that Aglaya contrived in order to impress the Prince of Ganya's supposed love of her: "'He loves me more than his life. He burnt his hand in front of me to show me that he loved me more than his life'" (p. 471). The power she imagines is precisely that which a skeptic would require in order to test knowledge in a "best case" scenario. To expect Ganya to burn his hand is to ask the inhuman of him, but this is a function of the will to knowledge as power: for Aglaya to require this test must mean that she does not see Ganya as human, and cannot love him as such. I can imagine that her motive might take the following form: Aglaya's fantasy of a proof of love beyond the bounds of the human condition indicates Aglaya's unwillingness to be *loved by* another human and her avoidance of the requirements which this would place on her.

The question of our ability to know another perfectly which is broached in this inconclusive episode between Aglaya and Prince Myshkin, and the question of the power which this would entail, is echoed in the following scenes of the novel. In the passage below, the Prince speaks of his knowledge of her as a "best case" of knowing, something worth his life; but, unlike Agalya in the earlier scene, he knows that his knowledge of her, conceived in such terms, can only be partial. This is because our knowledge of others depends not only on our willingness for love but also on their willingness for our love. It is for this reason that the knowledge of others, conceived as friendship or as love, must necessarily recognize the limits of our powers:

"Without Aglaya I—I must see her—I must. I—I shall soon die in my sleep. I thought I was going to die in my sleep last night. Oh, if only Aglaya knew—if she only knew everything—I mean, absolutely everything! Why is it we can never know *everything* about another person, when we ought to, when that other person is to blame!" (IV, 9; p. 627)

Radomsky replies to the Prince, invoking images of power and denial which we know from our earlier discussion of *The Idiot*: "'Aglaya loved like a woman, like a human being, and not like a— disembodied spirit! Do you know what I think, my poor Prince? Most likely you've never loved either of them!'"

What Radomsky says is terrifyingly true for the Prince, and in some respects it gives necessary expression to what he himself is gradually recognizing, and will finally admit (Radomsky says that these events show the Prince to himself "'as in a looking-glass,'" p. 623). The comment makes explicit the Prince's denial of Aglaya and it projects his final, catastrophic denial of Nastasya Filippovna as well. His denial of Aglaya is at least in part a consequence of his weak constitution; he is, as we have said, the image of a "beautiful soul" in the world, who is incapable of action and unable to make the personal responses necessary to bind him in love to a woman. If he reacts to Aglaya as a disembodied spirit—which is Radomsky's charge—this may be because he himself is nearly a spirit, in flight from his own finitude.

The Prince's relationship with Aglaya is complex because there are serious doubts about her ability to requite his love, even if he were capable of a human response to her. But certainly there are no doubts about Nastasya Filippovna's ability to love the Prince "like a woman." How is it, then, that the Prince is ignorant of that capacity and unresponsive to it? Myshkin returned to Petersburg from Switzerland primed for a life of action. He was immediately struck by Nastasya Filippovna's beauty, intrigued by her moral flaws and by her sometimes pitiable social status. But the question, which Radomsky puts as frankly as possible in the passage below, is whether the Prince was ever taken by anything more than the *idea* of Nastasya Filippovna. He is and remains a virgin, which testifies not just to his alleged "purity" but also to his avoidance of the finitude which attaches to human nature; as Radomsky says,

"You came here in the first flush of eagerness for action and, as it were, flung yourself into action! And then, on the very first day of your arrival, the sad and heart-rending story of a badly used woman is told to you—you, a knight-errant, a virgin—and about a woman! The very same day you saw the woman, you were bewitched by her beauty. . . . It's quite clear that, carried away by your enthusiasm, as it were, you pounced on the chance of publicly proclaiming your generous idea that, as a student of ancient lineage and as a clean-living man, you did not consider a woman dishonored who had fallen from virtue not through any fault of her own, but through the fault of a disgusting aristocratic libertine. Why, good Lord, it's quite understandable! But, my dear Prince, that's not the point. The point is whether your feeling was true, whether it was a genuine feeling, or whether it was nothing but an intellectual enthusiasm. What do you think?" (IV, 9; pp. 623–24)

The terms of Radomsky's sharp indictment recall Nietzsche's frank estimation of the human feelings. Radomsky pleads for honest emotions, for unembarrassed feelings. The idea is hardly romantic, for a romantic would on the contrary want the Prince to pity Nastasya, and Radomsky stands squarely against any love which masquerades under that guise: "'She deserves to be pited? Is that what you were going to say, my dear, kind-hearted fellow? But how could you, out of pity and for her satisfaction, put to shame another high-minded and pure girl, humiliate her in those disdainful and hateful eyes? Where will your pity lead you next?'" (p. 624). Pity resembles love, and, like love, draws on our willingness for it, which of course means that we have the power to withhold it as well. In the case of pity, this is accomplished under the *guise* of love, by subordinating others to our willingness to love them; pity thus humiliates them, and turns our willingness to love them into a manifestation of our will to power over them. Love, by contrast, would demand to be granted even where it might destroy our powers—without pity or stint.

These distinctions echo a concern voiced much earlier in the novel, in a dialogue between Rogozhin and Myshkin. At one point in Part II, Myshkin frankly admits that his attraction to Nastasya Filippovna stems from his pity for her: "'I loved her not because I was in love with her, but because I pitied her'" (II, 3; p. 240); the comment contrasts directly and explicitly with Dostoevsky's notations for the final scene, mentioned earlier ("The Prince . . . tells [Nastasya] why he loves her and that it is not merely from compassion . . . but from love"). Rogozhin is more blunt in his denial of Nastasya, but he is never blinded by his reactions to her in the way that Prince Myshkin is ("'Well, there ain't no such pity for her in me . . . your pity is much stronger than my love,'" he says, II, 3; p. 240). The Prince feels deeply for Nastasya, which is perhaps why he is blind to her; as Aglaya tells Nastasya at their meeting near the end of the novel, "'he told me that he had long since ceased to love you, that even the memory of you was painful to him, but that he was sorry for you and that every time he thought of you he felt as though his heart were pierced for ever'" (IV, 8; p. 611; Dostoevsky indicates in his notes that this should be spoken "calmly, *nobly and simply sorrowfully*").

The Prince's pity carries the action forward toward his final recognition of what he had in fact been meaning and saying, but it is
Rogozhin's "love" which plants crucial spurs in the plot. His "love"
finally bursts into action, while the Prince is paralyzed by his pity;
both ignore Nastasya Filippovna, although in radically different
ways. Already in the early parts of the novel, Rogozhin threatens to
murder her, and in the final scene his threats are made real, as an
image of his malicious love: "'Well,' the prince smiled, 'your love
cannot be distinguished from malice, and when it passes, there's
going to be even greater trouble perhaps. . . . Anyone is better than
you, for you really may murder her, and she realizes it perhaps now
all too well. That you love her so much? Well, perhaps it's that'"
(II, 3; p. 245). The comment recalls the description of Othello as
"one who loved not wisely but too well." Throughout the novel,
Dostoevsky is drawing out the consequences of the observation
made of Rogozhin early on: "'He might marry her tomorrow and,
perhaps, murder her a week later'" (I, 3; p. 62). Equally alarming is
the possibility that Nastasya may be unwilling for or incapable of
love by either Rogozhin or the Prince; indeed, Myshkin tells
Rogozhin that "'I've heard there are women who are looking for just
that kind of love.'" The inference I draw is that if love, like trust,
can only be granted, it can also be denied.

The context from which these crucial phrases are taken is central
to the themes of knowledge and power, and the motives which drive
them—not only for Rogozhin, but for Prince Myshkin as well.
Whereas Rogozhin is, terrifyingly, capable of marrying Nastasya
and also of killing her, the Prince is incapable of marrying her;
indeed, he is powerless to marry anyone ("'I can't marry anyone
. . . I'm a sick man'"). As the discussion earlier indicated, commitment to marriage would mean recognizing his flawed nature. We
know that this "beautiful" and otherwise perfect soul is an epileptic,
and his illness haunts him even after his return from the Swiss
sanitarium. Avoiding marriage to Nastasya Filippovna because he is
a "sick man" allows him to avoid the fact of his own human nature
and whatever limited powers this may grant.

From early in the novel, there are signs of the Prince's reluctance
to love Nastasya (i.e., to see in her what he avoids in himself). He
tries to know her as one would know an object of the external

world. He examines her portrait and wants to read in it the signs of a private, inward life which, he assumes, is hidden from view: "'A remarkable face! . . . And I'm sure her life has not been an ordinary one. Her face looks cheerful, but she has suffered a lot, hasn't she? Her eyes show it and her cheekbones, those two points under her eyes. It's a proud face, a terribly proud face, but what I can't tell is whether she is kind-hearted or not'" (I, 3; p. 62). The "heart" of the person, the soul to which the body is wed, is finally unknowable and is certainly insubmissible to empirical proof. One cannot tell whether she is kind-hearted simply by looking; one can tell only by renouncing the claim to knowledge by power, which here means offering her his love and asking for love in return.

The Prince's attempt to know Nastasya from her portrait recalls two other moments in this text, one with Aglaya after she falsely accuses him of setting a trap for her, and the other with Nastasya, near the end of the novel, after the Prince has decided to enter into marriage. Aglaya tries to conceal her feelings, but finds that they give evidence of themselves despite her wishes ("She did not blush, but turned pale as she uttered these words, and suddenly got up, as though not realizing what she was doing," III, 8; p. 470). Evidence like this—the signs that the body gives—may be the best basis we have for knowing another person; indeed it may be *all* we have, but that does not just mean that the Prince can know Aglaya's inner life from her facial expressions. If we take his later comments about Nastasya's face as any indication, he may not want to bear what this would require of him. Near the end of the novel, he glimpses what it might mean to look at another's face and actually to know that person (to know their "inner" life, their "hidden" feelings); he finds the prospect terrifying:

"Now I understand everything I didn't understand before—well, you see, when they [Aglaya and Nastasya] stood there facing each other, my dear fellow," he went on, lowering his voice mysteriously, "I've never told anyone about it—never—not even Aglaya, but I can't bear to see Nastasya Filippovna's face. . . . It was true what you said just now about that party at Nastasya Filippovna's, but there was one thing there you've missed because you don't know it: I looked at *her face!* That morning even—I mean, when I looked at her portrait, I could not bear it. . . . Vera Lebedev, for instance, has quite different eyes. I," he added with extraordinary terror, "I am afraid of her face!" (IV, 9; p. 626)

Apparently, the Prince has some idea of what it would mean to know Nastasya Filippovna, the responsibilities and admissions it would entail of him, and he shuns that knowledge. He does so not so much by denying her his love, not overtly at any rate, but by masking his denial of her in forms of behavior that look like love— in pity, for example. Thus in a single breath the Prince can proclaim his "love" for Nastasya and deny that she may be capable of receiving his love by calling her a child: "'Oh no, I love her with all my soul! Why, she's just a—a child, an absolute child!'" (IV, 9; p. 626). To say that she is a child is more evidence of his pity for her; it attests to his belief that she is a victim of her own human nature: "He had quite truthfully told Radomsky that he loved her truly and sincerely, and in his love for her there was an attraction to some sick, pathetic child whom it was difficult and even impossible to leave to its own devices" (p. 634). To say that she is a child is also to say that she cannot be the object of his love, certainly not of his mature, human, sexual love. Given the fact that she is a "fallen woman," this is laden with the irony that the Prince ends up denying the very thing which is most plainly obvious about her: her sexuality. It points up something ingenuous, rather than malicious, about him. He returned to Russia a virgin, and the insistent comparisons between him and Christ suggest that he is "immaculate," in somewhat the way that Nietzsche's Zarathustra found the "beautiful" worthy of contempt ("Your spirit has been persuaded to despise the earthly; . . . And that which permits itself to be touched by cowardly glances you would baptize 'beautiful'"[6]).

Prince Myshkin's denial of Nastasya Filippovna reaches its climax in the final episode of the novel; the murder of Nastasya, seized from the Prince on their wedding day, is the point to which the action has been moving ever since the intimation that Rogozhin might murder her; the Prince's silence beside the corpse suggests that he has, through his failings, been an equal factor in her death. Here, the comparisons with *Othello* are direct. In Shakespeare's play, it can be said that when love becomes caught in the grip of power it is projected as murder. In *The Idiot*, the actual murder is unseen, as if to suggest that the love which it images was never substantial at all. We see Nastasya not as a person but as a body, a corpse. Does she have any "inner" life? Dostoevsky suggests that we shall never know. Rogozhin says in confession that he pierced her with a knife (the description recalls Cervantes' story of the two friends), but she gave precious little evidence of what transpired at her death ("'you see, the knife only went in three or four inches— just under the left breast—and no more than half a tablespoon of blood came out on her chemise—not a drop more,'" p. 655). The Prince concludes that she must have died from severe internal hem- orrhage—which, given his reluctance or inability to know her "inner" life in any other way, is sadly ironic.

While the Prince searches for Nastasya Filippovna, he looks for tangible evidence, for "ocular proof"; when he finds her (or rather, her corpse) she is described, exactly like Desdemona in *Othello*, as a statue, as marble, inert:

The sleeper was covered, from head to foot, with a white sheet, but the limbs were, somehow, only faintly visible; only from the raised outlines was it possible to make out that a human being was lying there stretched out full length. . . . At the foot of the bed some sort of lace lay in a crumpled heap, and on the white lace, protruding from under the sheet, the tip of a bare foot could be made out; it seemed as though it were carved out of marble, and it was dreadfully still. (p. 656)

The image of the other as marble, as sculpted stone, captures the will to know their existence as one would know the existence of an object of the external world. The will to knowledge projects a power over others which in effect turns them to stone. In *The Idiot*, Prince Myshkin's prior denials of Nastasya Filippovna, his failure to love her, find expression in this form of skepticism and this demand for knowledge—as if to say that this tragedy is not only an expression of the power of knowledge, but knowledge an expression of the will to power. Our demand to know others as one would know the exis- tence of the external world (or the skeptical claim that we cannot know them so) is thus a harrowing expression of the more basic will to power which it is part of human nature to abet.

FLAUBERT

"'I am to be pitied—not to be sold'"
—*Madame Bovary*

AS PRINCE MYSHKIN SEARCHES through Nastasya Filippovna's rooms, he finds an open book, and a turned-down page; his fiancée, it seems, had been reading *Madame Bovary* just before she died. Dostoevsky does not discuss Flaubert in his notes for the novel, but there is evidence from his wife's diary that he was reading *Madame Bovary* during the course of his work on *The Idiot*. Critics have seen the mention of *Madame Bovary* here as a signal of the tragic dimension of Dostoevsky's novel, in contrast to the comic rhythm of *Don Quixote*, which is cited near the beginning of the work. There is a striking resemblance between *The Idiot* and *Madame Bovary*—the vigils over Nastasya Filippovna's dead body and over Emma's corpse—which suggests that the relationship between these two works is substantial and deep.[7] No less than Cervantes, Dostoevsky, or Shakespeare, Flaubert is concerned with the alliance between power and knowledge and with the possibility that knowledge may fail. Here, I shall discuss the mutual ignorance that plagues the relationship of Emma and Charles in light of the scene around Emma's corpse. I want to suggest that this scene takes up the problem of skepticism with respect to our knowledge of other persons as modeled in texts we have been seeing so far. More specifically, it shows the truth of our outsideness to one another and the consequences of any attempt to gain absolute power over them.

In terms of overall structure or form, there are similarities between Cervantes' tale of the two friends, *The Idiot*, and *Madame Bovary* which are worthy of mention. In them we see a movement from marriage to death, the scene of death being some function of the avoidance of conjugal love. In *Madame Bovary*, the relationship between marriage and death is anticipated from the earliest descriptions of Charles' marriage to his first wife. Like Emma, his first wife dies, and it is only at her death (i.e., once it is too late) that he realizes her love for him. As Charles returns from her funeral ("in a sorrowful reverie") he comes to what seems an astonishing conclusion: "She had loved him after all" (I, 2; p. 14). There is abundant irony in that observation, and there is potential tragedy in it as well. Yet more important, I think, it points up a fact about his love for her: if he realizes her love for him only now, this late, then in life he could not have loved her very deeply at all. As in Cervantes' tale, there is reason to believe that Charles had not loved his first wife in a conjugal way. At the celebration of his wedding to Emma, for instance, Charles is embarrassed by certain innuendos in the comments his guests make ("He answered feebly to the puns, *doubles entendres*, compliments," p. 21). Flaubert is gathering force for the suggestion that Charles was a virgin at the time of his marriage to Emma:

The next day, on the other hand, he seemed another man. It was he who might rather have been taken for the virgin of the evening before, whilst the bride gave no sign that revealed anything. The shrewdest did not know what to make of it, and they looked at her when she passed near them with an unbounded concentration of mind. But Charles concealed nothing. He called her "my wife," addressed her by the familiar "tu," asked for her of everyone, looked for her everywhere, and often he dragged her into the yards, where he could be seen from far between the trees, putting his arm around her waist, and walking half-bending over her, ruffling the collar of her blouse with his head. (I, 4; p. 21)

Both *The Idiot* and Cervantes' story of the two friends are dominated by the demand to know the existence of the other by the power of reason, in order to recognize or conceal the limits of human power. In Flaubert's text, however, we see the mutual denials which lead to Emma's death, yet none of the insistence on the "ocular proof" that we find in Shakespeare or Cervantes. Flaubert, like Dostoevsky, works the other side of the relationship of tragedy and skepticism: tragedy is not the product of an epistemological demand which goes unmet because unmeetable; rather, skepticism shows up—in Emma's escapes from the ordinary world, for instance—as stemming from some potentially tragic facts about us, which it might serve to mask or conceal. What distinguishes Emma Bovary from Prince Myshkin in this regard is that Emma recognizes these facts—her apartness and her finitude, for instance—and accepts them for herself when she swallows the poison.

From the start of their marriage, Emma grows increasingly estranged from Charles. Her pursuit of extramarital love is just one indication of a flaw in her love for Charles. But especially toward the end of the novel, she avoids Charles because there is something about her relationship to him, something which the fact of her dependence on him in marriage tells her, which she would not face: she takes the daughter she has had by him as a sign of her own finite nature. At the announcement that she has given birth to a girl—proclaimed, with full irony, at dawn on a Sunday—Emma faints. When she visits her daughter at the nurse's and finds Léon present, she is mortally embarrassed; worse still, the baby is sick on Léon's clean collar. Late in the novel, as Emma is about to die, she calls for the child to be brought to her, and she is filled with a loathing, a veritable disgust—not so much with the child as with herself; she sees in the child a sign of her own human limitations, proof that she is of frail flesh: "At the mention of this name, that carried her back to the memory of her adulteries and her calamities, Madame Bovary turned away her head, as at the loathing of another bitterer poison that rose to her mouth. But Berthe remained perched on the bed. 'Oh, how big your eyes are, mamma! How pale you are! how you sweat!'" (III, 8; pp. 232–33).

Emma's virtual hatred of the fruits of her love, despite her craving for passion, seems all the more pathetic because of Charles' ignorance. Yet he is equally to blame for the failure of their love. Emma has an enormous potential for passion and warmth; her imagination finds expression in overtly aesthetic ways, but Charles is unreceptive. Emma may not succeed in communicating with him because her passion exceeds words, but his sensibilities are so vastly different from hers that he would always be unable to hear what she means:

Perhaps she would have liked to confide all these things to some one. But how tell an undefinable uneasiness, changing as the clouds, unstable as the winds? Words failed her and, by the same token, the opportunity, the courage.

If Charles had but wished it, if he had guessed, if his look had but once met her thought, it seemed to her that a sudden bounty would have come from her heart, as the fruit falls from a tree when shaken by a hand. But as the intimacy of their life became deeper, the greater became the gulf that kept them apart. (I, 7; p. 29)

Charles suffers from a defect opposite that of Emma. His communicative lapses, which contribute to their marital silence, are signs of a dearth of genuine imagination, feeling, or thought; if he fails to talk, it is because he has nothing to say. His remarkably ordinary language indicates a lack of interest in the world, and is part of what I called a "crisis of the commonplace" ("Charles's conversation was commonplace as street pavement, and everyone's ideas trooped through it in their everyday garb, without exciting emotion, laughter, or thought").

Nietzsche once said that marriage is, or ought to be, a long and successful conversation: "When marrying, one should ask oneself the question: Do you believe that you will be able to converse well with this woman into your old age? Everything else in marriage is transitory, but the most time during the association belongs to conversation."[8] Charles' and Emma's marital failings show up especially well in their inability to achieve meaningful conversation. Their failure to converse—to understand the other and to make themselves understood—means that Emma and Charles have not, in marriage, adequately *known* one another. The expression "conversation" still retains some of its older sexual connotations, as does the word "communication," but the failure of conversation in *Madame Bovary* is of course not itself a sign that Emma and Charles did not consummate their marriage; it could not be, since after their wedding night Charles leads us to suspect that he has lost his virginity. Nonetheless it suggests certain deficiencies in their common life: even an active sexual life would be meaningless if they had no other conversation; it would mean that they still did not know one another in any significant way.

If the purpose of marriage is conversation, and if Emma and Charles fail in this regard, then we can well understand Emma's

question about her reasons for marrying ("'Why did I marry?'").
She asks herself this question because no satisfactory conversation
with Charles has been found. If Emma then seeks love outside of
marriage, denying Charles her love and refusing his love (could he
give it to her), Charles is unable to share in the full range of
emotion that Emma feels, and is unable to receive her love. One
might expect that marriage, and the opportunity for dialogue that it
provides, might offer a way for these characters to escape the will to
power, and in one sense it does. Charles finds something like a will
to *submission*, but this too is placed in the service of the more
corrosive power at work here, the denial of love. He will act as a
child, which in effect disqualifies him as an object of Emma's love:
"He could not keep from constantly touching her comb, her rings,
her scarf; sometimes he gave her great sounding kisses with all his
mouth on her cheeks, or else little kisses in a row all along her bare
arms from the tip of her fingers up to her shoulder" (I, 5; p. 24).
Emma, for her part, treats Charles as a child, as Prince Myshkin
treats Nastasya Filippovna, as one incapable of responding to her
love: "She put him away half-smiling, half-annoyed, as one does
with a clinging child." Together, the patterns of their affection fall
into the staid cadences of habit: "[Charles'] outbursts [of affection]
became regular; he embraced her at certain fixed times. It was one
habit among other habits, like a familiar dessert after the monotony
of dinner" (I, 7; p. 31).

   In *Madame Bovary* there is no final reconciliation, hence no
sense that Charles' and Emma's marriage could withstand either the
threats of power or the dullness of submission. Unlike *Don Quixote*,
which is a comic novel and which while repudiating the romances
of chivalry is also a romance, this novel is no comedy and their
marriage is no romance. Their failure to know one another as adult
human beings shows up in the hollowness of their marital conversation, in the emptiness of its ring. Their conversation, such as it is,
is incapable of binding them together in love (recall the remark
that "[Emma] even confided many a thing to her greyhound! She
would have done so to the logs in the fireplace or to the pendulum
of the clock," I, 9; p. 44). In *Don Quixote*, by contrast, Cervantes
portrayed a relationship in which dialogue was a mode of knowledge

and language a shared "form of life." In *Madame Bovary*, however, words have lost the power of communication, so that conversation is no longer a viable way of life. But still words are the expression of *some* power, as if to suggest that we wield power over others *especially* where we are ignorant of them. Indeed, we see such power at work in this novel through what might be thought of as indirect effects, e.g., in Charles' infantile expressions of emotion, which correspond to his essential submissiveness.

Charles' and Emma's mutual silence is capped at the scene of her death; Flaubert describes Emma as lifeless, inert: "Pale as a statue, and with eyes red as fire"; "Emma's head was turned towards her right shoulder, the corner of her mouth, which was open, seemed like a black hole at the lower part of her face; her two thumbs were bent into the palms of her hands; a kind of white dust besprinkled her lashes, and her eyes were beginning to disappear in a viscous pallor, as if covered by a spiderweb. The sheet sunk in from her breast to her knees, and then rose at the tips of her toes, and it seemed to Charles that infinite masses, an enormous load, were weighing upon her" (III, 9; pp. 236, 241). Charles is as reluctant to believe in his wife's death (presumably for what it would mean about his ignorance of her) as he was, during their marriage, to recognize her life. The narrator reflects, half-musing with Charles: "Someone's death always causes a kind of stupefaction; so difficult it is to grasp this advent of nothingness and to resign ourselves to the fact that it has actually taken place" (p. 238). Charles did not adequately know Emma while she was living, and so has trouble telling what it means for her to be dead. Stanley Cavell half jokingly speculated that such knowledge is the business of anyone with an instinctual sense for the human, perhaps even a dog. The priest in Madame Bovary makes a closely related remark when he notes that "'People say they smell the dead. . . . It's like bees; they leave their hives when there is a death in the neighborhood'" (p. 243).[9] If this is indeed so, then it speaks a sad commentary on our (in)capacity as humans to know the human in others, and therefore in ourselves. On some accounts of human evolution we have lost the instinct for what is human *because* of our gift of human reason. Unwilling or unable to see that Emma is dead, Charles wonders if he might not revive her by some form of magic or might of will: "He recalled stories of catalepsy, the marvels of magnetism, and he said to himself that by willing it with all his force he might perhaps succeed in reviving her. Once he bent towards her, and cried in a low voice, 'Emma! Emma!'" (p. 241). If he thinks that Emma could be revived by magnetism, he must not, cannot, know what it would mean to know her as alive.

If Emma and Charles are equally to blame for their failure to know one another as humans, for their failure to achieve meaningful conversation in their marriage, for their failure to be faithful to their marriage bond (not to say their vows), then why does Emma seem heroic while Charles appears pathetic? We respond to him with pity, but to her with admiration, which is not to say that together they make for a tragic fate. Emma is plagued by her sensuality, by her fiercely burning passions, and she feels called on to experience life with the same intensity she imagines of the exotic characters about whom she has read. This fervid aestheticism will not allow her to fail to see for herself what other characters seek to avoid; one senses that if she had more time, she might be willing for love. Certainly, the bases for love, and the possibility that she might remain faithful in it, are in place at the end of the novel. Emma reaches for the poison, showing that she at least has it in her power to accept the limits of human power. She has come to terms with pity, clearly distinguishing it from love. Accordingly, she does not solicit our pity; she may be a fallen woman, fallen to the power of her passions (which is what the Prince saw in Nastasya Filippovna), but she thus proves herself worthy of finite, human life. She has some of what Nietzsche would have admired as the courage of her sensibilities; she recognizes her independence from others— which is a consequence of her outsideness to others—over and above her dependence on them. Recall once again her reaction near the end of the novel, where she is in dire financial straits. She asks the notary for the loan of a thousand *écus,* and in reply he solicits her love: "'You shamelessly take advantage of my distress, sir! I am to be pitied—not to be sold'" (III, 7; p. 221). She knows the meaning of pity, just as she knows the meaning of love, and if she does not gain our pity, neither does she win love. In some other age,

[269]

Emma Bovary might be tragic. Here she is plainly human, not to say ordinarily so, which is precisely what she loathed to find out about herself. Unlike Charles, however, she knows before she dies that no voice, no magic, no power of will or wishing, will bring her back.

Notes

I. CERVANTES

Skepticism and the Problem of Criteria

1. These views, too numerous to mention individually, are largely indebted to Ortega y Gasset, *Meditaciones del "Quijote"* (1914).

2. I cite the *Quixote* according to the translation of Samuel Putnam (New York: Modern Library, 1949), giving Part and chapter.

3. "Linguistic Perspectivism in the *Don Quijote*," in *Linguistics and Literary History* (1948; rpt. Princeton: Princeton University Press, 1974), pp. 59, 68. He says that "the real protagonist of this novel is not Quijote, with his continual misrepresentation of reality, or Sancho with his skeptical half-endorsement of quixotism—and surely not any of the central figures of the illusionistic by-stories: the hero is Cervantes, the artist himself, who combines a critical and illusionistic art according to his free will" (p. 69). This glorification of the artist dilutes much of what he has to say about the linguistic "perspectivism" of the *Quixote*.

4. Ludwig Wittgenstein, *Philosophical Investigations*, trans. G. E. M. Anscombe (New York: Macmillan, 1953), II, p. 195e.

5. *Meditations on "Quixote,"* trans. Evelyn Rugg and Diego Marín (New York: W. W. Norton, 1961), p. 141.

6. See Gilbert Ryle, *The Concept of Mind* (New York: Barnes and Noble, 1949) and, for the pragmatist angle, Richard Rorty, *Philosophy and the Mirror of Nature* (Princeton: Princeton University Press, 1979), and *Consequences of Pragmatism* (Minneapolis: University of Minnesota Press, 1982).

7. "'It is plain to see,' said Don Quixote, 'that you have had little experience in this matter of adventures'" (I, 8). The key word here, I take it, is "experience," which in the original cannot mean what the British empiricist tradition means ("no estás *cursado* en esto de las aventuras").

8. In *El pensamiento de Cervantes* (Barcelona: Noguer, 1972), Américo Castro cites Cervantes' *Persiles* (I, 14) to this effect: "La experiencia en todas las cosas es la mejor maestra de las artes" ("Experience is the best teacher of all subjects").

9. This is the point of Saul Kripke, *Wittgenstein on Rules and Private Language* (Cambridge, Mass.: Harvard University Press, 1983).

[271]

10. Stanley Cavell gives this formulation in *The Claim of Reason* (New York: Oxford University Press, 1979), p. 45. Cavell is preceded by Roman Ingarden, in *The Literary Work of Art*.

11. "Other Minds," in *Philosophical Papers*, 2d ed., ed. J. O. Urmson and G. J. Warnock (Oxford: Oxford University Press, 1970), p. 79.

The Conditions of Body and Mind

1. Ian Watt, *The Rise of the Novel* (1957; rpt. Berkeley: University of California Press, 1974), and "Some Reflections on *The Rise of the Novel*," *Novel: A Forum on Fiction* (1968), 1:205–18.

2. Marthe Robert, *The Old and the New: From "Don Quixote" to Kafka*, trans. Carol Cosman (Berkeley: University of California Press, 1977), pp. 38, 39.

3. The principal references are: Descartes, *Meditations* and *Discourse on Method*; Locke, *Essay Concerning Human Understanding*; Reid, *Essays on the Intellectual Powers of Man* (Watt names Reid but does not cite his work). For a recent discussion and critique of this tradition, one to which I am indebted, see Richard Rorty, *Philosophy and the Mirror of Nature* (Princeton: Princeton University Press, 1979).

4. Rorty, *Philosophy and the Mirror of Nature*, p. 50. See also Wallace Matson, "Why Isn't the Mind-Body Problem Ancient?" in *Mind, Matter and Method: Essays in Philosophy and Science in Honor of Herbert Feigl*, ed. Paul Feyerabend and Grover Maxwell (Minneapolis: University of Minnesota Press, 1966), pp. 92–102.

5. Descartes, *Meditations on First Philosophy* (Third Meditation), in *The Philosophical Works of Descartes*, I, trans. Elizabeth S. Haldane and G. R. T. Ross (1911; rpt. Cambridge: Cambridge University Press, 1975), p. 160.

6. Stanley Cavell discusses this problem in *The Claim of Reason* (New York: Oxford University Press, 1979), pp. 417–18. He suggests that there are limits to what we will allow such an Outsider to know: "if the coherence in imagining the Outsider with respect to me and the external world turns on his being invoked just to tell an antecedently clear difference or to make an antecedently clear comparison, then suppose I invoke an Outsider with respect to me and other minds just to make a comparison between, say, what I feel when I say I feel pain and what others feel when they say so, and between what I see when I say I see red and what others see when they say so." He says that we will allow the Outsider to discover that each of us sees different things as red, and would accept that I might be mistaken in what I see, but not that I might be mistaken in what I feel as pain. Descartes's fiction of the evil demon (an Outsider) can be described in the same terms: there are thinkers who would say that Descartes was not thorough enough or serious enough in this fiction, because he would not allow it to subvert the existence of the subject (i.e., the thinking thing who will not tolerate the idea of a mistake about its being, for instance, in pain). The point is that on the one hand we should have to require the Outsider to be located within us, while on the other we will not tolerate such self-subversion.

[272]

NOTES

7. Alexander Welsh, *Reflections on the Hero as Quixote* (Princeton: Princeton University Press, 1981), pp. 87–88.

8. Stanley Cavell, "What Becomes of Things on Film?" *Philosophy and Literature* (1978), 2:251; my italics.

9. I follow the translation of Harriet de Onís, in *Six Exemplary Novels* (Woodbury, N.Y.: Barron's Educational Series, 1961), here, p. 70. For a recent discussion of this text in the context of Renaissance skepticism, see Alban Forcione, *Cervantes and the Humanist Vision* (Princeton: Princeton University Press, 1983).

10. *The Praise of Folly*, trans. John P. Dolan, in *The Essential Erasmus* (New York: Mentor Books, 1964), p. 170.

11. The notion has become a prominent concern in recent work on the philosophy of mind, as for example in Richard Rorty's influential *Philosophy and the Mirror of Nature*. But the phrase was current among Shakespeare and Bacon (in *Measure for Measure* and *The Advancement of Learning*, respectively). It was first invoked for modern philosophy by C. S. Peirce, but can be traced to ancient ideas about the nature of (Greek) *nous*. On this see Rorty, pp. 42–43.

12. As Wittgenstein said, "a soul which some body *has*," *Philosophical Investigations*, §283. I am indebted here to Cavell, *The Claim of Reason*, pp. 370-496 *passim*, especially p. 383.

Personal Identity: The Moral Ground

1. The same (rationalist) tradition of thought on the question of personal identity informs E. C. Riley's study "Who's Who in *Don Quixote*? Or an Approach to the Problem of Identity," *MLN* (1966), 81:113–20.

2. *The Tragic Sense of Life in Men and Nations*, trans. Anthony Kerrigan (1972; rpt. Princeton: Princeton University Press, 1977), p. 352.

3. *The Theory of the Novel*, trans. Anna Bostock (1971; rpt. Cambridge, Mass.: The MIT Press, 1977), p. 104.

4. Américo Castro, Introduction to *La vida de Lazarillo de Tormes*, ed. Everett W. Hesse and Harry F. Williams (Madison: University of Wisconsin Press, 1948). p. v.

5. *Fictions of the Self: 1550–1800* (Princeton: Princeton University Press, 1981), pp. 20–31.

6. "The Death of Lazarillo de Tormes," *PMLA* (1966), 81:149–66.

7. I have discussed the structure of the book further in this light in "The Rhetoric of Defense in the *Guzmán de Alfarache*," *Neophilologus* (1979), 63:380–88.

8. G. E. Moore, "Proof of an External World," *Proceedings of the British Academy* (1939), 25:273–300; Ludwig Wittgenstein, *On Certainty*, ed. G. E. M. Anscombe and G. H. von Wright, trans. Denis Paul and G. E. M. Anscombe (New York: Harper Torchbooks, 1972).

9. *Beyond Good and Evil*, trans. R. J. Hollingdale (1973; rpt. Harmondsworth: Penguin Books, 1979), pp. 28–29 (section 17).

10. See Américo Castro, "Incarnation in *Don Quixote*," in *An Idea of History*, trans. Stephen Gilman and Edmund L. King (Columbus: Ohio State University Press, 1977), pp. 23–76.

11. Marthe Robert said that "The suppression of this distance has the serious inconvenience, among others, of transforming Don Quixote into a caricature and reducing the novel to the proportions of a pleasant but limited satire"; as she points out, this is what tends to occur in theatrical adaptations of the book. (*The Old and the New*, p. 23.)

12. See also Juan Bautista Avalle-Arce, "Conocimiento y vida en Cervantes," *Deslindes cervantinos* (Madrid: Edhigar, 1961), pp. 15–80.

13. I develop this in "The Logic of Moods: An Essay on Emerson and Rousseau," *Studies in Romanticism*, (1985), vol.24. I am indebted to Stanley Cavell's "Thinking of Emerson," in *The Senses of Walden* (Berkeley: North Point Press, 1981), pp. 125ff for the germ of this idea. The canonical texts involved are Heidegger, *Being and Time*, 134–39, and Kierkegaard, *The Concept of Anxiety*.

14. This is the "quijotización" of Sancho and the "sanchificación" of Don Quixote. See Madariaga's *Guía del lector del "Quijote"* (1926; rpt. Madrid: Espasa-Calpe, 1976).

15. *After Virtue: A Study in Moral Theory* (Notre Dame: University of Notre Dame Press, 1981), p. 24.

16. Appropriate readings are H. L. A. Hart, *The Concept of Law* (1961; rpt. Oxford: The Clarendon Press, 1965); John Rawls, *A Theory of Justice* (Cambridge, Mass.: The Belknap Press of Harvard University Press, 1971); Robert Nozick, *Anarchy, State, and Utopia* (New York: Basic Books, 1974).

17. See, for instance, Robert Paul Wolff, *Understanding Rawls: A Reconstruction and Critique of "A Theory of Justice"* (Princeton: Princeton University Press, 1977).

18. *Right and Wrong* (Cambridge, Mass.: Harvard University Press, 1978), p. 9.

II. DOSTOEVSKY

The Contradictions of Skepticism: Existence and Execution

1. I follow the translation of A. V. Miller (1977; rpt. Oxford: Oxford University Press, 1981), p. 120.

2. See Hans-Georg Gadamer, "Hegel's Dialectic of Self-Consciousness," in his *Hegel's Dialectic*, trans. P. Christopher Smith (New Haven: Yale University Press, 1976), pp. 54–74.

3. *Concluding Unscientific Postscript*, trans. David P. Swenson and Walter Lowrie (1941; rpt. Princeton: Princeton University Press, 1974), p. 176.

4. *Concluding Unscientific Postscript*, p. 275.

5. Kierkegaard writes in the *Postscript* that "Don Quixote is the prototype for a subjective madness, in which the passion of inwardness embraces a particular finite fixed idea" (p. 175).

NOTES

6. I follow the translation of David Magarshack (1955; rpt. Harmondsworth: Penguin Books, 1977), here I, 2; p. 46.

7. *Reflections on the Hero as Quixote* (Princeton: Princeton University Press, 1981), p. 204.

8. Quentin Lauer, S. J., *A Reading of Hegel's "Phenomenology of Spirit"* (New York: Fordham University Press, 1976), p. 115.

9. *Fear and Trembling*, trans. Walter Lowrie (1941; rpt. Princeton: Princeton University Press, 1968), p. 56.

10. *Parables and Paradoxes* (1946; rpt. New York: Schocken Books, 1958), p. 43; Clement Greenberg is responsible for the translation of this story.

11. I follow the translation of Willa and Edwin Muir, revised, with additional material translated by E. M. Butler (1937; rpt. New York: Vintage Books, 1968), p. 3.

12. I follow the translation of Stuart Gilbert (1946; rpt. New York: Vintage Books, 1956), pp. 142–43.

13. *The Art of Dostoevsky* (Princeton: Princeton University Press, 1981), pp. 149–50.

14. The significance of "alienation" to the process of self-understanding outlined in *The Stranger* is suggested by the alternate rendering of *L'Etranger* into English as *The Outsider*.

Crime and Conviction

1. I cite the translation by David Magarshack (1951; rpt. Harmondsworth: Penguin Books, 1970); here, IV, 2; p. 467.

2. "Character and Consciousness," *New Literary History* (1974), 5:234.

3. *The Art of Dostoevsky* (Princeton: Princeton University Press, 1981), p. 198; italics added. See also F. I. Evnin, *Tvorchestvo Dostoevskogo* (Moscow, 1948), pp. 165–72, translated by Natalie Beinstock as "Plot Structure and Raskolnikov's Oscillations," in *Crime and Punishment: The Coulson Translation*, ed. George Gibian (1964; rpt. New York: W. W. Norton, 1975), pp. 656–57.

4. *The Notebooks for Crime and Punishment*, ed. and trans. Edward Wasiolek (Chicago: University of Chicago Press, 1971), p. 56.

5. *Dostoevksy and the Novel* (Princeton: Princeton University Press, 1977), pp. 88–89.

6. "Dostoevsky in *Crime and Punishment*," in *Dostoevsky: A Collection of Critical Essays*, ed. René Wellek (Englewood Cliffs, N.J.: Prentice-Hall, 1962), pp. 35–36; originally published in *Partisan Review* (1960), vol. 27.

7. *The Triumph of the Novel* (New York: Oxford University Press, 1976), p. 175.

8. Letter to Katkov, cited in Konstantin Mochulsky, *Dostoevsky: His Life and Work*, trans. Michael Minihan (1967; rpt. Princeton: Princeton University Press, 1973), p. 272.

9. "Crime for Punishment: The Tenor of Part One," *Hudson Review* (1960), 13:203.

10. Letter to Katkov, cited in Mochulsky, *Dostoevsky*, p. 273.

11. *The Brothers Karamazov*, trans. Constance Garnett, revised by Ralph E. Matlaw (New York: W. W. Norton, 1976), VIII, 2; p. 352. Further references are to this edition and are included in the text.

12. *The Vision of Tragedy*, new edition (New Haven: Yale University Press, 1980), p. 114.

13. This can be stated in more analytic terms. In Robert Nozick's formulation, "we know that *p* when our belief that *p* is a true belief and tracks the fact that *p*. Knowledge is a real (subjunctive) relationship to (and in) the world" (*Philosophical Explanations* [Cambridge, Mass.: The Belknap Press of Harvard University Press, 1981], p. 524).

14. "The Theme of the Double in Dostoevsky," in René Wellek, ed., *Dostoevsky: A Collection of Critical Essays* (Englewood Cliffs: Prentice-Hall, 1962), p. 126.

15. *The Will to Power*, trans. Walter Kaufmann and R. J. Hollingdale (1967; rpt. New York: Vintage Books, 1968), §552, p. 298.

16. "Dostoevsky's 'Idiot': The Curse of Saintliness," from *The Tragic Vision* (New York: Holt, Reinhart, and Winston, 1960), pp. 209–27; I cite according to the text in Wellek, ed., *Dostoevsky*, pp. 39–52.

17. *Journeys to Selfhood: Hegel and Kierkegaard* (Berkeley: University of California Press, 1980), p. 216.

Outsiders

1. The argument is developed in Stanley Cavell, *The Claim of Reason* (New York: Oxford University Press, 1979), p. 443.

2. In *The Philosophical Works of Descartes*, I, trans. Elizabeth S. Haldane and G. R. T. Ross (1911; rpt. Cambridge: Cambridge University Press, 1975), p. 160 (from Meditation III).

3. "Cogito and the History of Madness," in *Writing and Difference*, trans. Alan Bass (Chicago: University of Chicago Press, 1978), pp. 31–63.

4. *The Antichrist*, section 16, in Walter Kaufmann, ed. and trans., *The Portable Nietzsche* (1954; rpt. New York: Penguin Books, 1981), p. 583.

5. See, for example, his own remark in I, 3: "'I'm an invalid and I've never had any regular education'" (p. 52).

6. This reference is adduced by Konstantin Mochulsky, *Dostoevsky: His Life and Work*, trans. Michael A. Minihan (1967; rpt. Princeton: Princeton University Press, 1973), p. 367.

7. Letter to Maikov, January 12, 1868, cited in Mochulsky, *Dostoevsky*, p. 344.

8. Letter to S. A. Ivanovna (Dostoevsky's niece), January 1/13 [sic], 1868, cited in Mochulsky, *Dostoevsky*, p. 345.

9. *The Antichrist*, section 15, in *The Portable Nietzsche*, p. 582.

10. *Philosophical Investigations*, trans. G. E. M. Anscombe (New York: Macmillan, 1953), §297.

11. Cavell, *The Claim of Reason*, p. 286.

NOTES

III. FLAUBERT

The Female Quixote: Aesthetics and Seduction

1. Søren Kierkegaard, *Either/Or*, vol. I, trans. David F. Swenson and Lillian Marvin Swenson, revised by Howard A. Johnson (1959; rpt. Princeton: Princeton University Press, 1971), p. 255.

2. *The Gates of Horn: A Study of Five French Realists* (1963; rpt. New York: Oxford University Press, 1966), p. 248.

3. *Concluding Unscientific Postscript*, trans. David F. Swenson and Walter Lowrie (1941; rpt. Princeton: Princeton University Press, 1974), p. 262.

4. *The Theory of the Novel*, trans. Anna Bostock (1971; rpt. Cambridge, Mass.: The MIT Press, 1977), p. 29.

5. I cite according to the translation by Paul de Man (New York: W. W. Norton, 1965), here III, 6; p. 206. Further references will be incorporated into the text.

6. Here I amend the de Man translation to correspond more closely with the French, which reads "'nous nous entendrons plus tard; avec les dames je me suis toujours arrangé'" (*Oeuvres complètes de Flaubert*, I, ed. Jean Bruneau [Paris: Editions du Seuil, 1964], p. 609b).

7. *Either/Or*, vol. II, trans. Walter Lowrie, revised by Howard A. Johnson (1959; rpt. Princeton: Princeton University Press, 1971), p. 12.

8. *Sartre and Flaubert* (Chicago: The University of Chicago Press, 1981), p. 360.

9. *The Novels of Flaubert* (Princeton: Princeton University Press, 1966), p. 85.

10. *Kierkegaard: A Kind of Poet* (Philadelphia: University of Pennsylvania Press, 1971), p. 5.

11. *Phenomenology of Spirit*, trans. A. V. Miller (1977; rpt. New York: Oxford University Press, 1981), §90–91, p. 58.

12. Josiah Royce, *Lectures on Modern Idealism* (New Haven: Yale University Press, 1919), pp. 147ff; M. H. Abrams, *Natural Supernaturalism* (New York: W. W. Norton, 1971), pp. 225–37.

13. *Beyond Good and Evil*, trans. R. J. Hollingdale (1973; rpt. Harmondsworth: Penguin Books, 1979), §123, p. 80.

14. Charles Baudelaire, "Madame Bovary," in *L'Art Romantique, Oeuvres complètes* (Paris: Gallimard, Bibliothèque de la Pléiade, 1961), pp. 444–50.

Social Epistemology: The Marriage Contract

1. Dominick LaCapra, *"Madame Bovary" on Trial* (Ithaca: Cornell University Press, 1982), p. 56; Hans Robert Jauss, "Literary History as a Challenge to Literary Theory," *New Literary History* (1970), 2:7–37.

2. *Adultery in the Novel: Contract and Transgression* (Baltimore: The Johns Hopkins University Press, 1979), pp. 362–63.

3. *The Claim of Reason* (New York: Oxford University Press, 1979), p. 25.

4. David Hume, "Of the Original Contract," in *Social Contract*, ed. Sir Ernest

Barker (New York: Oxford University Press, 1962), p. 149; Cavell discusses this passage in *The Claim of Reason*, p. 22.

5. *The Social Contract*, trans. Lester G. Crocker (based on the anonymous 1761 translation) (1967; rpt. New York: Washington Square Press, 1974), pp. 22–23.

6. Søren Kierkegaard, *Stages on Life's Way*, trans. Walter Lowrie (Princeton: Princeton University Press, 1967), p. 121.

7. The essay appears in a translation by Matthew J. O'Connell in *Critical Theory* (New York: Herder and Herder, 1972), p. 126.

8. *The Claim of Reason*, p. 27.

Moral Education

1. *Sentimental Education*, trans. Robert Baldick (1964; rpt. Harmondsworth: Penguin Books, 1969); here III, 1; p. 328.

2. Flaubert, *Correspondance*, 9 vols. (Paris: Conard, 1926-33); here V, 158.

3. David Hume, *An Enquiry Concerning the Principles of Morals*, 1777 ed. (1902; rpt. Oxford: The Clarendon Press, 1972), p. 170.

4. I cite according to the translation of William H. Payne (New York: D. Appleton, 1908); here IV, p. 211.

5. *Correspondance* III, 349, and I, 47.

6. Victor Brombert, *The Novels of Flaubert*; Jean-Paul Sartre, *L'Idiot de la famille*, 3 vols. (Paris: Gallimard, 1971-72); Jonathan Culler, *Flaubert: The Uses of Uncertainty* (London: Paul Elek, 1974).

7. See Hazel E. Barnes, *Sartre and Flaubert*, pp. 334, 386.

8. *Deceit, Desire and the Novel*, trans. Yvonne Freccero (Baltimore: The Johns Hopkins University Press, 1965), p. 151.

9. *The Senses of Walden*, expanded ed. (San Francisco: North Point Press, 1981), pp. 85–86.

10. The formulation is that of John Rawls, *A Theory of Justice* (Cambridge, Mass.: The Belknap Press of Harvard University Press, 1971), p. 549.

11. *An Essay Concerning Human Understanding* (New York: New American Library, 1964), p. 174.

12. I owe this reference to Garry Wills, *Inventing America* (1978; rpt. New York: Vintage Books, 1979), p. 250.

13. *An Inquiry into the Original of Our Ideas of Beauty and Virtue* (1725), pp. 250–51; cited in Wills, *Inventing America*, pp. 251–52.

The Abuses of Certainty

1. "Flaubert's Last Testament," in *The Opposing Self* (1955; rpt. New York: Harcourt, Brace, Jovanovich, 1979), p. 158.

2. Victor Brombert, *The Novels of Flaubert*, p. 269.

3. *Lettres inédites à Raoul-Duval*, ed. Georges Normandy (Paris: Michel, 1950), p. 211. I owe this reference to Harry Levin, *The Gates of Horn*, p. 293.

NOTES

4. *Bouvard and Pécuchet*, trans. A. J. Krailsheimer (1976; rpt. Harmondsworth: Penguin Books, 1978), here VIII, p. 204, italics added. All further references will be incorporated into the text.

5. The translation is that of Donald M. Frame (New York: New American Library, 1961), p. 16.

6. See Eugenio Donato, "The Museum's Furnace," in *Textual Strategies*, ed. Josué Harari (Ithaca: Cornell University Press, 1979), pp. 213–38.

7. Flaubert, *Correspondance*, VI, 183–85; see Brombert, *The Novels of Flaubert*, p. 268.

8. If one accepts this reading of Flaubert vis-à-vis the Enlightenment, he becomes a version of what Richard Rorty would call the "culture critic," committed to the idea of truth as correspondence *among representations* rather than truth as correspondence to *nonrepresentations*. See the essays in Rorty's *Consequences of Pragmatism* (Minneapolis: University of Minnesota Press, 1982), and my review in *Philosophy and Literature* (1983), vol. 7.

IV. KNOWLEDGE AND POWER

1. The reading of *Othello* referred to here was prompted by Stanley Cavell's analysis of that play in the final pages of *The Claim of Reason* (New York: Oxford University Press, 1979). It draws on the related essay "The Avoidance of Love," in *Must We Mean What We Say?* (1969; rpt. Cambridge: Cambridge University Press, 1976), pp. 267–353. My remarks about *Pygmalion* were prompted by Paul de Man's discussion of Rousseau's version of it, in *Allegories of Reading* (New Haven: Yale University Press, 1979).

2. I follow the edition of Alice Walker and John Dover Wilson for The New Shakespeare (1957; rpt. Cambridge: Cambridge University Press, 1976), here V.ii.4–5. See *The Claim of Reason*, p. 482.

3. Cf. the episode of Marcela and Grisóstomo, discussed earlier, where Grisóstomo commits suicide because of Marcela's *hardness of heart*.

4. "Othello: An Essay to Illustrate a Method," in *Perspectives by Incongruity*, ed. Stanley Edgar Hyman (Bloomington: Indiana University Press, 1964), p. 187. Cf. his earlier comments in this direction regarding Iago: "Iago is a function of the following embarrassment: Once such privacy has been made the norm, its denial can be but promiscuity. Hence his ruttish imagery, in which he signalizes one aspect of a total fascination" (p. 157).

5. *The Notebooks for The Idiot*, ed. Edward Wasiolek, trans. Katharine Strelsky (Chicago: The University of Chicago Press, 1976), p. 224.

6. Trans. Walter Kaufmann, in *The Portable Nietzsche* (1954; rpt. Harmondsworth: Penguin Books, 1981), pp. 234–35.

7. See Robin Feuer Miller, *Dostoevsky and The Idiot* (Cambridge, Mass.: Harvard University Press, 1981), p. 157.

8. *Human, All-Too-Human*, §406, trans. Walter Kaufmann, in *The Portable Nietzsche*, p. 59.

9. Anyone who knows Victor Erice's film *El espíritu de la colmena (The Spirit of the Beehive)* will recognize here its principal theme.

Index

INDEX

DATE DUE